From Badgers to Nighthawks: Adventures of a Wildlife Ranger

By Malcolm J Ingham

Published by

Greenock Scotland
http://www.beul-aithris-publishing.com

Copyright © by Malcolm J Ingham

First Edition Published 2019

ISBN 978-0-9957784-4-3

List of Illustrations

Chapter 1:   View of Waddow Hall from River Ribble

Chapter 3:   William the Razorbill

Chapter 4:   Nigel the Nighthawk taking a pinkie

Chapter 5:   Barn Owl eggs & chick in Bell Tower, Royden Park

Chapter 6:   Toby & Pickles – 2 tiny badger cubs

Chapter 6:   Toby on the bottle

Chapter 6:   Toby, Pickles, Cassie & Kippy in their shed

Chapter 6:   Kippy in the garden pond

Chapter 7:   Mike chased up the old Scots Pine (Mike Jackson sketch)

Chapter 8:   Ann & Basil the badger in the garden

Chapter 9:   Mike McCartney & the Chip Shop Boys

Chapter 9:   The new Wildlife Hospital Unit

Chapter 10:   Muffles the fox in the grass

Chapter 10:   Velvet the fox

Chapter 10:   Hamish the Scottish Wildcat

Chapter 10:   The Beached Whale (Mike Jackson sketch)

I dedicate this book to all the wild creatures that have enriched my life with their presence and allowed me the privilege of getting to know them.

A particular mention must go to Muffles & Velvet, two of the gentlest foxes you could ever wish to meet.

To Basil, Toby, Pickles, Cassie, Millie and Kippy, six badgers who charmed us with their presence and antics.

To Elsie, my dear departed mum-in-law who was an avid animal lover and offered great encouragement in the idea of putting pen to paper. She would have loved to have seen the finished article!

Also to my parents, John and Mary for allowing me the freedom as a grubby kneed kid to explore the wonders of the countryside.

Finally to Ann my wife, for her patience, tolerance and support during my quest to become a ranger followed by my continued ambitions to pursue my chosen career to its limits.

Contents

Acknowledgments 1

Foreword by ex-Scaffolder (Thank U Very Much) Mike McCartney 2

Preface 4

Chapter One: The Beginning - A Lapwing & Peg O' Nell . 5

Chapter Two: From Dunsop & a Whistling Fox to Wirral 22

Chapter Three: From a Rook to a Razorbill 52

Chapter Four: Operation Nighthawk 76

Chapter Five: Deer Hunting in Birkenhead, Barn Owls in a Bell Tower & a Weasel in the Bathroom 101

Chapter Six: Toby, Pickles, Cassie, Millie and Kippy - Five Badgers that took over our lives 126

Chapter Seven: Trials & Tribulations of a Badger Release. 153

Chapter Eight: Barney & Podge Spikes Attack & Basil from Bridgemere 210

Chapter Nine: A Student from Helsinki, a Saker Falcon in the Depths of an Iranian Ship & a Few Scaffold Songs Raise Money For a New Unit 235

Chapter Ten: Muffles & Velvet, a Walk on the Wild Side, Hamish the Scottish Wildcat & a Beached Whale 251

Chapter Eleven: On the Trail of a Big Cat, Confronting Badger Diggers, & Time to Hang Up My Boots 268

Acknowledgments

My first and foremost acknowledgment must be to my wife Ann who has shared my passion for wildlife and conservation over many years and for her invaluable help and support at the Wildlife Rehabilitation Unit. I must also thank her for the endless hours of proof reading to ensure that the book resembled at least some form of legible reading. (Any mistakes, blame her!!)

A big thanks also to Mike McCartney for reading my first draft, his invaluable advice, and for agreeing to write the foreword, and last but not least, for his encouragement and support in my endeavours to get it published plus his unstinting friendship over many years. Thank U Very Much Mike!! Much appreciated!!

A big thanks also to Mike Jackson, not only for allowing me to use his sketches and excerpts from his notes made during the badger release, but for his dogged determination to stick it out during the release of Toby, Millie, Kippy and Cassie under conditions above and beyond the call of duty despite Toby's efforts to persuade him otherwise. And of course for the many laughs and unforgettable memories we shared during our time in the woods. I must also express my thanks to Dr Bevyl Cowan for allowing us free range of her estate for the release.

To Peter McElroy BVSc MRCVS for his valued help & support during the initial years of the Wildlife Rehabilitation Unit and to Brian Coles BVSc MRCVS for his advice and expertise in the field of avian medicine.

And finally to all the animals that have made the writing of this book possible – without them, there would be no book!

Foreword by
Mike McCartney
Ex-Scaffolder
Current musician, Author &
Photographer
Thank U Very Much!

"Malcolm J Ingham, Head Ranger and Wildlife Officer...now there's a statement for you!"

The majority of professions in our society are pretty straight forward...photographer, surgeon, binman, etc. The photographer captures his images, the surgeon slices his skin and the binman empties his bin. All professions under your control, but how do you control a wild, free living animal or bird? Not so easy...you need a special type of person to be an animal man...to tend, mend, and care for wild animals is a whole new box of tricks, particularly the way mankind has treated nature over the years, resulting in wildlife becoming increasingly wary and afraid of us humans...and no wonder!! Nature just wants to be natural, living free and wild.

But what happens when things go wrong and a creature becomes sick or injured, often through the carelessness or downright cruelty of us humans!

This is when that special unique person is needed, and Malcolm J. Ingham is that person.

I was introduced to Clitheroe lad Mal (and his luvly wife Ann) when I was doing research for my ecological children's book, *Sonny Joe and the Ringdom Rhymes* in 1987 but then over the years got to know and admire him, not only for his lifelong dedication and love of creatures (particularly badgers!) but also because he's such a nice bloke. He tells his stories in an informative, fascinating and often humorous way which allows us to conjure up pictures of the places, events and sometimes drama that he's experienced over the years. In the following pages you'll find out all about Malcolm's many adventures with nature.

When the Inghams finally settled in North Wales, the previous owners of the cottage were at first reluctant to mention that they had badgers in their garden in case the new owners were not too wildlife friendly, but once they realised who the new owners were, they finally revealed their secret. "Don't worry" said Mal I'm sure we'll cope with a few badgers in the garden!...and not only that, their new home was only three miles from where they had released their own badgers some years before.

Please settle back to enjoy Mal's marvellous stories...I certainly did!

Mike McCartney

Preface

For as far back as I can remember I have felt a deep connection with nature and wildlife. I have vivid memories of escaping from my primary school playground by scaling the high wall to discover on the other side another world, a magical mysterious place full of nature, a stream full of sticklebacks and minnows, its banks a mass of wild primroses and cowslips. Of butterflies and bees flitting from flower to flower and if I was really lucky, I would catch a glimpse of the electric blue flash of a kingfisher as it darted low over the water to alight on its favourite perch to watch for a passing minnow. Of being told off for being late back into class because the world I had entered didn't have school bells and teachers, just fascinating creatures that filled my mind full of wonder and sowed the seeds of my ambition to work with wildlife.

An ambition that I was eventually to fulfil: not only in becoming a Countryside Ranger, but also a Wildlife Officer and ultimately a Head Ranger. A life that would lead me into a world of caring for, and rehabilitating many species of wildlife from owls to foxes and badgers and even an electric blue kingfisher! A world of lecturing and television, the adventures of returning hand reared badger cubs back the wild and to flying an American Nighthawk to Belize.

But the most cherished memories are of the animals that I have been privileged to regard as friends. Muffles and Velvet my foxes, Basil the badger rescued from a life of misery in a dilapidated zoo; Hamish my Scottish Wildcat, plus many others who, over the years have rewarded me with their trust and friendship often continuing into the wild.

I hope that by the telling of these stories the memories of these creatures will live on and also inspire anyone wanting to pursue a career in conservation to continually push forward and not let go of the dream to achieve what may seem the unachievable.

Chapter One
The Beginning
A Lapwing and Peg O' Nell

"Malcolm! How much longer is this damn bird going to be in my greenhouse? It's messing all over my tomatoes!"

The now familiar cry came from somewhere within the conglomeration of tomato plants, seed trays and other garden paraphernalia that was to be found in my father's pride and joy, his greenhouse come shed. His patience was beginning to fray a little. Rabbits and budgies he could cope with, but a lapwing on the loose in his beloved greenhouse was something else. I had come across the bird one day whilst on one of my many explorations into the nearby countryside.

We lived, 'we' being my parents, my two younger brothers, Michael and Stephen, and of course me, on a council estate in the small East Lancashire market town of Clitheroe nestled in the rural Ribble Valley under the shadow of Pendle Hill, famed for its connection with the infamous Pendle Witches and the witch trials of 1612. Names such as Demdike and Chattox, two of the most notorious members of this band of so-called witches, were still whispered within the ancient villages set amongst the slopes of the old hill.

We kids spent many a happy day roaming the rough grassy slopes of Pendle serenaded by the haunting cry of the curlew and many a night was spent searching for the infamous remains of the witches den 'Malkin Tower.' Needless to say we never did find it, but we had a few scary nights trying! When we weren't tramping around Pendle we would be roaming the local woods and fields in search of bird's eggs to add to our collection. One particular egg was destined not for the collection but for the frying pan. The Lapwing or Peewit egg as we called it was fried along with chunks of eel obtained from a recent overnight fishing spree at our favourite spot just below Brungerly Bridge on the river Ribble between Waddington and Clitheroe. This spot was even scarier than searching for the Witches den 'Malkin Tower'. It was on a stretch of the river just above the weir opposite the old 17th century mansion house Waddow Hall, now a girl guides centre and said to be haunted by the ghost of Peg O' Nell. According to legend, Peg had been a maid at the hall and whilst collecting water from a well by the river bank had slipped and broken her neck. Because of this untimely death Peg had haunted the place ever since and felt the irresistible urge to drown something or someone every seven years.

The story also went on to say that the only way to appease this seven yearly craving was to sacrifice a chicken on the river bank by the well. It may all sound very far-fetched but as kids we were brought up listening to these stories of witches and ghosts. They were so deeply ingrained in the local folklore and history that we believed every word of it without question. After all, if our grandparents and even parents believed it then it must be true! We spent many memorable nights on this riverbank but one in particular is unforgettable.

It was around midnight and the four of us me, Trevor, Patrick and Eric, better known as Horlicks (Yes, Horlicks! don't ask me why, I never did get around to asking him) all had our fishing rods leaning on their rests, line weighted down out in the river and hooks baited with a huge mass of big fat juicy lobworms. We were huddled around the fire with sleepy eyes stinging from wood smoke trying to focus on the tip of our respective rods in the hope that it would suddenly jerk sharply and violently downwards as our big bunch of lob worms was carried off by some monster of the deep. The only sounds to disturb our drowsy concentration were that of the river as it tumbled over the weir below, the hoot of a tawny owl, or the dull splash of a sea trout or salmon as it leapt out of the water. Daubenton's bats would skim across the surface of the water in search of insects occasionally just missing our rod tips as they darted over the surface, their dark shapes silhouetted against the full moon that hung above Waddow Hall.

View of Waddow Hall from the river Ribble - taken from a 1950's postcard

The old Hall, backlit against the full moon, looked eerie as dark shadows were cast down the far bank and across the water towards us. A rod tip quivered as something investigated the bait, Trev leapt up from the fire to hover over his rod ready for the strike, but nothing, it fell still again and he settled back down by the fire. The moon had now risen high above the hall with the far bank a fusion of moonlight and wispy dancing shadows. All was peaceful as we huddled around the fire, its embers glowing red occasionally sending sparks dancing around our feet as a log disintegrated into a dozen burning pieces. A couple of us talked in hushed tones about who was going out with who to the latest Cliff Richards record or this new Liverpool group, the Beatles, whilst another would be quietly dozing off.

Abruptly our peace was shattered as Horlicks suddenly jumped up and pointing across the river to the far bank screamed, "What's that?!!"

We leapt up in a muddle of rude awakenings and bewilderment to see what all the commotion was about as we dashed towards the bank tripping over fishing rods in the process.

Horlicks was frantically pointing across to the far bank shouting, "There, it's over there."

A hazy damp mist was now rising from the river adding to an already eerie atmosphere as we scanned across to the far bank.

"What are we looking for?" we enquired.

All Horlicks could nervously splutter was, "There it is, it's coming towards us!!!"

We couldn't see anything and began to accuse him of playing one of his pranks when all of a sudden there it was! Flitting from bush to bush was a dark eerie shadow, one minute silhouetted against the moonlight, the next gone only to reappear again even closer. The dark ghostly figure was heading directly towards us as if floating effortlessly down from the Hall towards the well and the bank directly opposite us.

Horlicks screamed, "Told you so!" followed by Trev screaming, "Bloody hell, its Peg O' Nell!"

Despite the fact that there was an expanse of river between us didn't do anything to abate our worst fears that we were about to come face to face with the ghostly spectre of old Peg herself as she glided silently across the misty moonlit water to pick out her next victim. I remember myself, Trev and Pat pushing Horlicks to the front muttering nervous and barely coherent ramblings about how long it had been since she was reputed to have claimed her last victim and, to make matters worse, we didn't even have a sacrificial chicken to save us!! We just stood there, eyes agape like rabbits caught in the headlights of an oncoming car, entranced by this thing that was getting closer and closer to the far bank and the water's edge.

All of a sudden a voice interrupted our trance like state with, "We'll soon find out if it's a ghost or not!" followed by an almighty bang and a flash as Pat, now back to logical thinking, let off his dads old 410 shotgun in the general direction of old Peg.

As lead shot, not quite reaching the far bank, plopped

one by one into the water, old Peg did an about turn with her dark ghostly shadow last seen off like the clappers zig zagging back up the grassy hill towards Waddow Hall! Had it been a 12 bore she, or whoever it was, would have been picking lead shot out of their backside for some time!! Needless to say she never attempted to gate crash our all night fishing parties again! But I digress, back to the lapwing and my dad's greenhouse.

One day I was at one of my favourite haunts, the local sewerage farm of all places. It's main attraction being that it was a haven for wildlife with moorhens scuttling through the marshy pools, grey and pied wagtails flitting from stone to stone bobbing their tails and lapwings (peewits) tumbling and twisting overhead giving off their distinctive calls of "peer-wit, pee-wit, weep." I first spotted the lapwing as it stumbled over the shingle beds dragging one of its wings along the ground. Lapwings are ground nesting birds laying their stone to buff coloured eggs, tinted with browns and olives in shallow scrapes amongst gravel or stone and will often feign injury including a broken wing in an attempt to lure a predator away from the nest site. But this one seemed to be genuinely injured and in need of attention, its feathers were soiled and grubby and it looked exhausted as it struggled to get away. Capture was easy; it put up a half-hearted attempt at escape but eventually just lay there on its side staring up at me with a mixture of fear and trepidation.

I gently picked it up ignoring its feeble attempts at pecking my hand and wrapping it in my jacket ran across the fields back home. Here I was able to take a closer look and soon came to the conclusion that the wing was broken, it was also very thin with its breast bone sharply protruding through the feathers. I wasn't quite sure what I could do to help the poor bird but remembered having read somewhere that the best treatment for a broken wing was to strap it to the bird's side for a few weeks and all would be well. After rummaging through my mums cupboards and kitchen drawers, I found some bandage and a roll of Elastoplast. Armed with my medical kit I proceeded to place the wing in its normal resting position and strapped it to its body. Much to my surprise, it took all this manhandling totally in its stride as if somehow realising that I meant it no harm and was soon tucking into a dish of freshly dug earthworms. The next problem was where to keep it?

Dad's greenhouse seemed to be the ideal place, it had a natural earth floor that was home to a wide variety of worms, bugs and other insects and with a little persuasion he finally consented to it having free range of his beloved inner sanctum. And so it came to pass that my very first wildlife patient spent its weeks of recuperation in my dad's greenhouse feeding happily on a diet of earthworms and anything else it could find. It made a comical sight as it slowly flitted between the tomato plants and geraniums. Eyes transfixed downwards with crest held high, it would pause for a second, rather like an African Secretary Bird stalking a snake on the African plains, and then suddenly it would plunge its bill into the soft fertile soil to emerge with its prize, a long slimy worm! I watched with wonder as it patrolled between the plants with the sun filtering through the dusty cobweb clustered panes highlighting its beautiful green plumage.

The bird gained weight quickly and at long last it was time to remove the strapping. I slowly peeled away the by now very grubby bit of Elastoplast and bandage that had served to keep the wing held firmly by its side. It came off quite easily albeit with bits of feather stuck to it but nothing too drastic. Once the strapping was off, I placed the bird on the floor and watched with trepidation as it looked around, walked a few paces, gave a good shake of its feathers and proceeded to preen the injured wing. It looked good; it was still drooping slightly but looked much better. After another a week of feeding, bathing and preening it looked much stronger as it jumped up and down with flapping wings and to my delight was soon taking a few short flights around the greenhouse.

The time had come and to my dad's relief release was imminent. The following weekend I was legging it across the fields towards the sewerage farm clutching my now mended patient to my chest eager to release it back from whence it came. I carefully placed it down onto the shingle bed close to where I had found it. It looked around for a few seconds and then set off like the clappers only to vanish into the reeds without so much as a thank you or a final goodbye wave of a wing! I never gave a thought as to whether it could really fly or not, I just it took it for granted that it could. As far as I was concerned, it was mended, its eyes were bright and shiny, its plumage looked fine and it had put on loads of weight and in my naivety that was good enough for me. Dad wasn't going to argue; he was master of his own domain once more and could carry on with the business of tending his tomatoes without tripping over an indignant lapwing and sliding around on bird poo.

I missed my patient, the greenhouse now seemed strangely empty and I missed not having a creature to care for. But I needn't have worried for very soon patient number two was waiting in the wings so to speak. A jackdaw that appeared to have flown into something was soon to be the benefactor of my new-found skills. No greenhouse for this black beauty, my dad had reclaimed his pride and joy and he wasn't going to relinquish it again so easily a second time around. What was I to do? Another patient in need of my expertise and no facilities!

The problem was soon solved; I acquired a large old parrot cage rescued from the local council rubbish dump. It was custom built for a needy jackdaw, but where to put it? Mum, bless her, took pity on me and allowed my jackdaw, incarcerated in its rather dilapidated cage to take pride of place in the living room.

Unfortunately this arrangement wasn't to last too long before once again I was to be subjected to cries of, "Malcolm! Will you please do something about that blessed bird?"

All members of the Corvid family are renowned for their intelligence and my jackdaw was no exception and he very quickly became adept at opening the cage door and taking himself walkabout or, in his case, fly about around the Ingham household. The final straw came one day when, upon returning home from school, I discovered mum frantically trying to entice my beloved jackdaw back into its cage. Finally, after umpteen laps of the living room and much raucous screaming (from both the bird and my mum) he was rugby tackled and banished once more into the security of his parrot cage. The living room was a mess; it looked as though World War Three had just taken place. There were shiny black feathers floating sedately back to earth, broken ornaments lay about the floor and the settee looked as though it had fallen foul to some ghastly disease with great spots of black and white jackdaw poo intermingled within the floral pattern. Needless to say release number two was about to take place! This time my patient was only too eager to fly the coop and flew off over the roof tops without a second glance, glad to be free from the restraints of its old rusty parrot cage.

The years that were to follow brought many other pressing priorities into my life but my interest in wildlife never lay dormant for very long. Occasionally some circumstance would find me briefly once more caring for some injured creature whether it is a humble sparrow, pigeon or magpie. My fascination with wildlife tended to grow rather than diminish with time and during my latter years at school my only real interest was the countryside and wildlife and I knew from an early age that that was how I wanted to earn my living. I was very fortunate to have been allowed the freedom to explore the countryside by my home. It was a natural part of my life and I was always at my happiest when fishing in the river or stream or exploring the fields and woods.

One of my fondest and most vivid memories is of walking along the banks of a narrow overgrown canal known locally as the 'cut'. It was in fact an old mill race that began its life at a large wooden sluice gate above the weir on the River Ribble at Brungerly by Waddow Hall. It was originally constructed in early Victorian times to supply water from the river to power the great iron water wheels of the now long gone cotton mill at Low Moor village on the outskirts of town. Now its banks were overgrown with willow, alder and reeds, it's still dark waters home to an abundance of wildlife from giant eels to water vole, moorhen, coot, heron and kingfisher.

I was going fishing, and whilst walking along the bank of the 'cut' towards the weir, a heron silently and gracefully took off from the reed beds, its great grey wings carrying it across the weir to the far river bank. I heard the distinctive plop of a water vole as it entered the water but I wasn't prepared for what I saw next. An otter! It was on the edge of a reed bed by the big damp moss covered wooden sluice gate. I remember it vividly to this day my eyes wide open in wonderment frozen to the spot with fishing rod in hand hardly daring to breath as I stared in awe at this mysterious creature that previously I had only ever seen pictures of in my well-thumbed copy of *The Observers Book of Wild Animals*. Standing upright with its broad flat head with small dark eyes staring back at me I was transfixed, it was as though everything around me had stopped and fallen silent. Eventually after what seemed an age the spell was broken as it slid gracefully and silently into the depths of the dark deep water leaving nothing but a trail of bubbles popping up to the surface as it went. I would watch salmon as they struggled to make their way through the white foaming rapids to the concrete salmon steps that helped them to negotiate the fast flowing waters to the top of the weir and on to their spawning grounds.

I listened intently as the local Clitheroe characters related tales of the many mysterious and unbelievable sights they claimed to have witnessed by various nocturnal creatures whilst out poaching rabbit with long nets and running dogs, or casting nightlines for sea trout and salmon.

One of the more famous Clitheroe characters was a gentleman by the name of Royal King who had departed this world in the early 1950s but whose name still lived on and was synonymous with local wildlife and folklore.

Royal King was his real name, his parents being either very royalist or had a strange sense of humour; I'm not quite sure which. He was the uncle of a friend and also a relation of a step uncle of mine. I can remember as a 10 or 11-year-old visiting his widow's cottage situated on the edge of town. It was a place of absolute wonder and mystery! I would sit at the old scrubbed pine kitchen table and gaze around the room in awe at the assortment of stuffed animals and birds staring out from their old display cases. I remember being allowed to hold an enormous ostrich egg and feeling the soft velvet fur of moleskins and staring in awe at all the other strange animal orientated paraphernalia that seemed to be everywhere you looked. Fox, badger and otter heads with grotesquely over exaggerated savage expressions upon their faces mounted on wooden plaques hanging on the walls. Despite their fearful appearance I hoped one day to be able to see these creatures for myself, not dead with heads mounted upon a wall, but alive and living free in the wild. The outside was festooned with a conglomeration of hen pens, pigsties and various other assortments of sheds and enclosures that had at one time been home to a variety of domestic and wild creatures including badgers. His widow still kept a few chickens and some fearsome looking turkeys that would emit a guttural "gobble, gobble, gobble" as they came charging at you from across the cobbled yard. Once again, this experience only served to feed my fascination with wild creatures and the mysteries and wonders of nature.

Many years later I was given a copy of his obituary from the local paper the 'Clitheroe Advertiser and Times.' It read as follows: - 'Like Mowgli in the Jungle Book and Androcles of the Bible, Royal King had a strange affinity for animals but, unlike them, he was as much a killer as a friend. Some he cherished; others he hounded with cunning matching that of his prey. He bred mice, ferrets, goats, pigs, terriers and even owls. He exhibited bantams and trained one to do amusing tricks. But most of all he was known for his hunting; especially rats. In one year he accounted for

5,000 of them. Nearly all of Royal Kings life was spent in the fields and woods of Ribblesdale and Bowland. Many of his weekends were spent hunting badgers or moles; he would make waistcoats and belts out the pelts out of the latter.'

The obituary concludes with, 'Today the East Lancashire countryside lost its most colourful character.' It included a photograph entitled – 'Royal King with an outsize rat he caught in the Ribble Valley.' It depicted him holding up by the tail a very large rat-like animal that was in fact not a rat at all but a Coypu, a large South American rodent sometimes farmed in England for their pelts. Some are known to have either escaped or been released, but these were mainly on the fens of Norfolk, not Lancashire!

The years went by and other priorities and events other than wildlife took up my time with the most notable of these being the evening I met Ann, my wife to be. That evening myself and my old fishing mate, Patrick of Peg O' Nell and 410 shotgun fame were loitering around the gates of Clitheroe Castle in the town centre trying to decide which lucky hostelry would next have the pleasure of our company. Ann and a friend walked by and rather than grace another pub with our presence we decided instead to practise our chat up lines and the rest is history! We eventually married and before too long our two sons Derek and Gary came along, but the passion for wildlife was never very far away and it only took a spark to re-ignite it once again.

One such spark came one October evening as we were driving along a narrow country lane on the outskirts of the centuries old picturesque village of Bolton-by-Bowland tucked away deep within the ancient Forest of Bowland. Once a royal hunting ground and now designated an 'Area of Outstanding Natural Beauty' and noted for its herd of wild Japanese Sika deer. Dusk was falling and we were hoping to catch a glimpse of them as they left the cover of the woodland to come out to feed in the open fields. The rutting season was well underway and the stags were full of themselves constantly groaning, whistling and challenging each other for dominance. We were slowly driving along; eyes scanning the fields in the hope of catching a glimpse of them silhouetted against the skyline in the rapidly fading light when suddenly a large stag bounded over the fence and into the path of the car. As I stopped and caught him in the headlights he turned and purposely walked towards us finally stopping only a few inches from the front bumper whereupon he proceeded to paw the ground whilst shaking his head and tossing his huge antlers from side to side. He looked magnificent, the absolute epitome of strength and wildness! Suddenly our little Austin Mini seemed very small indeed! We sat there totally in awe of this imposing beast until he decided that he had intimidated us sufficiently and were now duly respectful of his presence and with one last toss of his head and a snort he leapt over the hedge to vanish once more into the night.

We were actually on our way to visit some friends who rented an old farmhouse a few miles outside Bolton-by-Bowland. The house was set quite a way up from the road and accessible only by a long potholed track that meandered its way through rough damp pasture interspersed with small patches of woodland of twisted oaks, rowan, birch and pine. The land was poor and farmed mainly for sheep and beef cattle with the odd horse or pony intermingled amongst them.

This was the land of the curlew, lapwing, hare, fox, roe and sika deer. It was classic hunting country. If you didn't hunt, shoot or fish you were considered to be rather abnormal and missing out on the pleasures of life. Hunting took on many forms, from coursing hare with long dogs up on the rough pastures to the traditional hunting of the fox. This was carried out on foot with hounds along the bracken-covered hills or on horseback through the more fertile lowlands of the valley and woods, whilst the terrier men would dig out fox and badger from their earths and setts. Poachers would take the game fish from the rivers. The Kendal & District Otter Hounds would travel south from their home at Dallam Tower, Milnthorpe to hunt the waters of the Hodder and Ribble. The farmer would be out shooting rabbits and crows whilst the gamekeepers shot, trapped or snared any creature they considered a threat to their pheasants or grouse.

Our friends fitted in well, they bought and sold horses which they would break in for riding or train them to the harness to pull a gig around the narrow lanes. Once broken in they would either be sold on at the annual gipsy horse fair in Appleby in Cumberland or the Clitheroe horse sales.

Once a month the cattle market in the centre of town would be taken over by horse dealers from far and wide who would show off their horses and ponies to prospective buyers by riding them bareback or pulling sulkies at speed up and down the adjacent road. (Sulkies are a light two-wheeled horse drawn vehicle used mainly in trotting races.) Most deals were sealed by a spit in the palm of the hand followed by a handshake and the exchange of a large wad of notes.

Occasionally whilst at our friends we would be offered the chance to put a horse through its paces by riding it bareback through the rough pastures. On one occasion I was riding our Arab cross thoroughbred mare bareback whereupon after jumping across a wide gulley and reaching the other side decided that she was bored with my company and proceeded to try and unseat me. I was thrown about like some rodeo rider much to the amusement of Ann and our friends but I managed to retain my dignity and stay on - but only just! Other times I would leap cowboy style onto a horse from behind, how I managed not to be propelled onto the house roof by an almighty kick I don't know!

The farm consisted of a wide assortment of outbuildings from old pigsties to stables with an even wider assortment of animals living amongst them. Chickens and peacocks roamed freely around the place whilst various breeds of dog from terriers to collies barked at you excitedly from the old pigsties now serving as their kennels, whilst the ever-present collection of horses and ponies grazed in the fields or peered at you from over their old stable doors. On more than one occasion, I would walk into one of the outbuildings to be confronted by the result of a successful nights poaching. This was usually in the form of a pheasant or hare but on one occasion it was a sika deer hind hanging by its hind legs from the beam hooks. Its stomach was cut wide open with its bloody and twisted intestines gruesomely sitting in a bowl on the floor, a practise known as gralloching which was meant to stop the meat from spoiling. Not a pretty sight! On another occasion, there was even a fighting cock complete with spurs strutting around in a wooden crate. With a wink and a nod I was told that the bird was a prize-fighter and worth a bob or two. Bullocks would peer at you through the window above the kitchen sink whilst a canary would sing its little heart out from within its cage hanging from a beam above the fireplace. The terriers were used for fox or badger digging, usually both. It was through these people that Ann and I saw our very first badger cub, it was being kept in a small concrete enclosure at a farm a couple of miles away. It had been taken from the wild during a badger dig with the intention of keeping it as a pet. I remember us both being enthralled by the sight of it but at the same time feeling very sorry for it and wanting to help but not knowing how. I doubt very much that it survived for long all alone and incarcerated in its alien concrete environment. Little did we know then what lay in store for us years ahead and the joys and sorrows we would have with badgers; my friend often told me that he never actually killed a badger. He would, he said, respond to a farmers request to remove them from the land by digging them out with dogs and spades only to release them again elsewhere.

Royal King was very similar; he hunted badger and yet kept badgers as so-called pets, with one of his females even giving birth to cubs. A copy of a 1949 magazine entitled 'The Animals Friends Magazine' had a photograph of him proudly holding a dead boar badger by the scruff of the neck whilst another depicted him bottle-feeding a cub.

These people didn't consider themselves cruel or heartless; on the contrary, they regarded themselves as animal lovers. Their lives revolved around animals whether it is hunting them for so-called sport, for the pot, as pets, or for making a quick bob or two. It didn't really matter which so long as their lives revolved around animals. Theirs was a life entwined around old country ways and travelling people, it was a life chosen by choice and devastating when brought to a sudden end by circumstances beyond their control.

Little did our friends realise just how devastating this could be until one day they were informed that their home was to be sold and as they had no formal tenancy agreement purely a verbal one and a shake of the hand, their way of life was about to change dramatically. They eventually bought a small terraced house in Clitheroe situated on a main road with their only access to land being a small narrow garden with a shed. They found it difficult to adapt and for some time spent their weekends living in a converted Sherpa van on a country lane within sight of their old farm. However, being ever resilient, their garden shed was converted into a small stable and a horse was purchased which was tethered on waste ground during the day and housed in the converted shed at night. Ann and I went round one day with Guy our Welsh cob and without the slightest hesitation they took us, (us being Ann, me and Guy the pony!) through the hallway, into the living room and out through the kitchen into the tiny garden to look at their shed-come-stable and their new horse. In time, they let go and reluctantly settled into town life but they were never quite the same people again. Knowing them and experiencing a little of their way of life is an experience I would not have wanted to have missed. I may not have agreed with, or have wanted to participate in all of it, but they were not bad or cruel people. At the opposite end of the spectrum are the real cruel and callous individuals I would later encounter who took great pleasure in inflicting pain and suffering on any animal, wild or otherwise.

Over the years I have had the displeasure of coming into

contact with more than my fair share of them, particularly badger diggers and baiters, but I have also had the great pleasure of acting as expert witness for the prosecution on many occasions and taken great delight in seeing them found guilty and given a custodial sentence. The look of horror and disbelief on their faces when they are handcuffed and taken away is worth every hour of unrelenting defence cross-examination. But all of this was yet to come.

One individual in particular was well known around the Ribble Valley for his digging exploits. He worked as a factory foreman from Monday to Friday and was an avid and zealously cruel badger digger in his free time. He and his equally sadistic cronies would travel many miles into the counties of Cheshire and beyond to carry out their sickening pastime. No matter where the venue one thing was certain, it was going to be a spectacle of unadulterated bloody terror for the badger and quite often the dogs themselves faired not much better. The badger in his single minded attempt at survival will fight to the death whilst the gutsy little Lakeland and Patterdale terriers, egged on by their masters laughing and jeering above them, enters the badgers labyrinth of tunnels and chambers time and time again to do battle with this formidable adversary. Eventually dog and badger come face to face, the badger with nowhere to go, has no choice but to fight for his life. The men above, on hearing the snarls and excited barking of the dogs dig down with spades and picks into the badgers retreat. Finally, the digging over, the gutsy and bloody little terrier is hoisted free from the now exposed chamber. Next comes out old brock, his coat caked with dirt and blood, exhausted and injured but with still a flame of spirited defiance keeping the spark of life going within him, suffering the final indignity as he is held firmly by the tail whilst his skull is crushed with the blows of a spade.

Both badger and dogs would suffer terrible injuries and regardless of where this spectacle of sadistic debauchery took place, the outcome would be the same, death! The only exception to this would be if they wanted a live badger for a badger baiting session. Then old brock is taken, albeit injured but alive and kept at a secret location until the day came when he is thrown into a pit or some other inescapable enclosure. There dogs would be entered, sometimes two or three at a time whilst their masters goad them on and take bets on whose dog will fare the best. The atmosphere is tense and noisy with much shouting, laughing and cheering, dogs barking furiously and the sickening smell of blood intermingled with cigarette smoke and ale. Finally after many hours of torture the badger is dead. His bloody torn carcase is either dumped by the side of the road to look like road kill or just left somewhere to rot. Some of the dogs will have suffered terrible injuries themselves and either be crudely stitched up by their owners or just disposed of. Even if the badger is spared the horrific ordeal of a baiting session, his fate is still a prolonged slow painful death. These people have no respect for man or beast, as far as they are concerned the countryside is there simply for them to carry out their sadistic bloodthirsty pleasures.

These experiences only served to strengthen my resolve to work within the countryside, not to kill wildlife and destroy habitats through disregard and ignorance, but to conserve and in some way if possible to fight against the badger diggers and other like-minded individuals who viewed the countryside purely as a means of satisfying their cruel pleasures. As yet I had no idea as to how that might be possible or how to go about it!

I had left Ribblesdale Secondary School with no qualifications other than what my fifteen years of life of living in the Ribble Valley and its countryside had given me. I remember vividly my school careers officer asking me what job I might be considering upon leaving the inner sanctum of Ribblesdale Secondary School. I told him that I wanted to work in conservation and with wildlife to which he replied rather abruptly that my chances of doing any such thing were virtually impossible and I should consider something more realistic!

Chapter Two
From Dunsop and a Whistling Fox to Wirral

I had tried my hand at a number of jobs since leaving school including an apprentice painter and decorator, my mum's idea not mine! I had no interest whatsoever in being a painter and decorator. I remember turning up on my first day wearing pristine white bib and brace overalls feeling like a fish out of water. I endured two years of painting, slapping paste onto the back of wallpaper and suffering raw finger tips from sanding down old paintwork, not to mention the feeling of complete nausea whilst travelling in the back of the bosses Austin 45 van amidst a variety of paint cans and other decorating paraphernalia while he puffed away merrily on his pipe.

I would emerge from this fetid smoke filled tin can on wheels amidst a cloud of blue smoke, green at the gills and smelling strongly of a mixture of Old Condor pipe tobacco and paint. Not a good combination! The only respite from this dreary existence was my one-day a week attendance at the Accrington College of Art as part of my apprenticeship. Actually there was more messing about done than any serious work and a group of us probably spent more time in the 60's era café round the corner drinking frothy coffee and blasting out Beatles and Rolling Stones tunes on the juke box. Finally, I could endure no more and persuaded my dad to get me a job at his place of work, the Limmer & Trinidad Asphalt Works situated on the outskirts of town.

It had the unenviable reputation for being a place of hard men and equally hard work but at least it was outdoors. The job consisted of being one of a two-man team loading heavy asphalt blocks onto the back of flat backed wagons. We each had to lift and throw a square solid block of asphalt weighing around 55 lbs onto the back of the wagon until it had reached its designated load which was usually around

10 to 20 tons with each wagon having to be loaded as quickly as possible; otherwise you had a backlog of impatient wagon drivers waiting their turn.

On my first day my loading partner, a stocky guy with the strength of a cart horse gave me these reassuring words, "This is hard graft, and I'm not working for two, I'll pull you through for a week then you're on your own."

Thankfully after a few weeks of aching muscles and calloused hands I soon got into the job and even enjoyed it. It certainly beat sitting in the back of a smoke contaminated Austin A45 van every day!

I also did a stint in the Territorial Army which occasionally took me to Devizes in Wiltshire or to the wilds of Scotland on training exercises. Scotland was my favourite, I enjoyed being out on night manoeuvres and tramping around the Scottish hills, it brought back happy memories of my days as a kid spending nights on Pendle Hill looking for the infamous 'Malkin Tower'. We would be dropped off at various locations in small groups, cap badges removed along with anything else that might reflect light or give away information if caught and with faces all camouflaged, off we would go to spy on the enemy. Our brief was to cross into enemy territory under cover of darkness and gather information on their positions and any other intelligence that we may come across and, of course, the all-important not to be seen or captured. We would lie low during the day and sneak around in twos and threes after dark. This would go on for a couple of days or so before heading back to a pick up point to be taken back to camp for a debrief followed by a hot drink and much needed shower.

I remember vividly one dark night myself and another chap stumbled upon enemy HQ. I say stumbled! You couldn't really miss it! It was a large camouflaged army tent lit up like Blackpool illuminations with Tilley paraffin lamps burning away all over the place. We watched, hidden in the heather as various enemy big wigs (The Red Team) came and went. We were so close that we could even hear snatches of conversation as they discussed battle tactics.

The temptation to go in and capture them was almost overwhelming as we whispered, "Just think of it! The two of us capturing enemy HQ all on our very own, we would be the heroes of Blue Team." (That was us, the goodies!)

"We could have all their maps and battle plans plus the odd Major or two and perhaps even a General if we're lucky!"

We had the element of surprise on our side: they hadn't a clue we were there, we could lob in a few fire cracker flares and go charging in shouting and hollering, "Hands up the lot you, the games over for you sirs, hand over those maps."

It was a nice thought while it lasted! But the reality of the situation slowly dawned upon us that we there just to observe and report back, not to play the hero. Apart from that there was just the two of us and at least a dozen of them and to complicate matters even more they were all senior NCO's and officers and we would have got an almighty rollicking for not playing fair! At least we had the consolation of knowing their location and we hadn't been caught!

It was all good fun but one unforgettable occasion brought it home to us that we weren't playing war games just for the fun of it when one night we were suddenly and unexpectedly shaken from our slumbers in the early hours. All of a sudden there was an air of seriousness and urgency, gone was the usual barrack room banter as we were ordered to get dressed and make our way to a particular building as quickly as possible. As the clatter of boots made their way across the parade ground and entered the building, we were told to line up in an orderly fashion and ask no questions.

Eventually our orderly if not totally silent queue began to shuffle along, firstly to a table where a medic armed with an impressive array of syringes and bottles barked, "Roll your sleeve up," whereupon he proceeded to fill a number of syringes from his collection of bottles only to empty them again in our now exposed arms.

At the end of the line and with arms red and stinging, we

were then ushered one by one into a small office at which point, a Warrant Officer thrust various official looking papers into our hands followed by, "Sit yourself down there and fill these in, make sure you sign each one and hand them in to the Sergeant as you leave."

One guy, as he took the forms enquired, "What's going on, Sir?" The reply was simply, "Don't worry, it will all be explained shortly, now move on."

The forms requested name, rank and army number plus details of next of kin etc. with the final one being a last will and testament. With forms duly signed we were then marched off to the quartermasters store and armoury to be kitted out, after which we were told that we were now on full alert and a complete briefing would be given only if, and when, deployment became imminent. Thankfully, deployment never came and after 24 hours of mixed emotions from eager anticipation to the fear of the unknown we were finally stood down. A few days later we were informed that the exercise was over and I was soon travelling south again to Clitheroe. We were told nothing more about the possible deployment or what it would have involved; we could only assume that we would have been sneaking around after dark in some foreign land trying not to be caught.

I was soon back at my full-time job at Limmer & Trinidad and even though it was hard physical work and out in all weathers, I enjoyed it, but rumours were floating around that its days may be numbered and closure could be looming around the corner. I now had a family to provide for and needed to find something else to do and quickly, but what? Working in conservation was still my ultimate goal, but how? It seemed an impossible dream and I was beginning to think that my school careers officer might have been right after all and maybe I should resign myself to spending my life doing what was considered to be a normal job for a working class lad from a council estate. Was ditching my apprenticeship as a painter & decorator a wise decision after all? At least I would have had a trade behind me; somebody always needed their living room decorated! As it was, I had nothing to fall back on other than labouring or factory work and began to scan the vacant jobs column in the local paper.

One day I spotted an advert for a process worker come laboratory assistant in a plastics laminating factory. It was a million miles away from working at Limmer but it was only a five-minute walk from home and the money was good. I duly applied and much to my surprise, I got the job! Little did I realise then that fate had just taken pity on me and was about to put me on the first rung of the conservation ladder.

One of my main duties was quality control and one morning as I walked into the laboratory, one the of the girls handed me a copy of the Clitheroe Advertiser & Times followed by, "There's a job in there Malcolm that's just up your street, Lancashire County Council are advertising for volunteer rangers, just suit you down to the ground!"

I eagerly scanned the advert, which gave a brief description of what they were looking for and the telephone number of the Head Ranger, a Mr J. Peel. But my heart sank when I spotted the closing date, it was two days ago! What the heck I thought, ring him anyway, he can only say, "Sorry you're too late!" I dialled the number there and then, no answer! I tried again a few hours later, still no answer! A week later and I was still trying and still no answer!! By now I was pretty convinced that I had no chance at all of getting one of the posts. I was even beginning to wonder if the Head Ranger even existed and was merely a fictional character dreamt up by some sadistic entity purely to build up my hopes only to take great pleasure in seeing them dashed to nothing! But I persisted and eventually my perseverance paid off when at long last someone actually picked up the receiver.

"Hello is that Mr Peel the L.C.C. Head Ranger?" I enquired.

"Yes it is, "What can I do for you?"

I explained that I wished to apply for one of the volunteer ranger posts also explaining that I had been trying to get hold of him for over a week.

"Ha, I've been on holiday, this is my first day back in work, I'm sorry but the closing date has been and gone and we now have our full quota."

My heart sank once again!

"Can you not take one more? I really would love to do this," I pleaded. There was an ominous silence at the other end of the line.

Finally he said, "Where do you live?"

"Clitheroe," I replied.

He responded with a few more questions before saying, "What are you doing this Sunday?"

My heart jumped a beat, was he going to relent? "Nothing in particular," I replied.

"Ok," he said, "Do you know Quernmore?"

"No," I replied resisting the temptation to say never heard of it!

"Right, have you got a pen handy?"

"Yes," I replied.

"Ok, write this down."

He then proceeded to give me an eight-figure grid reference after which he said. "Be there at 9 am sharp and be prepared for a day on the moors."

End of conversation!

That evening I scanned my Ordinance Survey map and worked out the grid reference. It led me through the Trough of Bowland and down a single track lane leading into Quernmore car park at the foot of the wide expanse of wild moorland above Lancaster.

Sunday finally arrived; I was up bright and early, my rucksack was brimming with all the necessary items ready for a day's hill walking. I double checked the contents one last time, waterproofs, check! Map and compass, check! Flask and butties check! Satisfied that I was duly equipped I was on my way at last. The morning was fine and clear with high wispy clouds as I drove out of Clitheroe and headed over Waddington Fell towards the Trough of Bowland. The weather was perfect. I was looking forward to my day on the moors and if everything went well I could be putting my foot on the very first of many rungs of that long ladder to achieving my ambition. It was a pleasant drive as I passed through the tiny rural villages of Waddington, Newton and Dunsop Bridge with the latter leading me into the Trough of Bowland with its winding narrow road meandering its way over the heather clad fells. Before long I was driving over the highest point of my journey overlooking the city of Lancaster and Morecambe Bay. I drove down a steep winding hill to the village of Quernmore where I took a right turn on to a single-track winding lane.

After a couple of miles, I finally drove into the small potholed car park and found the awaiting, if not illusive Mr J. Peel. He was casually leaning against a pale blue Land Rover adorned with a large roof-rack decorated with a couple of long handled fire-beaters attached to either side of it and at the front, a large official looking sign stating, 'Lancashire County Council Countryside Ranger.' I couldn't help but think to myself, 'That could be me one day!'

As I parked up and began to unload my rucksack and boots he wandered over to greet me and with a wry smile shook my hand followed by the words, "Can I just check your gear? Need to be sure you're properly equipped, never know what the weather's going to be up there."

He then proceeded to go through the contents of my rucksack, gave a few enquiring glances at my attire and fired a few questions at me. He appeared to be duly satisfied that I was reasonably well equipped and with a "Right follow me," proceeded to climb a ladder stile on to a narrow winding path that climbed steadily up on to the moorland meandering its way through tall straggly heather and dark expanses of peat bog. The minute his boots touched the ground he was off like a rabbit with a ferret at its backside! After a couple of hours of rapid pace and breathless conversation he stopped and said, "Ok son time for a butty," as he proceeded to take off his rucksack.

It was a bright clear day and as we sat in the heather

eating our sandwiches the view over Lancaster and beyond to Morecambe Bay was stunning, you could even make out the distant peaks of the Lake District. Between taking lumps out of his sandwich he fired more questions at me and explained that if taken on I would be expected to take a rigorous eight-week course in navigation culminating in a written exam, plus a practical navigation test on the moors in poor weather, if it could be arranged! After which, with one last gulp of coffee he proceeded to don his rucksack and off we went once again finally arriving back at the car park some hours later.

He took off his rucksack and as he unceremoniously tossed it into the back of his Land Rover said, "Well I suppose one more volunteer won't go amiss, not all make it through the course anyway. You will get conformation in the post along with the course details," whereupon he jumped in his Land Rover and sped off leaving a cloud of car park dust swirling behind him.

As I drove home through the rugged Bowland scenery, face glowing from the sun and legs a little weary, I was ecstatic! I had got my foot on the very first rung of the ladder, I was a ranger! Albeit a volunteer, but a ranger none the less and I would build on this. I was on my way at last!

The following week an envelope bearing the Lancashire County Council logo popped through the letterbox. I quickly tore it open to reveal a letter confirming my appointment and that I was booked to attend the Ranger Training Course at Beacon Fell Country Park at 9.30 am the following Sunday morning. After what seemed an age of anticipation Sunday finally arrived and I found myself sat in the lecture theatre at the Beacon Fell Country Park Visitor Centre along with about a dozen other new volunteers all sat around an assortment of tables and chairs arranged to face the front of the room. The Head Ranger welcomed everyone to the course and introduced us to the three full-time rangers who would be assisting him, followed by explaining that everyone would be expected to attend all the classes and be fully committed to the course after which, if we passed, equally committed to the role of Lancashire County Council Volunteer Ranger Service.

It was a fairly intense course focusing very much on advanced navigation plus radio and emergency procedure with a smattering of mountain rescue thrown in for good measure. The weeks flew by and before I knew it, it was assessment time; we were given a short written exam consisting of various questions covering all the elements of the course followed by a full-day practical navigation test on the moors. This was carried out individually rather than in a group and assessed by either the Head Ranger or one of the full-time rangers. Finally, my day of reckoning arrived and my assessor turned out to be none other than Mr J. Peel himself, just my luck I thought! He had a reputation for being a bit of a stickler and not allowing much leeway for error and so once again I found myself on the remote Quernmore car park and true to his word he'd arranged the weather as promised with a thick damp mist enveloping the hills above. I couldn't help but think, 'Mess this up and I'm gone!'

But any thoughts of doom and gloom were soon interrupted as he said, "Right lad, here's where you're on your own," as he handed me a small weather proof O.S. map, a two way radio with my call sign, Lima 1, plus a piece of paper with an eight figure grid reference written upon it.

He went on to explain that before setting off I needed to find my present position on the map and using the grid reference work out my route, which should lead me to a six-inch high wooden stake hidden way up there in the heather amid the swirling mist and peat bogs. Attached to the stake would be a clear plastic envelope containing a second piece of paper with another grid reference. So it went on until after several grid references later I should eventually arrive at my pick up point some ten miles away in the far valley. I would be expected to note down all my navigation calculations with routes taken from one point to the next, along with any detours made due to unforeseen obstacles etc. The map, along with calculations had to be handed in at the end where they would be scrutinised for accuracy to determine if luck had played any part in my journey across the misty moors. At around the halfway point I would make radio contact stating the time and my position with an eight-figure grid reference after which I would be allowed a 30-minute break for butties. I would make radio contact once again just prior to restarting giving the time and my intended direction. If I had not arrived at my pick up point by 17.00 hours I would be allowed an extra 30 minutes after which I would be contacted by radio and if I could not give my exact position would be deemed lost and in need of rescue. Even just being out of time could mean failure due to you being considered not totally proficient in your navigation or simply not fit enough. The thought of that alone was bad enough, but to be rescued as well!! That wasn't even worth contemplating!

At last, the briefing was over and I was off, I had worked out my route and headed off into the mist, compass and map in hand, carefully pacing out my steps and distance. Some thirty minutes later I came across the first of my many six-inch stakes well and truly hidden in the heather. I quickly retrieved my second grid reference, plotted my route and was off again. By the time I had reached the halfway point, the mist was even thicker with visibility down to no more than a couple of metres at the most and getting worse. Eventually I came across a large rocky outcrop and decided that it would be a good spot for my break.

I checked my position and proceeded to radio it through, "Lima 1 to Lima 2, do you receive, over?"

No reply! I tried again, "Lima 1 to Lima 2, do you receive, over?"

At last through the static came the crackly voice of Mr Peel. "Receiving Lima 1, what's your position, over?"

With formalities out of the way, I sat myself down in the heather and with back against the boulder proceeded to munch away on my butties and have a welcome hot drink. Suddenly I thought I heard a noise. All was deathly quiet up there in the mist, but there it was again. I peered towards where the sound seemed to have come from, I couldn't see anything other than the damp, cold mist swirling around like thick pea soup then all of a sudden I could just make out what appeared to be a figure emerging.

I sat there very quietly as Mr J. Peel like some ghostly spectre of the moors emerged from the mist. He stopped briefly no more than a couple of metres from me and with compass in hand checked his bearings; he looked around for a few moments as if looking for something before setting off again. I watched as his figure was soon enveloped in mist once more and then he was gone. He'd been no more than a couple of metres from me and I couldn't help but smile to myself as I thought, 'the crafty so and so is trying to keep tabs on me.' With butties scoffed, I donned my rucksack and made crackly radio contact with the ghostly Mr Peel once more before setting off again on the second leg of my trail. Around ten miles and countless grid references later I eventually made it to the pick-up point in plenty of time and was able to enjoy the last of my butties while waiting for my lift back.

Ten minutes later I heard the distinctive sound of a Land Rover as it came bouncing up the track and as I sat myself down the ranger enquired as to how my day had been followed by, "Let's get you back, the lord and master is waiting for you."

Thirty or so minutes later and we arrived back at the car park and the waiting Mr Peel.

"Well son, how do you think you have done?" He asked.

"I've enjoyed it, and I think I did ok."

"Well we'll soon find out, let's have your map and calculations."

The following day I was informed that I had passed and was now officially a volunteer countryside ranger! He never did let on that he'd also been up there and due to the fact that he hadn't come across me probably assumed that I had gone off track somewhere but recalculated and got back on course. I also thought it tactful to keep quiet over the fact that he'd walked closely by within a couple of metres of me without knowing it! I did wonder though that once he had worked out my route calculations, along with my radio position and timings, he must have realised that he had been very close to me during my butty stop. If he did, he kept it to himself.

Anyway, I passed and was soon on the weekend rota for patrolling the moorland access areas around Bowland and experiencing the hills in all their moods, from hot sunny days with blue cloudless skies, to rain, mist, and winter snow. Even though I had now been accepted into this elite band of volunteers, training was never quite over. When not on patrol we would be out on the moors carrying out Search and Rescue exercises, Land Rover 4x4 training or indeed anything our leader thought applicable.

I remember one particular training session very well indeed! It was a winters evening and the exercise was in the forest plantation areas of Beacon Fell Country Park. The exercise consisted of assisting the police in searching for an imaginary escaped prisoner who was last seen in the area and thought to be hiding out within the woods. My role was to drive around in a Land Rover checking all the isolated spots within the forest that could be accessed along various rough tracks. If I came across anything suspicious such as a vehicle parked in an out of the way place, or indeed anything out of the ordinary, I was to radio through the location and wait for back up in the form of a search patrol. Now that was fine but I hadn't taken into account that the role of the escaped prisoner was being played by Mr J. Peel, our illustrious and very devious Head Ranger.

I was driving out of one of the tucked away picnic areas after disturbing my umpteenth courting couple in a steamed up rocking car when the radio crackled into life asking me to check out a particular out of the way place deep in the woods following a report of a possible sighting. I checked the location on the map and off I went, eventually finding myself driving along a narrow winding forest track. It was very dark and quiet with the only sound being the tree branches as they scraped against the sides of the vehicle. Suddenly I came to a clearing and decided to pull up; I wound the window down and listened. All was silent, then I heard a rustling coming from somewhere within the dense conifers. It was difficult to make anything out apart from the dark shadows of the trees, which appeared to be enveloping the tiny clearing and swallowing it up. I decided to investigate on foot and headed off in the general direction of the sound, my torch beam cutting a narrow dim light through the darkness.

I had left the engine running on the Land Rover and the headlights on full beam which at least illuminated some of the area but away from this it was difficult to make anything out at all other than the tall dark trees with their branches like twisted fingers sending shadows dancing around in the dimness of my torch light. I listened again; all was quiet except for the calming sound of the Land Rover's engine as it slowly ticked away reassuring me that I wasn't completely alone. Then more rustling, my first thoughts were that it was probably a deer or some other nocturnal creature, anyway, I decided that rather than radio through and waste everyone's time by coming out to carry out a fruitless search, I would investigate it myself. A very foolish thing to do! And so with torch in hand, I proceeded deeper into the blackness of the wood. I had only gone a very short distance when I heard another sound, but this time coming from the direction of my Land Rover!

I immediately did an about turn and with branches whipping my face I ran like the clappers back from whence I came. As I entered the clearing I spotted this dark figure legging it like mad towards the Land Rover; it was the escapee, Mr J. Peel! Our sneaky, conniving Head Ranger! The crafty so and so was trying to nick it and leave me stranded! Luckily, I got there first, jumped in and drove off at speed cursing myself for almost falling into his trap. All I could do now was to radio through his position in the hope that he would be caught and more importantly, keep his mouth shut. Needless to say neither happened! He wasn't caught and he also found it extremely amusing to relate the tale of how he very nearly nicked my Land Rover to leave me stranded on my own in the woods and in the dark. His only regret being that he didn't succeed!

Over the next couple of years or so, I patrolled those moors on a regular basis and I loved it! Particularly on a crisp, clear winters day with pale blue skies when the horizon seemed never to end. On other days, the mist would be swirling around so thick that I would be constantly checking my compass bearings. No sounds to disturb your thoughts other than the rapid drumming of wing beats and alarm call of a grouse flushed from the heather at my approach. I felt at peace up there and yearned for a home in the countryside. Our little two up two down terraced house in Clitheroe was ok but it was still in town and in 1975, Ann and I began scouring the local paper for a country cottage to rent.

One day we spotted an advert saying that the Duchy of Lancaster had a cottage to let in the tiny hamlet of Dunsop Bridge in the Trough of Bowland and ideally were looking for a couple with young children. I drove through Dunsop Bridge on a regular basis while on my way to Quernmore to begin my moorland patrols and as such knew the village quite well. It sounded ideal and we wasted no time in applying. Eventually a letter popped through the door inviting us to an interview at the Duchy of Lancaster Offices at Forton in Bowland after which we were delighted to be offered the tenancy of 1 Holme Head Cottage, Dunsop Bridge, Forest of Bowland. We couldn't have wished for better! From now on I would not only be a ranger in Bowland but living there as well, it was a dream come true!

The cottage was the first of a row of four terraced cottages set half a mile back from the village at the start of a rugged river valley known as Whitendale with the river Dunsop flowing down from the hilltops only metres away from the back door as it meandered its way into the village to join the river Hodder. We wasted no time in preparing for the move. The house was quickly sold and within a few weeks we moved in. It came with its very own resident Muscovy duck, a drake called Charlie who, on our first day was sat on the doorstep to greet us. No one really owned Charlie; he was just part and parcel of the setting, he was always there, more conspicuous by his absence than his presence. Our immediate next-door neighbour was ex World War 2 RAF Squadron Leader Fenwick. He was very much a recluse who lived alone except for his three Golden Labradors and kept very much to himself refusing to socialise within the village and as such had developed a reputation for being a bit of an oddball.

One of the welcoming remarks to the village was, "You'll like it here, every one's very friendly, pity about your neighbour though; he's a right surly old bugger!"

Despite the warnings, we got on well with old Fenwick. His tall hunched figure became a daily sight as every morning and evening he would walk his dogs down the track, with his hands stuffed deep into the pockets of his faded and tatty Barbour jacket, his face the colour of scarlet with its usual gruff expression hiding the sparkle of devilment that lay beneath.

His main interests in life were his dogs, his home brew and his ongoing game of outwitting the local village bobby's attempts at catching him for his many motoring misdemeanours i.e.- no road tax, bald tyres and driving whilst under the influence! Last but not least, his total disdain for the gentleman in the end cottage who, in Fenwick's own words, "Had been a mere RAF mechanic corporal." The feeling between the two of them was quite mutual and often amusing to witness. I remember one such incident when Fenwick and myself were on the track sawing up the bounty of timber that had been washed down the valley in the latest spate of flood water and deposited on the river bank by the cottages when the 'mere corporal' came up the track in his car. Fenwick was busily sawing up a large branch that he had dragged into the middle of the track which meant that the 'mere corporal' could not get around him and on stopping proceeded to give a few blasts on the horn of his little Hillman Imp. Now Fenwick could, when the need arose, become extremely hard of hearing and decided that this provided the ideal opportunity for a bout of acute deafness and as such completely ignored all attempts by the 'mere corporal' to gain his attention, not even affording him the slightest cursory glance. Finally the 'mere corporal' out of sheer desperation and frustration had no alternative but to drive off the track and into the field in his attempt to continue his journey home followed by much cursing and swearing. Fenwick glanced up at me, his face alight with a wicked wry smile and a twinkle in his eye! He was one of those rare characters that if you're lucky, you come across once in a lifetime. His cottage always had the aroma of wet dogs intermingled with wood smoke and stale beer.

On a winters evening our two sons, Derek and Gary would sit around his fire, dogs by the hearth and his shotgun propped up in a corner. Pictures of Spitfires and Lancaster Bombers along with a row of medals hung above the fireplace whilst old faded black and white photographs of a much younger Fenwick in uniform adorned the mantelpiece. Here he would enthral them with tales of his wartime exploits or instructing them on the finer points of home brewing!

I remember one particular harsh winter; we were completely snowed in when suddenly there was an urgent knock at the door.

I opened it to find Fenwick standing there all red faced and a little breathless saying, "Do you fancy a walk down to Thorneyholme for a drink?"

Thorneyholme was at that time a rather posh country hotel on the edge of the village. I reminded him that the track was under two feet of snow and it was a fair old hike in those conditions, and in the dark! But he wasn't to be put off. The home brew had been consumed with the chance of acquiring further supplies soon totally out of the question and so I relented. The two of us wrapped up like Nanook of the North set off into the snow and darkness with only dim torches and Fenwick's face rapidly turning to a deep burgundy colour to light up the way. But he persevered and as he coughed and wheezed his way through the snow we eventually arrived at the hostelry. We swung open the big oak door and stumbled into a deserted public bar with a roaring log fire and as we stood there warming our backsides with rapidly melting snow forming a mucky wet patch around our feet a barman suddenly appeared. He looked totally flabbergasted at the fact that he actually had customers and enquired as to our preferred tipple. A few drams later we bade our farewells and made our merry way home once again. Fenwick was a changed person, gone was the coughing and wheezing, his face now back to its usual crimson and his step with a definite spring, albeit hampered a little by the snow and the odd dram or three!

The river Dunsop flowed down from the hilltops to within yards of the back door before making its way through the lower pastures under the little humpback bridge and into the River Hodder. From late spring and throughout the summer months the river would meander its way lazily down from the Whitendale Valley alive with brown trout rising to mayflies, dippers hopping from stone to stone and the iridescent blue flash of the kingfisher. From September onwards the rains would come and pour off the hills to turn this haven of tranquillity into a raging angry torrent held back from invading our cottage only by a concrete wall and the large limestone boulders strewn around below it. Many was the night we would be out with storm lamps in hand watching the dark peat stained waters rising to within a foot of the wall and wondering how long it would be before it came pouring over to flood us out. Thankfully it never did, although on more than one occasion we were cut off as the river broke its banks below the cottage to completely submerge our track and the surrounding fields. It was a strange sensation to gaze through your living room window and see a tree floating by. This was the time when the salmon and sea trout would battle their way upstream against the rapidly flowing waters in their desperate struggle to reach their spawning grounds.

Occasionally an osprey would follow the river before continuing on its journey north. The sound of the huntsman's horn and the baying of hounds would call from across the river as they scrambled on foot along the fell sides in their attempt to flush out a fox from the bracken. The heather clad fells were prime grouse shoots while the valley's woodland copses were the domain of the pheasant, all lorded over by the ever present all seeing God of all he surveys, the gamekeeper!

Our nearest keeper lived in a cottage just across the river from Holme Head. He was a belligerent sort of character whose general opinion of the countryside was that if it wasn't bred for shooting it shouldn't be there! A few hundred yards down from our cottage just by the river, he had a small pheasant release pen. He would rear pheasants in brooders by his cottage eventually moving them into the pen prior to the shooting season. By day they were allowed out to explore the fields and woods but before darkness fell he would entice them with his whistle and a bucket full of grain to return to the safety of the pen. Eventually they would be allowed to remain in the woods where, on the day of a shoot, the beaters would flush them out to fly over the heads of the waiting guns.

One day they were shooting just below the cottage, the beaters driving the pheasants out of cover and as they flew over the waiting guns, shots would ring out and dogs would scurry off to retrieve the birds. One or two of the birds would veer away from the guns to fly over the cottages. On this particular day a bird veered off, the guns let fly, feathers fluttered to the ground and falling shot pebble dashed Fenwick's bald head as he cleaned his car, and a pheasant dropped dead at our back door whereupon it was quickly snatched out of sight. Within minutes a couple of confused spaniels with frantically wagging tails were sniffing around the back door in a desperate attempt to retrieve the mysteriously vanishing pheasant before responding to their master's frantic calls and whistles only to return empty mouthed. That night we feasted upon roast pheasant!

One night I returned home quite late after enjoying a pint or two in the Hark to Bounty Inn in the village of Slaidburn and decided that before retiring to bed I would take Sally our whippet out for her last constitutional. It was turned midnight with a crystal clear starry sky and a full moon lighting up the track before me. I had walked down towards the village and was heading back in the direction of the cottage when I heard a whistling sound coming from the direction of the pheasant release pen. I stopped and listened more intently and for all the world it sounded exactly like the whistle the keeper made when scattering grain around to entice his young pheasants from the woods back into the safety of their pen for the night. The birds were familiar with the sound and associated it with food and would come half flying and half running from the woods to follow him into the pen to be securely locked in for the night. But that couldn't be, it was far too late, the only solution I could think of was the possibility of poachers.

I hurried home with Sally and telephoned the keeper's cottage, no reply; he was more than likely still propping up the bar at one of his many watering holes. Ann and I decided to investigate and quietly made our way down towards the pen being careful to keep in the shadows and hugging the river bank so as to approach from an unseen angle but with a good vantage point. The hilltops appeared as if floodlit with the full moon and the stars seemed so close that you could almost touch them. As we got closer to the pen we stopped and listened, the only sounds were the occasional bleating of sheep and the constant soothing sound of the river as it rippled gently over the stones and boulders, its waters glistening brightly in the moonlight. Occasionally there would be a splash followed by the rapid succession of excited quacks as a mallard duck left the stony bank for a midnight swim, but no whistling! All was quiet. Had I imagined it? We listened again and then there it was, unmistakably the keepers whistle, this was very strange!

We crept closer, now convinced that someone was about that shouldn't be and was up to no good. As we got even closer we had a good view of the pen now illuminated in the bright moonlight. We could clearly see the sheep grazing in the fields and even the pheasants slumbering away the night roosting in the higher branches of the small trees within their pen. The whistling, though intermittent was still there, but who was it? We couldn't see anybody, and then we noticed a slight movement in the shadows at the very outer edge of the pen. We inched a little closer; then we saw it, it made no rational sense whatsoever, there in the shadows sat on its haunches staring into the pen was a fox! The whistling was still audible and coming from the fox's direction. We could not believe our eyes or ears! If poachers had been around the fox would definitely not have been there. We watched for some time observing this strange inexplicable phenomenon. Finally the fox stood up, gave a long stretch and a yawn and quietly slipped away into the night. The whistling stopped! To this day I cannot explain the event, all I know is that it really happened and we didn't imagine it. Perhaps some of the poacher's tales I remember from my youth did have a hint of truth in them after all!

There wasn't a pub in the village but it did boast of another establishment other than Thorneyholme Hall in the form of Dunsop Bridge Working Men's Club. Sounds grand doesn't it! In fact, it was a tiny one up two down cottage over the little humpback bridge by the village Post Office. It consisted of one very small front room sparsely furnished with a few old wooden tables and chairs and a lumpy old armchair by an open fireplace. The one and only room upstairs boasted a full size snooker table and a cue rack hanging from the wall which held an assortment of slightly ancient and somewhat warped snooker cues.

The only source of heating was the small open fire downstairs. This meant that in the depths of winter a game of snooker upstairs was somewhat of an ordeal with woolly hat pulled down to your ears, scarf wrapped tightly around the neck, hands protected from frostbite by mitts and snooker balls constantly disappearing in the misty vapours of your freezing breath. The alternative to this was to stay downstairs by the fire and join in one of the ever constant games of dominoes. Unfortunately, this also had its drawbacks in the respect that if the wind was in the wrong direction the smoke came down the chimney making it difficult to see the dominoes through the smoky haze billowing from the fire with particles of black soot slowly drifting down from the ceiling to deposit themselves in your pint!

The bar was none existent; service was from a tiny back kitchen with a barrel sat on the flag floor and a pump clamped to a wooden shelf with brown sediment stained pipes connecting the two. You had the choice of a pint of bitter or a bottle of whatever was available at the time. Bar service was provided by whichever committee member could be persuaded to break from his game of dominoes to pop into the back kitchen and pull your pint. In this respect, your options were a little more varied than the choice of beverage. The average number of clientele on any one of the three opening nights was between six and eight, all committee members. The only exception to the rule being once a year when the membership and fishing club subscriptions were due, then you could hardly move for people not normally to be seen within a ten mile radius of the place all queuing up to hand over their hard earned cash.

The reason for this sudden liking for the club was that it leased a stretch of prime salmon fishing water off the Duchy of Lancaster estates on a peppercorn rent. To qualify for a permit you had to reside within a designated area of Dunsop and be a member of the club. For a mere five pounds per annum, you could have fishing rights on a delightful stretch of water that would normally cost you an arm and a leg. Needless to say on, permit and club membership renewal night the population of Dunsop miraculously increased three fold and extra barrels of bitter were ordered to accommodate the onslaught.

I remember my very first visit to this local den of iniquity. We had only been in the village a week and still being a keen fisherman at the time decided that if I wanted to fish this highly prized stretch of prime game fishing water I would have to join the club. The following evening, as it was one of the three nights the club was open, I decided to take the plunge and so made my way down the lane across the little humpback bridge to the black painted door bearing the small metal sign stating in white letters 'Dunsop Bridge Working Men's Club.' Now Dunsop Bridge is a very tiny hamlet with the community being very close knit and even clannish to a certain degree, which meant that I was taking a journey into the unknown. What would be the reaction of a stranger entering the inner sanctum? Yes I was a resident, but very much a newcomer and regarded with a little suspicion and to complicate matters I even appeared to be friendly with the local oddball, my neighbour Mr Fenwick! I paused for a second or two at the door and with some trepidation took a deep breath and went for it.

The door creaked open and I entered a tiny corridor. Directly ahead was a narrow steep staircase and to my right a wooden latch door. I could hear muffled voices coming from the other side. I took a second deep breath, lifted the latch and entered into the unknown. I was immediately met by the pungent smell of pipe tobacco intermingled with stale beer and coal soot. I stood there for a few seconds gazing through the haze; it was deathly silent, all the chatter had stopped. Four or five strange looking characters sat motionless, flat caps askew, pipes dangling precariously from mouths and dominoes suddenly in a state of limbo. All eyes were on me! Then I noticed what appeared to be a person of some authority sat in a tattered armchair by the fire. It was the local bobby, pint in hand and peaked cap sitting above on the mantelpiece. Eventually without a word, they slowly came back to life and the clatter of dominoes once more broke the silence. I stood around twiddling my thumbs for what seemed an age not daring to interrupt what appeared to be an internationally important game presided over by the local constabulary.

Finally after much cursing, swearing and clattering as dominoes were roughly thrown down, pints picked up and empty glasses banged back down onto the table a voice emitted out of the haze of soot and pipe smoke, "Suppose you want a pint do you?" it enquired.

"Yes please, a pint of mild if you don't mind," I replied.

"Don't have it, bitter or nowt."

"Bitter will be fine," I replied.

That night I enjoyed what was to be the first of many sooty pints on a cold winter's night in the 'Dunsop Bridge Working Men's Club'.

We soon began to settle into country life. Guy our little Welsh Cob pony that we had bought for a song a couple of years ago due to him, according to his previous owner, being unmanageable, grazed on the rough grass between the river and a copse at the back of the cottage. We had owned a couple of horses before Guy and had previously decided that those days were coming to an end due to the cost and time involved when out of the blue we got a call from our horse dealing friends saying that they knew of a three-year-old Welsh Cob going cheap.

Apparently his owner couldn't handle him and did we want him? We declined the offer but they were adamant that he was a good buy and some months later when we were told that he was still for sale we relented and went to see him. He was a 12.3 hands chestnut roan with a shaggy coat and a thick powerful neck. Ann rode him, liked him, and we took him home! So much for no more horses!

We were able to rent two pieces of land by the cottage from a neighbouring farmer, one for Guy the Welsh Cob and the other for a little 6-week-old white Saanen nanny goat kid that we christened Candy. We bought her from an elderly couple who lived in a caravan in the middle of a field with no electricity or running water and she had to be carried through three fields just to get back to the car! Her accommodation was all ready and waiting in the form of a paddock and a cosy goat shed. She was soon joined by a Golden Guernsey called Polly who eventually produced a kid of her own that we christened Tansy.

One day Fenwick returned home from a farm auction with some Muscovy ducks and to Charlie's delight released them into his front garden, needless to say our Muscovy duck population increased rapidly and added to the variety of inhabitants at Holme Head. Every year house martins nested under the eaves of the cottage and around April time, they would return from their wintering grounds in Africa to take up residence once more. Throughout the spring and summer months the evening skies would be alive with their constant chirruping as they soared and circled high above in pursuit of flying insects. At night, we slept with the bedroom window open to allow the clear crisp country air to circulate throughout the room and to listen to the sounds of the night. The call of a fox on the hillside or a tawny owl hooting from a nearby copse plus the constant chattering of the young martins as they shuffled around in the nest above the window.

One stormy night in mid-June we were in bed reading, the window was open as usual and the house martins seemed to be particularly restless when all of a sudden there was a flutter of wings and a young martin came in from the night, flew onto the lampshade above the bed, tucked its head under its wing and went to sleep! We carefully spread a towel over the bed to catch any little parcels that would undoubtedly be emitted from above, put the light out and attempted to get some sleep. Periodically the young martin would shuffle about a little, emit a few little chirrups and nod off again. At first light it awoke, ruffled its feathers, had a quick preen and flew out through the open window to catch its breakfast. The stormy weather persisted for the next few nights and our self-invited guest took advantage of our hospitality until all became calm and still once more.

I had been a volunteer ranger for some time now but by this time my full-time job was in a limestone quarry on the outskirts of Clitheroe. The hours were long and the job was dirty and noisy but it paid very well and was better than working within the confines of a factory. My ambition though was still to work full-time within conservation and to gain more experience, I had also become a volunteer ranger for the North West Water Authority Ranger Service. I had also now progressed from being a volunteer ranger for Lancashire County Council to being a paid part-time ranger. I was now applying for full-time ranger posts with invitations to interviews beginning to come through albeit in other parts of the country. I loved the Bowland area and didn't want to leave but full-time ranger vacancies in Lancashire just didn't happen. It was only a small service and no one ever left and if I wanted a full-time post I would have to look further afield.

The one aspect of living in Bowland that didn't appeal to me was the constant persecution of wildlife, both legally and illegally, and unfortunately all these years later as I write; it is still going on, particularly with the persecution of the rare Hen Harrier. I remember on one very memorable day while out on patrol on the Bowland fells. I had just sat myself down in the heather to have a break when suddenly a male Hen Harrier appeared and to my utter astonishment came closer and closer until he was literally only a couple of metres away. I could see that he was carrying prey in the form of a young rabbit. I froze as he started to descend until he was hovering a couple of metres above the heather when all of a sudden the female rose up flipped over and grabbed the prey before vanishing back into the heather again. I couldn't believe it; I had just witnessed a pair of Hen Harriers doing a food pass only metres away from me. I had been totally oblivious to the fact that I had sat myself down so close to their nest. I felt very privileged indeed to have witnessed this rare event and rather than risk disturbing them or giving their presence away I slowly crept off and left them in peace in the hope that they would survive and wouldn't fall prey to the keeper's gun, poison, or traps.

It infuriated me then as it does now, that too many gamekeepers believe they are above the law. In my experience they are the main culprits with regards to eradicating anything they consider a threat to their pheasant and grouse numbers. On more than one occasion, dead hen harriers were found on the fells having fallen prey to poison, pole traps or gunshot. Much of the moorland around Bowland is private land, owned by the very wealthy and heavily managed for commercial grouse shooting, a multi-million pound industry! Unfortunately the keepers are the ones whose main responsibility it is to ensure that their rich masters and often equally rich clients have a ready supply of grouse to be driven over their heads for them to take pot shots at. In this isolated private kingdom, the keeper is very much his own lord and master and can, if he so wishes, kill what he wants, when he wants, and by whatever method he wants, with very little chance of detection or retribution. His priority is to keep his master happy. To achieve this he is expected to rear good numbers of grouse or pheasant and won't tolerate wildlife in whatever shape or form, regardless of its protection status, to jeopardise it and as such will eradicate it! I'm sure that there are decent law-abiding keepers out there but unfortunately as yet I have to meet one.

It was now 1982 and I was still working as a part-time ranger. My brief had changed a little in that I was now also responsible for the Lancashire County Council's Spring Wood Picnic Site and adjoining woodland as well as the remote and historic Wycoller Country Park in Trawden coupled with being a volunteer ranger for the North West Water Authority. I had been for interviews for full-time posts in County Durham and the National Trusts Clumber Park on the edge of Sherwood Forest but as yet, without any luck. But I was getting interviews! The prospect of a full-time post in Lancashire still seemed very remote. Ranger jobs were difficult to come by regardless of where they may be with a single vacancy often attracting up to three or four hundred applicants. Competition was stiff to say the least! I was determined to achieve my goal and I knew that I would get there eventually, but when? One morning a letter arrived from Wirral Borough Council explaining that I had been short-listed and was invited to attend an interview

A couple weeks earlier I had been scanning the jobs vacant column in the environmental section of the Guardian and discovered a vacancy for a full-time countryside ranger at Wirral Country Park and had decided to apply. Prior to this we hadn't even heard of the Wirral and had to look it up on the map. We discovered that it was a long narrow peninsular squashed between the river Mersey with Liverpool on one side and the river Dee and the North Wales coast on the other. The park itself was one of the first designated country parks in the country and consisted of around 12 miles of linear footpaths and bridleways linking to other areas of countryside and coast. The main visitor and administration centre was based at Thurstaston by the Dee Estuary with views across to North Wales and this is where the post was to be based.

Even though we didn't think it the ideal location it was at least an interview and interview experience was valuable in its own right and so off we went. The interviews were to be held at the council offices in West Kirby with mine scheduled for 2 pm. All short-listed applicants were to arrive no later than 11am to allow time for a tour of the park and lunch. We gave ourselves plenty of time for the journey but got slightly lost once we hit Wirral necessitating a stop at a public telephone box to ring up and explain that we were lost and going to be a little late! Not a good start!

Eventually we found the place arriving just in time for the tour, and, along with five other shortlisted applicants were ushered into the back of two green canvas topped Land Rovers emblazoned with 'Wirral Countryside Ranger Service.' We were shown around the various areas of the park stopping occasionally for a short walkabout and an explanation of the area. Neither of us was particularly impressed with what we saw, it wasn't our type of area, it was too flat and over populated - even the rangers seemed to be of a different breed to the ones I'd been used to.

With grand tour and lunch over, we were ushered into a

room until our designated interview time. One by one names would be called with the recipient being nervously led away never to be seen again. At 2 p.m. on the dot, the door opened once again and I was led into a large oak panelled room to be confronted by the interview panel sat behind a large Victorian desk. This consisted of the Head Ranger, a very much larger than life character with a Liverpool accent and wearing the distinctive green uniform of the Wirral Ranger Service. He shook my hand and introduced himself as Wilf Watson, followed by the introduction of his boss, Assistant Director Mr David Brimley and invited to me take a seat and relax.

Ann and I had already decided that the post and the area weren't really what we wanted and as such I went into the interview totally relaxed with an attitude of 'What the hell! Give it your best shot, you've got nothing to lose, you don't really want the job anyway and at least the interview experience will be valuable.' They each had a copy of my application form along with other related documentation and my Lancashire County Council Ranger Service course certificate etc. They sat in silence for a few moments while they perused the documents interrupted only by occasional hushed snippets of conversation as they thumbed their way through them.

After a few moments Wilf Watson said, "Right Malcolm, they all look in order."

This was followed by the pair of them firing umpteen questions at me regarding various aspects of my work in Lancashire and why I thought that I was the right man for the job. They responded to each answer with more hushed conversation and nodding of heads.

Eventually Wilf Watson said, "Right son, anything you would like to ask us?"

I thought for a moment and then replied with, "If I was to be offered the post I would require the tenancy of the ranger's cottage that I understand has just become vacant."

This shocked them into a stunned silence until eventually they looked at each other before David Brimley said, "You do realise that we are looking to take on two appointments and there is only the one vacant cottage?"

I replied that I was aware of this and added that I would only be interested in the post if the cottage was also to be offered. I even had the cheek to ask if there was any land with the cottage because we had three goats and a pony that would also need to be accommodated.

After a few seconds of more stunned silence followed by a few low whispered exchanges it was confirmed that the cottage did indeed have a large garden that could be fenced off to accommodate our livestock, after which they stood up, thanked me for coming and said they would be in touch. The two-hour drive back home was ominously silent; I had a feeling about this one. I felt that despite my outspokenness the interview had gone well. Perhaps too well!

The following day I was back in the constant dust and noise of the quarry when I became aware of waving arms and a voice attempting to make itself heard over the din of the giant dumper trucks as they rumbled by transporting their massive loads of limestone boulders from the cliff face to the crushing plant.

The voice boomed, "There's a telephone call for you in the office, it's some bloke from Wirral asking for you."

My heart skipped a beat as I made my way into the office and picked up the receiver to hear, "Malcolm, Wilf Watson here from the Wirral Ranger Service, I'm pleased to say that I'm now in a position to offer you the post of Countryside Ranger at Wirral Country Park."

I didn't know what to say, my mind was in turmoil! The voice rang out again, "Hello Malcolm, you still there?"

"Yes, of course Mr Watson, thank you very much, can I have a few days to think it over?"

Rather taken aback by this unexpected retort he paused for a second or two before saying, "Well yes, but we need to know pretty quickly if you want the job or not."

"Yes I understand and thank you, I will confirm one way or the other once I've spoken to my wife," and as I put the receiver down I silently swore, my mind was all over the place. What was I to do? Was I going to a turn down a full-time ranger post after all this effort? What if this is my one and only chance? I had two choices, stay where I was and hope that a job with Lancashire Ranger Service turned up quickly which seemed extremely unlikely! Or go to the Wirral for a spell and then with a bit more experience under my belt, move on. First priority was to talk it over with Ann, secondly, think very long and hard, and thirdly, panic in utter indecisive confusion.

I asked Jeff Peel for his advice, he replied with his usual dryness, "Where? The Wirral! Cheshire isn't it? They're snobs down there, all ex. military and all that, the Head Rangers a Major somebody or other, isn't he? All flat as well, no hills you know!"

Thanks Jeff, big help! The lads in Dunsop Bridge Working Men's Club were not much better either responding with, "Wirral! Liverpool isn't it? What do want to go there for? It's not you, you won't settle, stay where you are lad."

In no time at all my days of indecisiveness were quickly ending, it was now make your mind up time. After much discussion and soul searching we decided to bite the bullet and go for it. It was very much a tongue in cheek decision but the following day I made the call to Wirral and the wheels were set in motion. We gave our notice on 1 Holme Head Cottage to Her Majesties Chancellor of the Duchy of Lancaster. I gave in my notice at the quarry, removal arrangements were made and after one last pint of sooty ale and final farewells we were on our way. I had realised my goal at last and I was now a full-time Countryside Ranger, but the elation was tempered somewhat by having to leave Dunsop Bridge. We would miss it something terrible, it was now our home and I was even on the committee at the Working Men's Club and could pull my own pints! But a new life and new challenges were waiting.

Chapter Three
From a Rook to a Razorbill

It was a fine September morning as we closed the door to 1 Holme Head Cottage for the very last time. Our little Renault 4 car was packed to the roof with cardboard boxes and suitcases as we drove silently down the lane towards the village. The removal van laden with our furniture had already set off on the journey to Wirral followed by a horsebox containing Guy the pony and our three goats, Polly, Candy and Tansy plus umpteen bales of straw and hay. What had we done? We were both thinking it but not daring to say it out loud.

The journey seemed to take forever but at last, we left the monotony of the M6 and M56 motorways behind us to join the A540 up to the Wirral once more. Some ten miles later, we reached our final destination, a three bedroomed centrally heated detached house consisting of a large open plan living room plus dining room and kitchen with an open staircase leading to the bedrooms and bathroom. This was the height of luxury compared to our house at Dunsop Bridge; there the central heating consisted of an open fire in the living room and draught excluders stuffed under the doors. The garden was made up of what had been, years before, an old cottage garden but now sadly neglected and wild and of course the all-important area of land for the goats and pony!

Despite being the last to leave we were the first to arrive followed shortly by the removal van and the horsebox. Our first task was to get the furniture inside followed by where to put the goats and the pony. With no fenced land or outbuildings to act as temporary stables or paddocks we were in a bit of a quandary. But where there's a will there's a way as my old grandma used to say and we set about quickly adapting the garage into a makeshift stable-come goat-shed. Before too long the animals were happily munching away on their hay nets and with liberal amounts of straw covering the concrete floor they contentedly bedded down for the night. We, on the other hand, were very much the opposite as by the time we'd got the animals sorted out it was far too late and we were far too tired to start putting a bed up and so we spent our first night sleeping on a mattress in the living room. Thankfully, we had a few days to sort ourselves out before I was due to report for duty on the coming Monday morning which gave us a little time to get the house organized and the animals more permanently settled.

Wilf Watson the Head Ranger was very much larger than life in both size and character and as I soon learnt, had a reputation for being a stickler for punctuality and making a statement one minute and contradicting it the next. We were on our second day and busy sorting out furniture when there was a hefty knock at the door, I opened it to find Wilf Watson's large portly frame completely filling the front porch. He made quite an imposing figure standing there in his green ranger uniform adorned with its badges and western style hat.

"Just thought I'd pop over to welcome you both and to see how you were settling in," he said in his rather loud blustery manner. "Anyway I'll let you get on and I'll see you in the office on Monday morning, there's no rush, wander in just after nine or so and we'll have a natter then."

Monday morning duly arrived and with it, my first step into a new world. I was now a full-time Countryside Ranger at last! It was only a five-minute walk to the Visitor Centre and as I crossed the wooden bridge over the pond to the main entrance I paused for a few seconds before entering to take a deep breath feeling like a nervous schoolboy on his first day. I walked down the long corridor past the various exhibits displaying the parks flora and fauna, eventually reaching the information desk. A small well-spoken lady with an air of authority about her bade me good morning and summoned me into the inner sanctum of the office saying, "Wilf's waiting for you, go on through," as she pointed to the Head Rangers office door. I knocked and walked in, it was around 9.15 am.

Wilf was at his desk having given the rangers their duties for the day and with a cursory glance at his watch said, "What time do you call this then? Never mind lad you're here now, you're with Jim today he'll show you the ropes."

I was about to say in my defence that he had actually said, 'No rush lad, just after nine will be fine,' when Jim arrived.

"Follow me" he said, "and we'll get you kitted out." A few minutes later, I was once more sat in a ranger Land Rover but this time rather than being given a guided tour I was being ferried off to the main stores. As I entered, Jim introduced me to a rather dapper looking character with a neatly trimmed pencil moustache that, in a strong scouse accent, proceeded to bombard me with the following questions, "Waist, collar, chest and shoe size please."

Once equipped with the required information and with clipboard in hand, he shuffled off along rows of neatly packed shelves occasionally stopping to retrieve an item. Finally, he reappeared; his arms piled high with an assortment of ranger attire topped off by a pair of size seven boots sitting precariously on top.

He placed them on the counter and began to methodically tick them off his list, "Two pairs of green trousers, check, two green shirts, check, one pair of boots, check, one Barbour jacket, check and three badges to be attached thereon, check."

Once satisfied that all the necessary items had been duly gathered up and accounted for he pushed a couple of forms under my nose with a, "Sign here please."

It was all very reminiscent of being back in the quartermaster's store at my old Territorial Army barracks and Jeff Peels' words came flooding back to haunt me, "They're all ex-military down there you know!"

The routine from that day on consisted of roll call at nine o' clock sharp and with jobs and areas allocated off you went in the canvas topped green Land Rovers to the various parts of this twelve miles of Country Park. I was a ranger at last but I didn't particularly feel like one, this was a million miles away from what I was accustomed to, I could have been on another planet! No patrolling the hills now, my days were spent repairing fences, cutting grass, shovelling gravel, litter picking and anything else that Wilf Watson and the senior ranger thought applicable to the management of the park and its surrounding areas. I could not help but ponder over the question is this, what I had strove so long for? And to add to the frustration, it soon became apparent that Wilf's idea of country park management and mine were poles apart! His appeared to be that visitors were able to stroll along neatly trimmed grassy banks and clean smooth footpaths without getting their shoes dirty rather than wildlife and conservation.

One day when seeing me with a pair of binoculars one of the rangers remarked "Wilf doesn't like us to take binoculars out with us."

"Why?"

"Because he says we should be working, not bird watching!"

It was becoming increasingly obvious that the park was managed more for people than wildlife but this was my lot now and I had to make the most of it, there was no going back. My plan of action was to stick it out, learn what I could and then apply for a post in a National Park, possibly the Lakes or the Peak District. After a few months of shovelling tons of limestone from the back of a tractor and trailer plus the endless grass cutting and fence repairing I decided that enough was enough, the job was more akin to labouring than being a ranger! The following morning I bit the bullet and after roll call told Wilf that I hadn't given up everything to be a ranger in title only. I had shovelled enough limestone in a quarry to last me a lifetime and I had no intentions of shovelling anymore and if things did not change quickly I would be looking for another post.

He sat there flabbergasted for a few minutes before spluttering, "Well it's all part of the job you know!"

"I'm well aware of that, but I'm not prepared to be a labourer on someone else's patch any longer."

He was visibly taken aback by my remarks saying, "I'll see what I can do."

To my surprise two weeks later I was given responsibility for my own patch. This consisted of a stretch of the Wirral Way and more importantly an area of land overlooking the Dee estuary that had, a few years previous, been an old landfill tip site and had a lot of potential for being managed as a nature reserve. It overlooked the Dee estuary and Welsh coast with a golf course, a small conifer plantation with open farmland and the country park making up the remaining borders. My first priority was to survey the area's flora and fauna in order to draw up a long-term management plan. It soon became obvious that the area had a lot to offer with an already rich and diverse number of species utilising the site. I soon became engrossed in my newfound freedom and wasted no time in compiling a management plan and forming a small band of enthusiastic volunteers to help out with the tasks of tree planting, fencing, grass cutting and the sowing of a wild flower meadow.

It was given the title 'The Dee Nature Reserve,' and many a hot summer's day was spent watering the previous winter plantings of alder, birch and willow from an old ex-army water bowser. More often than not, this would degenerate into a water fight between the volunteers who were themselves as diverse as the habitat they were helping to care for. Some were unemployed and looking for something to keep them occupied, whilst a couple would be killing time before going to university, one was even taking a degree in theology and destined for a life in the Catholic priesthood and had a particularly good aim with the water hose resulting in many a volunteer getting a good soaking. Others would be taking a two or three year course in conservation management and wanting to gain practical experience in their quest to become rangers.

One of the main distractions of working on the reserve

was the variety of wildlife; you would be knocking a fence post in one minute and then making a grab for the binoculars the next as some bird or other flew by. In spring, the reserve would resound to the distinctive melodious song of the skylark hovering high above the rough grassland, suddenly to fall silent and tumble to the ground only to climb again to renew its song from way up in the sky. The willow and hawthorn would be alive with warblers, blackbirds and thrushes whilst a kestrel hovered above, eyes scanning the grassland for any tell-tale movement of a field mouse or vole.

Farther down the estuary was the RSPB reserve at Parkgate with its vast expanse of salt marsh stretching out to North Wales. From here, from the old sandstone quayside where ships used to set sail for Dublin, you could, particularly on a high tide, watch short-eared owls, marsh harriers and merlin in pursuit of prey as mice and voles fled from the rising tidal waters as it washed over the marsh. Peregrine falcons would attempt to pluck a knot or a redshank from the sky as they twisted and turned in a dark dense flock above the rising tide.

I was beginning to think that perhaps the Wirral had a lot more to offer than I had first realised. I was discovering that it was a place of much diversity from lowland heath to estuary, woodland to marsh and open countryside to urban sprawl. Another major factor was that I was now making my mark and being given a free hand with regards to my own patch and habitat management, I was also now being nominated to attend various courses consisting of anything from Woodland Management to Public Speaking with the latter being the most terrifying!

The months flew by and with the passing of time our old life in Dunsop Bridge seemed a lifetime away but we still missed it and every once in a while felt the urge to return for a short visit. On one of these journeys of nostalgia we were driving past the Forestry Commission houses across the river from our old home when I spotted a familiar figure coming from one of the houses, flat cap askew, pipe dangling precariously from the corner of his mouth, fumbling in the pockets of his old tatty jacket for matches. It was ex fellow club committee member and domino playing partner, Jimmy Roscoe.

I pulled over and wound the window down as he ambled over saying, "Well would you see who we have here! You alright lad, settled in yet, how long you staying?"

"Just on a flying visit Jim."

"That's a pity; we're one short for domino doubles in the club tonight, never mind, next time maybe."

At that moment, I would have liked nothing better than to have spent the evening downing pints of sooty ale and playing dominoes in the club again, but our life in Dunsop Bridge was over and we were now carving out a new life on the Wirral. Ann was training to be a veterinary nurse and I was busy managing my section of the Wirral Way and nature reserve. But I still yearned to be back in the hills and had every intention of applying for another post at some point in the not too distant future but fate, or destiny, whatever you want to call it was about to intervene once more and take me along a totally different and unexpected route.

It was the 14th May 1983 and a member of the public walked into the Visitor Centre cradling what appeared to be a mucky old towel, which he gently placed on the counter to reveal, wrapped inside, an injured bird. He explained that he had found it whilst walking along the Wirral Way and could a ranger look after it? It was explained to him in somewhat abrupt terms that the park did not take injured wildlife and he should contact the RSPCA. I was within ear shot of the conversation and felt a little sorry for the guy; he was obviously in a quandary as to what to do next and before I knew it I was taking the towel from him and examining a rook with a badly broken wing. Suddenly my days as a Clitheroe urchin caring for an injured lapwing came flooding back and history was about to repeat itself as once again I found myself caring for an injured bird in a greenhouse.

Not in my dad's this time but in the old dilapidated one in the garden. As with the lapwing, I carefully strapped the wing and soon got it feeding but no release this time I'm afraid! Within a few days it succumbed to the trauma of the injury coupled with the shock of captivity and sadly faded away. At that point little did I realise that this was the beginning of something much bigger that would ultimately lead me into working with injured wildlife as part of my job and on occasions spotlighted in the media through the press, journals, radio and even television, but at this stage that had yet to come.

A few months later I was working on the reserve when my radio crackled into life with the rather cut-glass voice of the Senior Information Officer informing me that a member of the public had reported seeing an injured fox not too far from where I was working and could I help? After searching around for half an hour or so I found it in an area of tall scrubby grass on the edge of the reserve, it seemed totally lifeless but as I got closer I realised that it was alive, but only just! It was a young dog fox about three-quarters grown and with no visible signs of injury but was obviously a very sick animal and close to death. I carefully wrapped it in my jacket and placed it into the back of the Land Rover not really knowing what on earth I was going to do with it. I knew nothing whatsoever about caring for sick or injured wild foxes! Luckily someone told me of a vet in West Kirby who had been known, on occasions, to take in injured wildlife and I decided to give him a ring.

The vet in question was a Mr Peter McElroy and I gave a sigh of relief when he said, "Yes, I'll have a look at it, could you get it to the surgery?"

I replied that I could and would be there in about half an hour. Thirty minutes later, I was carrying the comatose animal through the waiting room and into the consulting room. He gave it a thorough examination and decided that all the symptoms pointed to some form of poisoning and placed it into one of the surgery cages on an intravenous saline drip. Three days later he rang me to say that the fox was looking much brighter and could I arrange to go along and collect it as it was now very snappy and smelling the place out! As soon as I entered the surgery recovery room I was immediately met by the overpowering pungent odour of dog fox.

"There he is in the bottom pen if you want to get him out," said Peter, and cowering in a corner was my patient and looking very much better.

With the aid of a dog grasper, I soon had him boxed and made my way back to the park and put him into a small wire enclosure that I had knocked up in the garden. He settled in well and was soon wolfing down dog food and the odd road kill rabbit. Not that I saw very much of him: he would hide away during the day only coming out after dark to devour his food, but of the glimpses I did have, he was looking well and shortly ready for release. This was going to done by leaving his enclosure door open one night but still leaving food there for a short while in case he returned.

One day I decided to show him off to my little band of faithful volunteers; unfortunately the fox wasn't too keen on this arrangement and slunk out of sight under a small bush. Undeterred by his bashfulness I was determined to show off my newly acquired animal handling skills and entered the enclosure. As I approached he slunk deeper into his refuge but undeterred I stuck my hand into the depths of the bush with the intention of grabbing him by the back of the neck and retrieving him from his hiding place but as I went to grab him he spun around with lightning speed and attached himself to my hand. I felt a horrible bone crushing sensation and let out a blood curdling scream!

I instinctively quickly withdrew my throbbing hand from the bush only to find the fox still attached to it and refusing to let go! With my free hand I attempted to retrieve my captive hand from his vice-like grip and while in the process of doing this he twisted around, sat on my lap, and peed all over me! The sight of their illustrious leader emerging from the enclosure face pale with shock, hand spurting blood, dripping with fox pee and smelling like nothing on earth was just too much for them and they all fell about in fits of uncontrollable laughter. That night my patient decided that he had had enough of my hospitality and dug his way out under the door and vanished into the night never to be seen again!

I had finally been able to fence off a section of the garden with some scavenged old chestnut paling fencing which now meant that Polly, Candy and Tansy, our three goats, could have some freedom at last along with a nice cosy shelter in case in rained. Goats being goats, they occasionally decided that the grass was greener on the other side and jumped over it to be off down the banking and into the park browsing on as many trees as they could fit in before being herded back into the garden.

Guy, our pony, was now living in a nearby field that we rented from a local livery stable and even he decided to test the resolve of any fence designed to contain him! Even though he'd been gelded (castrated), he still thought himself capable of charming the local mares and procreating. When these inclinations were upon him no fence was high enough and no ditch wide enough to stop him from rounding up all the mares in the adjoining fields that he thought would be responsive to his amorous intentions. This caused more than a little consternation particularly when an owner turned up to take Tulip out for a quiet hack only find that 15.2 hands Tulip was being romantically wined and dined three fields away by a little 12.3 hands chestnut roan gelding who thought he was God's gift to mares!

It was the 5th March 1984 and I had just returned from the reserve to find a member of the public in the Visitor Centre cradling a cardboard box containing what he described as an oiled penguin. He explained that he had been walking out to Hilbre Island off West Kirby and discovered the bird badly oiled hunched up by some rocks. Now I was well aware that the island and the estuary were renowned for their ornithological importance and could lay claim to an extensive list of recorded species but a penguin! Now that would be a first! I opened the box and peeped in and there peering back up at me was not a penguin but a very sorry looking razorbill.

Razorbills are attractive black and white seabirds with a distinctive heavy bill and said to be one of the deepest diving birds in the world and to anyone not ever having seen one before I suppose that they could be mistaken for a very small penguin, particularly if seen on land as they do have the similar comical shuffling walk. They could be seen quite often around Hilbre Island with the nearest breeding colony being not too many miles away on Puffin Island and on the cliffs of the Great Orme off Llandudno on the North Wales coast. I could see that it was quite badly oiled with thick, black, foul smelling sticky gunge plastered along its body and it appeared very weak.

For any seabird to be oiled is paramount to certain death, either through ingesting the oil whilst preening, starvation or drowning; even if found and cleaned the process can be very traumatic and success is anything but guaranteed. Prior to release back into the wild, any seabird has to be totally fit, with the plumage thoroughly waterproof. Misjudge any of these factors and the chances of survival are very slim indeed. To confound matters even more, in a captive situation a bird, once treated, can quite soon begin to look fit and healthy, even to the extent of seeming to be totally waterproof and in pristine condition. This can be very deceptive as once released and having to face the harsh elements of its natural environment, can rapidly spiral downhill again and very quickly die from either starvation, hyperthermia or drowning, probably a combination of all three.

My first priority was to treat it for shock; to have attempted to clean it at this stage could easily have tipped it over the edge and accelerated the process of shock and eventual death. It was put into a cardboard box lined with a thick layer of newspaper to soak up any oily residue and then placed into a dark, quiet and warm environment - the airing cupboard! Upon checking early the following morning I fully expected to find a lifeless razorbill but to my astonishment it was still alive and if anything even a little brighter. We decided that the time was right to attempt a wash; but we had no previous experience of doing this. And to complicate matters further the process of cleaning and aftercare of contaminated seabirds was, at that time, still a bit of a hit and miss affair and considered not to be particularly successful. I remembered reading in a journal that an organisation in Scandinavia had achieved some success in cleaning oiled birds using Fairy washing-up liquid in water at about 42 degrees centigrade. The idea was to place the bird in the water whilst methodically working the washing-up liquid into the plumage and other contaminated areas after which, the bird would be showered with a fairly strong jet of water of the same temperature until the water began to roll off in droplets like water off a duck's back.

It was all we had to work on and decided to give it a go and as soon as we placed the bird in the water it almost immediately turned black as globules of greasy sticky oil began to float to the surface. It was a very slow laborious procedure as we worked the washing-up liquid into every nook and cranny of his body and after an hour and umpteen water changes later, we had merely succeeded in removing some of the surface oil, the thick glutinous stuff still remained and clung like thick glue to the poor bird's inner feathers and legs. Finally, we showered him off with warm clean water to wash out the washing-up liquid, followed by allowing him to rest for a few hours in the airing cupboard before attempting to get some food into him.

The diet of the razorbill consists primarily of sand eels but with no sand eels at hand, strips of herring would have to suffice and three hours later, we gently attempted to feed him. He was far too weak to feed himself and even if he could, he would have been far too stressed to do so, leaving us with no choice but to gently prise his beak open and pop a small amount of herring down his throat. Once he had swallowed and it was in his belly we repeated the process. We only attempted small amounts with the idea being a little and often so long as we thought him strong enough to take it. He made a pathetic sight as he stood there on a towel, eyes half closed, breast bone protruding and feathers stuck together with the thick black oily tar. Surely he couldn't survive but despite all that he had gone through, there was still a spark in there that told us we shouldn't give up on him. Early the next morning we gave him a second wash, followed by another feed before returning him to the airing cupboard for a few hours rest.

In between times, I decided to ring the vet in West Kirby, Peter McElroy, who had kindly treated the fox for me. He explained that birds were not really his strong point but suggested I contact another vet that specialised in avian medicine and who was perhaps able to offer more help. Unfortunately, I hit a blank here also. He explained that parrots and birds of prey were his speciality not oiled seabirds and as such could not really offer any positive advice.

Day 3 arrived and to our amazement he was still with us and actually looking brighter, but he was still a long way from being clean. I was also worried that he may have ingested oil whilst attempting to preen which, if he had, could cause serious damage to his internal organs. I had now managed to get hold of some fresh sand eels, sprats and whitebait from a fishmongers stall on Birkenhead market which meant that at least now he would be on a more natural and nutritious diet if nothing else.

On day four, I decided to give the RSPCA a ring at their wildlife unit in Somerset explaining the situation and what we had done so far. Unfortunately they could not recommend anything that we had not already tried. Finally they suggested that as this was a particularly difficult problem it would probably be the best to have him put to sleep. I fully understood the reasoning behind their comments; he was, after all, in a sorry state and at the end of the day were we merely prolonging his suffering? We decided to persevere at least for another few days before finally deciding on the best course of action. He wasn't showing any obvious signs of stress and he did seem a little brighter.

The following morning as I prepared to force-feed him once again, I placed a small dish containing a mixture of pieces of sand eel and sprats next to his towel. I then went through the normal routine of sitting him on the towel, opening his beak and taking a piece of fish in my fingers ready to pop it down his throat but he had other ideas and completely surprised me by taking the fish from my fingers and swallowing it! He then proceeded to stand up, albeit a little wobbly and having to sit back on his haunches and use his wings to prop himself up but he was standing, and even better, he began to feed himself from the dish! Eureka! I couldn't help but feel pleased for him as he stood there like a wobbly little penguin wolfing down pieces of sand eel and sprat. Two days later he was strong enough to withstand a more prolonged wash after which, at long last, all traces of the obnoxious oil appeared to be gone! Finally he was showered until the water began to run off his feathers in tiny sparkling droplets.

We were now on the 9th March, five days since his arrival, it had been a hard slog but it was now looking as though we could see light at the end of the tunnel. He was free of the obnoxious stinking black oil; he was feeding well and getting stronger by the day.

On the 11th March we decided that 'William,' as he was now known, needed to have somewhere where he could have a good swim around, not only for his wellbeing but we could also observe the effects of him being in water for a prolonged period of time. The only thing we had that was large and deep enough was the household bath, so in he went! We filled it almost to the brim with warm water and gently lowered him in; the response was immediate, he was in his element! He swam around and around on his side propelling himself along with his stubby little wings; occasionally standing upright to rapidly beat his wings sending water cascading around the bathroom. He dived to the bottom only to pop back up like a cork out of a bottle.

He was looking good but then after about fifteen minutes or so wet patches began to appear on his plumage and slowly but surely, he began to lose buoyancy, a sure indication that he was not totally waterproof. But the exercise had done its job and from that day on bath time became a daily routine along with his three daily feeds. He was now going through copious amounts of sand eels, sprats and whitebait daily and this, combined with his daily bath, appeared to be working wonders: he looked fit, bright and full of energy and as such needed something more substantial than a cardboard box and an airing cupboard to call home.

William the Razorbill

For the past two weeks, I'd been busy constructing an enclosure for him in the garden which included a pool bordered by rocks placed to mimic a mini cliff. On the 18th March, although he still wasn't completely waterproof we decided that he was ready for the move. The aviary had shelter, a pool, rocks to sit on and he was a good healthy bodyweight. We carried him outside and popped him down by the pool; he waddled to the edge, looked around for a few moments then took the plunge. Just like in the bath, he swam and dived eventually jumping out onto one of the rocks to sit and preen his feathers. It was now the 24th

March and he was very content in his enclosure, he was feeding well and his plumage looked good, when he came out of the pool the water ran off him in tiny glistening droplets - like water off a duck's back!

He was an endearing bird and amusing to watch as he waddled around his enclosure occasionally emitting his throaty "goarrr, goarrr, goarrr" call. It was difficult to believe that he was in fact a totally wild seagoing bird that until being oiled, had in all probability never been in human contact before. He was totally trusting and seemed completely at home in his captive environment.

He'd been in his outdoor enclosure now for about three weeks and we started to give some serious thought to his release back into the wild. When I spoke to the RSPCA, they told me that members of the Auk family, i.e. Razorbills, Guillemots, Puffins and Auklets did not do well in captivity and would, over a period of time, develop various health problems all directly related to their captive environment. As such, we felt that time was of the essence and he had to go while he was still fit.

Plans were quickly put into action with the chosen release site being the Great Orme in Llandudno. A few days later, after a favourable long-range weather forecast, we set off for the north wales coast and Williams' last day of captivity. The weather was good as we drove along the coast road; the sea was calm with the waves gently lapping onto the rocky shore. At last, we reached our destination; we parked in a lay-by next to the beach and clambered down the grassy banking to the stony shore. Seagulls soared and called raucously overhead, a cormorant flew by skimming the surface of the water.

William was getting restless in his carrying box; it was as though he could sense the closeness of the sea and freedom. There was a cluster of large rocks leading out from the beach into the sea for a little way and it was decided that this would be a good place to release him. We carried him out to the farthermost large rock as he paddled around impatiently within the confines of his box. Upon reaching the farthest outcrop, Ann took him from his box and sat him on top of the rock giving him a good view of his surroundings and providing him with a good launch pad to freedom. We waited with baited breath; he just sat there on his haunches staring out to sea for what seemed an age. Every now and again, a light sea breeze would flurry through his feathers and he would stand erect, stretching his body and neck as far as he could with a flap of his stubby penguin like wings, emitting his now familiar call of "goarrr, goarrr, goarrr".

As the time went on he was becoming more restless; he obviously wanted to go but seemed hesitant as though trying to build up his confidence, then it happened! He finally launched himself into the air and with wings flapping rapidly he began to fly eventually dropping to within a couple of metres above the water. We watched as he flew farther and farther away from us and beyond the point of no return. Our minds were full off trepidation, would he be strong and fit enough to survive the harshness of his world once more and once in the water would he be totally waterproof? Only time would tell.

Eventually the inevitable happened as he belly flopped into the sea. We watched him through binoculars as he splashed around on his side just as he had in the bath. He dived under the waves only to pop back up again a few seconds later like a buoyant cork suddenly freed from the seabed. Thankfully he seemed to be doing well and enjoying himself, even rolling around on the surface and preening, but with a combination of his swimming and the current he was vanishing farther and farther out to sea until finally he was reduced to a tiny black dot on the horizon. He was being swallowed up into the vastness of the Irish Sea and it was becoming increasingly difficult to keep tabs on him: one minute he would on the crest of a wave and then totally vanish from view only to appear again a little farther away. Some 30 minutes had passed now and he was virtually lost from view. Even if something was to go wrong now, he would be too far out for us to be able to do anything about it, he was on his own.

All we could do was to wish him luck and head back home. With one last glance back out to sea we headed up the grassy embankment back to the car. Once we reached the top of the embankment we were quite a bit higher than we had been on the beach and as a consequence had a better view out to sea. And that was when we spotted the gulls!! About a half a dozen or so, they were a long way out and seemed to be swooping down on something. I quickly grabbed the binoculars and there way out in the distance I could just make out a tiny black speck that appeared to be the focus of the gulls' attention. At first I couldn't make out what it was, perhaps a bit of flotsam thrown overboard from a passing ship, but then I saw it move! A horrible feeling of desperation crept over me as I thought, surely it can't be William? Then our hearts sank as we realised that it was and he was in serious trouble and struggling to stay afloat and to add to his problems the gulls were taking full advantage of his precarious situation and mobbing him. We felt totally helpless, he was too far out to even to consider a rescue; all we could do was watch as he struggled to avoid the constant onslaught of the gulls as their attacks became ever more persistent. He was obviously waterlogged and in great danger of either drowning or being badly injured by the constant mobbing of the gulls.

It was awful to watch, he was becoming more and more waterlogged and as the water penetrated deeper into his plumage he began to sink lower into the water. We were now resigned to the awful fact that he was drowning and we couldn't do a thing about it. Rescue was out of the question and yet we couldn't just leave him to his fate but in the stark reality of the situation that was all we could do. Just watch until he finally vanished beneath the waves. And then the unbelievable happened! He was turning around and making for the shore, frantically paddling away with those stubby little wings. Surely he couldn't make it? He was a long way out and exhausted but he was making headway. Unable to contain ourselves we shouted encouragement, "Come on

William, you can make it," willing him to battle on against the sheer exhaustion that must have been tugging away at him with every stroke of his wings and the relentless mobbing of the gulls.

They would take it in turns to dive bomb him missing him by inches. Every now and again he would vanish as a wave washed over him, but his spirit to survive was far greater than the exhaustion or the gulls. He was fighting against the odds for survival and appeared to be winning. Our hearts were in our mouths, we just couldn't believe the determination of this little bird after all he'd been through and he was still fighting! After what seemed like an eternity, he finally made it to within a couple of metres of the shore. Ann, unable to contain herself, dashed into the oncoming waves and with the sea lapping above her knees snatched William from the water. He was absolutely soaked through with not a dry feather on his body. He was wet, cold and exhausted, but he was back, he had defied the odds and made it. We dried him off as best we could and wrapped him in a towel and with Ann cradling him we headed for home.

The big question was what now? If all the advice I had been given was correct then William, despite all his efforts to survive the oiling, the trauma of the washings, the force feeding, and now this, his future appeared very bleak indeed.

As we drove home we went through all the options; we could wash him again but that seemed a pointless exercise as he was already clean. We could keep him in captivity until he had completely moulted out in the hope that his new feathers would be watertight, but that would take a long time and by then it could be too late anyway! The only other option would be to take the RSPCA's advice and have him put to sleep. We knew that we were clutching at straws and the chances of long-term survival for this little fighter didn't look too good but he had made it quite obvious on more than one occasion that he wasn't ready to throw in the towel just yet! Fortunately within a couple of days he seemed to have recovered from his ordeal and was back to his normal contented self, bathing, preening and feeding.

The following week I rang the Wildfowl Trust at Martin Mere to see if they could offer any advice. They told me that they had been in a similar situation with a little auk, a close cousin of the razorbill, who had in fact become totally waterproof again after two months. They recommended adding vitamin supplements in the form of Vionate multivitamin powder and vitamin B12 to his food but concluded with, "We haven't tried it ourselves, but have heard that it works."

Over the coming weeks I sought advice from many different areas of expertise but it all varied tremendously and most of it had either already been done or was in the process of being done.

By the 10th April he was still looking wet after prolonged bathing but he was feeding well and seemed very content with his lot. Upon entering his enclosure he would come and waddle up to you with that funny little gait of his, flapping his stubby wings and emitting his usual guttural "goarrr, goarrr, goarrr" greeting. His endearing friendly nature won over all who met him and they found it difficult to believe that he was in fact a truly wild bird.

Over the coming weeks and months we tried just about everything that was recommended in the hope that something might miraculously give William back his well-earned freedom but nothing seemed to have any real long term effect. In a secure captive environment he looked a picture of health and vitality, but our last attempt at release taught us only too graphically that appearances can be very deceiving.

The 18th April brought another setback; he went off his food and started to lose condition. On the 21st April I had to resort to force-feeding him again but within minutes of getting food down him he brought it back up again. The following day I decided to ring the RSPCA at Little Creech again and upon relating the symptoms, they told me that this was a very common problem with members of the Auk family in captivity. Firstly loss of appetite, secondly loss of condition and thirdly death! Not what I wanted to hear! I'd heard it all before and thought, okay if he dies it won't be through lack of effort on our part and certainly not on his! We decided to battle on and on the 23rd April I tube fed him a solution of glucose and seawater blended with a mixture of Complan, sprats and herring.

To be honest the use of seawater instead of ordinary tap water, at least so far as we knew, shouldn't have made any difference at all but we were desperately grasping at straws. He was tube fed six or seven times a day and kept in a warm environment until at last on the 25th April he took some pieces of sprat from my fingers. This was the turning point and within four days he was eating as though there was no tomorrow and began to gain weight and condition.

On the 5th May, Peter McElroy the vet in West Kirby and myself attended a lecture at Martin Mere by a renowned specialist in avian medicine and author of many books on the subject. After the lecture we managed to corner the eminent professor and explained William's problems both past and present. Once again, everything he suggested we had already tried and ended by saying that we had done everything possible and unfortunately there was nothing else we could do. I was amazed that so little seemed to be known about the cleaning and rehabilitation of oiled sea birds and thought, 'we've done everything that can be done but what now?' Another attempt at release was out of the question we would merely be giving him a death sentence! We were now pretty well convinced that he would never again be fit enough to survive for long in his natural environment and after much deliberation we decided that as long as he had a decent quality of life and appeared to be happy and content, we would keep him in captivity.

Over the next six years, William enjoyed a full and healthy life, albeit a captive one and appeared to be completely happy and content with his lot. On numerous occasions over the coming years, he found himself sharing his enclosure and pool with recuperating guillemots, fulmars and kittiwakes. He challenged the expert's prognosis of his long-term survival in captivity by living a healthy life for another six years. He was an adult bird when he first arrived and, in the end, it was not pollution or illness that finally ended his life but old age. He passed away naturally and peacefully and we like to think that he's now chasing sand eels in the big ocean in the sky!

Over the years, a great deal more has been learnt about treating the casualties of oil contamination. In the aftermath of the Torrey Canyon disaster off Lands End in 1967 very little was known about the methods of washing casualties and the effects of ingesting oil, plus all the other associated problems and in particular the survival rate of released birds. Since that horrific disaster, we have been given ample opportunity to extend our knowledge and hone the skills necessary to deal a little better with the mass contamination of wildlife that inevitably follows any oil spillage disaster.

On the 24th March 1989, the Exxon Valdez spilled 232,000 barrels of oil into Prince William Sound in Alaska. In 1991 came the Gulf war and Saddam Hussain let loose an environmental oil disaster of unprecedented horror. On the 5th June 1993, the Brear tanker ran aground off Sumburgh Head in the Shetlands followed by the Sea Empress on the 15th February in 1996 in South Wales. The poisoning of our seas and oceans is ever present: ships illegally washing their tanks out at sea, a spillage from a local oil refinery or chemical plant. Whatever or wherever pollution occurs and whatever the scale, you can guarantee that wildlife in one form or another will suffer the consequences. Thankfully, we are now more aware of the effects of oil pollution on the environment and we have gained a wider knowledge in saving at least a small percentage of its casualties. But the lesson we refuse to learn is that the natural environment is a far more valuable commodity than oil and I fear that by the time it is learnt it will be too late!

Not too many years later, I was to find myself involved in a serious oil pollution disaster in the River Mersey that would entail me having to handle and treat many more severely oiled sea birds. This also led to a media frenzy with me being filmed handling some horrifically contaminated birds plus interviews on various TV channels, national newspapers and magazines.

Hello magazine even ran a full page article on the disaster with a picture of me holding a dead cormorant that looked more like a big lump of black tar than a bird. At times, I found it difficult to juggle between trying to help the casualties and deal with all the media attention but at least I was able to voice my frustration at such a sad and sorry tragedy.

Ironically, shortly after this sad episode and despite my condemnation of them in the media, I was contacted by Shell UK at their Stanlow Oil Refinery in Cheshire. These were the people directly responsible for the disaster and subsequently had been fined a large sum of money. They asked if I would consider carrying out a full flora and fauna survey of the refinery including making recommendations as to how they could maintain any existing wildlife areas within the refinery and the feasibility of creating new ones. My findings and recommendations would then be published in an eye-catching format that would tell all and sundry what Shell UK was doing to preserve wildlife in the biggest oil refinery in the UK. It was to be distributed throughout Shell both at home and abroad.

My first thoughts were 'What on earth am I going to find in a giant oil refinery other than pollution?' and my second was that this was nothing more than a public relations exercise in an effort to try and win back a few brownie points. But I said yes and much to my surprise discovered that there was indeed an abundance of wildlife living within the security boundaries of Stanlow. I discovered large areas of derelict land that nature had reclaimed and were now home to a varied and diverse mixture of flora and fauna from breeding peregrine falcons, kestrels, barn owls, ravens, little ringed plovers and lapwings. The list seemed endless: orchids grew in profusion, foxes took scraps of food from the night shift workers and badgers thrived.

Finally my report was published and yes it was a PR exercise, but it was also a working conservation management plan for the site listing all existing flora and fauna plus various recommendations for creating new habitats. My visits to Stanlow carried on for many years and I took great satisfaction from the fact that many of my proposals were in fact implemented including the creation of a very large pond that became home to a variety of avian and aquatic species. Although not achieving all of my goals I did see a marked difference in managerial attitudes towards wildlife both within and beyond the refinery. Quite often, I would be invited to sit in on managerial meetings in order to highlight and give advice on any adverse effects that the proposals being discussed may have for wildlife.

None of what they implemented within Stanlow could ever make up for the tragic loss of life caused by their oil spill but it did benefit wildlife, not only from creating new habitats but also from highlighting and taking positive actions to ensure that the preservation of flora and fauna within the refinery and beyond was high on the agenda.

Chapter Four
Operation Nighthawk

It was five o' clock on Friday the 11th October 1985 and I had just arrived home from the reserve. It had been one of those days; what with the tractor getting bogged down in the mud whilst scraping out a new pond and the sledge hammer head flying off the shaft as I was hammering in a fence post almost braining my volunteer John the would be priest in the process. We reckoned it was nothing short of divine intervention that saved him!

The Ingham wildlife menagerie was growing and if I wasn't feeding something I would be out knocking up a new enclosure or aviary for some furred or feathered creature. I was about to make myself a coffee before checking on a couple of sick gulls, the kettle was just coming to the boil and I was about to put a spoonful of coffee in the mug when the inevitable knock came at the door. You could guarantee that to sit down for a meal or to put the kettle on would automatically generate a response from either the telephone or the front door.

Cursing to myself at the intrusion I opened it to see a gentleman standing there clutching a shoebox tightly to his chest.

"Sorry to bother you," he said apologetically, "but the RSPCA said I should bring it to you."

"That's fine, what have you got?"

"I was in the garden when I found it, I took it to a pet shop in Moreton and they told me it was a bird of prey and to ring the RSPCA and as I explained they told me to bring it to you," he said as he thrust the box towards me.

Before leaving he hurriedly scribbled his name and address down on a piece of crumpled paper saying, "You will let me know how it gets on won't you?"

I promised that I would and once back in the house I laid the box down on the dining room table, re-boiled the kettle and made that desperately needed mug of coffee. With my caffeine levels replenished I slowly lifted the lid of the box just enough to be able to peer inside fully expecting to find a blackbird or thrush but as I peeked in I couldn't believe my eyes.

I called to Ann, "My God I think it's a nightjar!!"

Nightjars hadn't been recorded on Wirral for many years but here I was peeking in at what, to all intents and purposes, definitely appeared to be a nightjar. I carefully removed the lid and gently took it out of the box to take a closer look, immediately realizing that yes this was indeed a nightjar, but not of the European variety! It was about nine and a half inches in length with grey-brown mottled plumage, long pointed wings with bold white bars, a slightly forked tail, a large head and mouth, which seemed to be out of proportion to the rest of its body and two enormous black eyes. In some respects it was similar in appearance to that of a small falcon hence the confusion at the pet shop. It was a handsome looking bird but it was in a bad way. The breastbone was sharp and protruding with those two big black eyes half closed and glazed. I gave it a quick examination but couldn't find any visible injuries; it was obviously starving and appeared to be totally exhausted. The first priority was to treat it for shock and after placing it into a more suitable box lined with an old towel we popped it into the darkness and warmth of the airing cupboard for a few hours on the concept that if it worked for a razorbill then why not for a nightjar?

After treating it for shock the second priority was food and the third was to identify it as a species, at this point it was a UFO (unidentified flying object), albeit of the nightjar variety. After a couple of hours in the airing cupboard we decided to try him with a bit of minced beef rolled into tiny sausages dampened with a little glucose and water and dipped into insectivorous food. We also had a few live mealworms leftover from feeding a robin a few days earlier and decided to try to get a couple of these down him also. We had used this diet with some success on swallows, swifts and house martins, and as these birds feed on various flying insects and catch their prey on the wing, as do nightjars, it seemed the most obvious choice.

Before attempting the first feed, we weighed him and he was a mere 46 grams, not a lot for a bird of his size, estimating that he should ideally be in the region of about 55 to 60 grams. However, before we could determine his normal healthy bodyweight we would have to identify him as a species followed by his natural diet and where he should rightly be, which obviously was not Wirral! But first things first, food was the number one priority right now. If we didn't get something into him soon, he stood a very real chance of literally starving to death. We tried to tempt him by gently popping the food into his mouth but it came as no great surprise when he completely refused to accept all of our culinary offerings and spat them out followed by clamping his beak tightly shut. This left us with no choice, but to resort to force-feeding as we did with William.

I don't like having to resort to this method, it's stressful for the bird and time consuming for the carer but sometimes it's the only way to get vital nourishment into a starving bird. Very gently we opened his beak to reveal an enormous cavernous gape designed to catch and swallow large moths and other nocturnal flying insects. We placed a small sausage shaped morsel of food at the very back of his throat above the tongue and gently pushed it down into the depths then closed his beak and massaged the throat until the food had been swallowed repeating the process a couple of times before allowing him to rest. After a few more feeds he began to swallow the food voluntarily but we still had to resort to gently forcibly opening his mouth and popping the food in. It was a huge step forward; he was at least taking food without the indignation of having a finger pushed down his throat. At around midnight, we decided that he should now at least be able to survive the night without the danger of fading away from starvation. We placed him carefully back into his box and back into the warmth of the airing cupboard for the night. At around 6 am the following morning I decided to check on him and with some trepidation took the box from the airing cupboard. To be honest we didn't hold out too much hope and fully expected him to have passed away through a combination of starvation and exhaustion but, like William, this little bird had more resolve than I gave him credit for and as I peeked in I saw those two big black eyes staring back at me. He was looking remarkably perky considering his condition but it soon became obvious that feeding was still going to be a battle of wills with him clamping his beak tightly shut but with perseverance we managed to get more food into him.

The true identity of the bird still baffled me and the following day I rang the local RSPB warden explaining that I had a rather unusual looking nightjar that required a second opinion with regards to a positive identification. After much deliberation and going through the pages of countless bird books we finally decided that we had a male common nighthawk (*Chordeiles minor*). He was described in the books as a bird that occupies open lowland areas over much of North America roosting on tree branches, rooftops, fence posts and on the ground, feeding on flying insects active during early morning and late evening and migrates south for the winter. We concluded that he was an immature bird, possibly on his first migration to Central or South America when he was blown a few thousand miles off course by hurricane 'Gloria': a hurricane that had been working its way through the southern states of the USA and Central America at that particular time and making headline news in the UK.

He was fed on average every two or three hours from early morning to around midnight spending his nights in the warmth of the airing cupboard. On day three he was looking fairly lethargic, he hadn't gained weight since arriving but on the positive side he hadn't lost any either. At least we were keeping him stable but his plumage was looking more jaded and his eyes duller. He was still losing condition and it wasn't going to improve unless we could get him on a more suitable diet and quickly. I spoke to people in the avian dept. at Jersey Zoo, London Zoo and Chester Zoo, all to no avail. I found it amazing that nobody appeared to be able to offer me any positive advice on caring for a common nighthawk in captivity.

They all said the same. "We've never had one, we don't know of anybody that has kept them in captivity."

Eventually I was a recommended a book called *Diets for Birds in Captivity* jointly written by Kenton C. and Alice Marie Lint. Prior to his retirement in 1976, Kenton C. Lint had been the Curator of Birds at San Diego Zoo in California and wrote the book to fill a vital gap in the aviculture market. It was said to be an indispensable book for anyone working with birds in private collections or zoos. It was certainly worth a try; after all, it was the only positive advice I had been given so far! Unfortunately I was also told that it wasn't a particularly easy book to get hold of in the UK and with no such thing as web browsing in those days it was a case of making numerous phone calls to book dealers up and down the country until I finally tracked down a copy. It was ordered without delay with a plea for urgency and dispatched the same day.

It was now day five; he was still battling on but losing condition far too rapidly. Despite all our efforts, he just wasn't getting enough food and what he was getting obviously wasn't nutritious enough to allow him to gain that vital weight. We had even considered tube feeding but I was sure that the stress would knock him over the edge and kill him.

On the morning of day six the postman arrived and a brown parcel slipped through the letterbox, I eagerly opened the package; it was the book at last, it had only taken two days to arrive but it felt an awful lot longer. I immediately began to thumb through the species index looking for common nighthawk. The list seemed endless with everything from the humble house sparrow to trumpeter swans and turkey vultures with individual listings of all their dietary requirements in captivity. But would you believe it - no mention of a nighthawk! I thought 'surely it must be there, it's got to be!' Then, after much searching I came across a family group called Caprimulgiformes which listed frogmouths, a close cousin of nightjars, and there at last on page 106 - Nightjars!! I couldn't find the common nighthawk but I did find a very close relative, the 'Dusky Poor-will' (*Phalaenoptilus nuttallii californicus*).

The recommended diet was three newborn mice or rats followed by three or four cockroaches or crickets hand fed three times a day at the following times: 7 am, 12 noon and 6 pm. I immediately set about the task of acquiring these rather unsavoury sounding dietary requirements. A local pet shop offered to supply the newborn mice in the form of frozen pinkies whilst Chester Zoo offered me a supply of live locusts, not exactly crickets but they would suffice. Cockroaches proved impossible to get hold of but I must admit to not being over bothered about that one, pinkies and locusts would have to do. At his next feed, I offered him his normal diet in the form of a mealworm lightly moistened and dipped in insectivorous food.

He responded in his normal uncooperative manner by clamping his beak tightly shut and turning his head away in disgust, then I offered him a live locust, he looked at it opened his mouth slightly and as he did so I quickly popped in the squirming insect, he swallowed it without hesitation! Eureka!! He had just voluntarily taken food for the very first time since he had been with us but now for the big test, a tiny pink bald mouse! I picked up the newly defrosted pinkie and dangled it in front of him. The response was amazing! He immediately opened his mouth to reveal a great gaping cavernous hole that up to now had only been opened very reluctantly to a mere fraction of its capacity. Before I could pop it in he grasped the pink lump from my fingers and in one gulp, it was gone. If he could have licked his lips I'm sure he would have.

We had just crossed a massive milestone and from that moment on there was no looking back. From thereon he accepted all offerings of food with great relish and rapidly began to gain weight and condition. His eyes lost that dull uninterested look and began to open wide and sparkle like two shiny black gems. His plumage gained a healthy sheen and he was soon looking a picture of health and vitality. His weight shot up from the original 46 grams to a far more respectable 56 grams.

We now found ourselves facing a totally unexpected problem in that our nighthawk was rapidly becoming something of a celebrity! Apparently he was a very rare bird for the UK with only very few ever being previously recorded, and so we were told, never been in captivity in the UK.

All the previous sightings had been mainly on the Scilly Isles with the records listing the following:

Two sightings on the Scilly Isles, September 17th 1927.
Two sightings on the Scilly Isles, September 28th 1955
Two sightings on the Scilly Isles, October 12th 1971
One sighting at Nottingham, October 8th 1971
A rare individual indeed!

We hadn't broadcast the fact that we were caring for a nighthawk and even more so once we realised what a rarity he actually was. The bird's welfare was paramount and if my past experiences of twitchers was anything to go by, and they got knowledge of his location, they would stop at nothing to try and add another tick to their little twitchers book. But it soon became obvious that if I was winning the battle with the bird, I was definitely losing it with the twitchers. Unfortunately, word got out and someone decided to advertise his whereabouts publicly on the various twitcher outlets and that was it. They descended in their droves!

One evening about fifty arrived by coach with binoculars and cameras dangling from around their necks clutching their twitchers tick list and with pencils at the ready came stomping up the drive to the front door demanding to see the 'Common Nighthawk!' Not a 'please can we' or a 'sorry to bother you' from a single one of them. So far as they were concerned it was their God given right to be allowed to see the bird regardless of what I thought about it. They didn't appear overly convinced when I told them that I had no idea what they were talking about and one or two even had the audacity to imply that I wasn't being entirely truthful provoking me to deliver a rather curt and not too polite reply. Finally even the thicker-skinned of the rabble got the message and after much grumbling and whingeing trudged off back down the drive to their awaiting coach minus that all important tick! Would you have fifty muddy booted binocular slung twitchers running loose in your living room? Not on your nelly, I bet!!

But that wasn't the end of it: over the coming days they kept on coming like flies to a jam pot, so much so that I even considered investing in a water cannon to wash them off the drive! I'm sorry to say that my opinion of twitchers is born from my many bad experiences of their total disregard for the well-being of their chosen quarry and the extremes to which they will lower themselves in pursuit of a tick in their little book. May they all suffer from fogged binoculars and lack of lead in their pencils!

Despite the many distractions thrust upon me by these tick chasers the nighthawk was in fact doing extremely well and now ready for release. But this was easier said than done. He should have been sunning himself in Central or South America not on Wirral, particularly in October and the oncoming winter. I was now facing perhaps an even bigger challenge. Okay, we had saved him from starvation and certain death, but what of his future? Somehow we had to get him back to where he should have been in the first place. Time wasn't on our side, even though he was now fit and healthy, the longer he remained in captivity the less likely his chances of survival were going to be, time was of the essence. We had to come up with something quickly but I had no idea what! By this time the national newspapers and TV were picking up on the story with the BBC ringing one day to say that they wanted to feature the bird on one of their topical news programmes and could they send a crew along to do some filming. I gave it some serious thought but declined even though it may have been a way of appealing for help in the release, I was unsure at that point how the bird would cope with the stress of the cameras and handling under that sort of situation and I wasn't prepared to risk it.

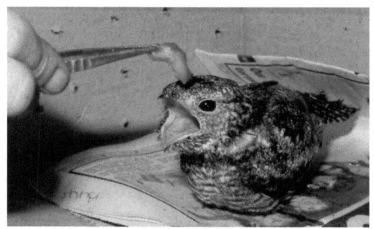

Nigel the Nighthawk taking a pinkie

Various national newspapers had also been in touch wanting to run the story then the Daily Mail rang to say that if they could have an exclusive they would, one way or another, assist in getting the nighthawk back to his rightful destination. How could I refuse, it sounded too good an opportunity to miss and to be honest theirs was the only positive offer of help, the other media outlets wanted the story but none of them actually offered any positive assistance. I stressed the importance of the time factor and that the wheels would have to start turning very quickly indeed. They said that they fully understood the urgency and would get things moving as quickly as was feasibly possible.

Initially they approached British Airways, who offered the bird a flight out to Rio de Janeiro in Brazil. I declined the offer for two reasons, firstly the destination wasn't ideal and secondly, they could only offer accommodation in the cargo hold which again was out of the question. Regardless of the destination, it was important that he be accompanied and monitored on such a long flight. He would require his five daily feeds; his travelling box would need to be kept clean and with someone to constantly check on his welfare. I had not done all this just for him to die of stress or neglect on an aeroplane!

On the afternoon of Tuesday the 15th October, Andrew Louden, a reporter with the Daily Mail arrived at the house along with Kevin Holt a photographer. Andrew busily jotted down the full story of the nighthawk whilst Kevin took several photographs.

Andrew paused from his writing and enquired, "Does he have a name?"

"Not really."

"Well he should have, it gives him an identity with the readers," and after much deliberation we decided upon 'Nigel'.

Why Nigel and not Fred or George is now lost in the realms of time but it seemed to suit him and Nigel didn't object. His diet now consisted of a one day old mouse, four live locusts and three mealworms fed five times a day with a sprinkling of vitamin supplement. His weight now peaked at a constant 54 grams, which was recorded as the normal healthy bodyweight for a male of his species and he seemed very content with his lot, not showing the slightest hint of stress during his photo session with Kevin, posing quite happily. The following day the Daily Mail ran a preview of the story and within a few days Andrew was on the phone saying that the RAF had been in touch and were offering to fly Nigel from Brize Norton to Belize. Belize was one of my ideal choices with Common Nighthawks being recorded there on their migration south and even better, the Belize Audubon Society had recorded them as a breeding species.

Brize Norton is the largest RAF station in the UK and the main base for their air transport capabilities and home to No.1 Parachute Training School. The flight was to be on one of their regular Wednesday morning VC10 flights out to Belmopan the capital of Belize with Nigel joining the various military personnel and their families all destined for a spell of service out there. They were even offering to allocate him his very own personal stewardess in the form of Flight Sgt Jill Corner to pander to his every whim and it was even hinted that I may even be allowed to go too. Needless to say I jumped at the offer! Anything for a free holiday!! From the moment I said yes things began to move quickly and the following plans were soon in place.

Upon arrival in Belize he was to be met by an RAF corporal who was also a British Trust for Ornithology bird ringer along with representatives from the Belize Audubon Society. He would be taken to Belize Zoo for a thorough check up, given five star overnight accommodation with bed and breakfast after which he would be released back into the wild with the option of staying in Belize or to continue upon his slightly interrupted migration. What more could a VIP bird ask for!   All we had to do now was to sort out a few simple formalities and he would be on his way. The RAF were all ready to go with the following Wednesday to be the day of departure. All was organized and ready at the Belize end and it was arranged that Andrew and myself with Nigel would drive down to Brize Norton on the Tuesday ready for the early Wednesday morning flight, or at least that was the plan!

The week prior to departure the phone rang, I picked up the receiver to hear Andrew saying, "Hello Malcolm, we have a problem, don't panic it can be resolved."

When I was able get a word in I enquired, "What sort of problem?"

He went on to explain that in order for Nigel to be able to leave our green and pleasant land he would have to conform to the requirements of the European Regulations 3626/82 and 3418/83!

"Conform to what?"

"Don't worry about it. The Daily Mail will sort it out."

In non-bureaucratic jargon it simply meant that he needed an export license and a vet's certificate of health. He also went on to explain that because of a ninety minute refuelling stop in Miami USA he would also require a license from the USA aviation authorities and a Federal Wildlife Permit plus an import license to enter Belize! Simple really!

Thankfully some influential people pulled a few influential strings and things began to move rather quickly with paper work that would normally take weeks coming through in days. Eventually the Daily Mail rang to say that all I needed now was to have Nigel issued with a vet's certificate of health and he would be on his way. The following day I rang Brian Coles the vet. who specialised in avian medicine and also happened to be a keen ornithologist and as such didn't hesitate at the chance to examine this little avian rarity. Nigel was given a thorough examination, pronounced fit and healthy and issued with the final piece of paper that would allow him to fly out to Belize. Or so we thought! The RAF had scheduled Wednesday 23rd October for the flight and made all the necessary arrangements including accommodation for Andrew Louden and myself in the officer's quarters. And then it happened!

Some bright spark in the USA Wildlife Service posed the question, "What is this bird going to be fed on during the flight?"

He was told dead day old mice and live locusts, which apparently created the response of, "What!! Live locusts!! We can't allow live locust to enter the US!!"

They then softened a little by asking, "Where and how are they to be kept on board the aircraft?" followed by asking themselves, 'can we permit this and if so do they need a licence?'

Thankfully, it was all resolved pretty quickly with the US officials finally relenting by saying, "OK under the circumstances, we will allow it just as long as they (the locusts) can't escape and are not taken off the aircraft."

At long last, we had the green light and were still on schedule for the 23rd October. I kept an ever-watchful eye on Nigel ensuring that he stayed fit and healthy and didn't totally embarrass me by popping his clogs or something silly.

All the birds we cared for and ultimately rehabilitated were given a British Trust for Ornithology (BTO) ring prior to release which meant that if the bird was found sick, injured or dead after release the details would filter back to me. It was an invaluable tool in determining the success of our releases; two notable recoveries were that of a heron found dead seven years after release and the second being a peregrine falcon taken into a vet in North Wales suffering slight concussion two years after release.

It was particularly important with regards to Nigel as he was the only common nighthawk ever to have been in care and rehabilitated from the UK and as such was given ring number BTO.RX72927.

Wednesday the 23rd October crept ever closer and I was running around like a headless chicken trying to ensure that I had everything under control and ready for the big day. My mind was full of nagging questions. 'Had I prepared enough food for the flight? Would his travelling box be suitable for such a long journey? Would he cope with the hustle and bustle of passengers embarking and the roar of the engines before take-off?'

It was now Tuesday 22nd October and it was going to be a very busy day! I was up bright and early to give Nigel his first feed of the day followed by organizing his food for the long journey ahead. It was imperative that the mice stay frozen until needed and the locust stay alive and fresh. It was going to be a long flight, first to Miami then onto Belize, it was vital that Nigel retained his healthy bodyweight and condition; he had to arrive in Belize as fit and healthy as he was when he left the UK. The Daily Mail had agreed for the story to be covered locally and at 10.30 am, a reporter and photographer arrived from the Liverpool Daily Post, followed shortly after by Granada Television to film a news item for Granada Reports. At mid-day, I gave Nigel another feed followed by making myself a badly needed mug of coffee and trying to grab a bit of free time before Andrew arrived for the long drive down to Brize

Norton. At 12.45 pm Andrew's BMW pulled up outside.

"Afternoon Malcolm," he greeted swiftly. "Everything ready, how's Nigel?"

"All ready to go, Nigel's fine," I said as I began to load the cool box of frozen mice and the container of live locusts into the boot. With Nigel bedded down in his cardboard travelling box and strapped securely to the back seat I did a last minute check to make sure nothing had been forgotten. Finally I said my farewells, grabbed my travel bag and at last we were on our way! As we drove off, Andrew began to fill me in on the itinerary once we arrived at Brize Norton. It sounded pretty hectic with photo shoots for the Daily Mail plus the RAF Public Relations people wanted interviews and photographs for their journal the 'RAF News.' After an uneventful journey, we arrived at Brize Norton pulling up to the main gate at 6 pm whereupon a heavily armed sentry requested our passes.

After checking them over he gave us directions to the main administration building informing us that someone would be there to meet us followed by, "How's the bird, Malcolm?"

"Just fine thanks," I replied.

He raised the security barrier and as he waved us through said, "Hope he makes it."

We thanked him and drove into the midst of a full-blown security exercise with military personnel running around all over the place all adorned in full combat gear and armed to the teeth as they attempted to ward off some mysterious non-existent breach of military security. I couldn't help but think, 'it's just like being back in the T. A.!' After dodging several security patrols, we pulled up outside the main admin. building totally unscathed and with not a single scratch or bullet hole to Andrew's beloved BMW. We were met by Flt. Lt. Strachen, the base Community Relations Officer. She escorted us to her office where over coffee and biscuits gave us a quick chat regarding security protocol whilst temporarily residing on a high security military air base.

With the security formalities over we were then escorted to our quarters at Gateway House, the RAF Air Transit Centre for Brize Norton, followed by a tour of the officer's mess and an invitation to make full use of the facilities. My main priority was to check on Nigel, it had been a long journey and he would be ready for a feed. I'd left him in my quarters at Gateway House and at the first available opportunity made my way back to check on him, he was fine and seemed totally unperturbed by the journey. I gently lifted him out of his box and sat him on the bed and offered him a pinkie, he immediately opened his beak to reveal that great gaping cavern of a mouth and swallowed it with relish. This was followed by a couple of locusts for desert after which he closed his eyes and nodded off in total contentment. I put the remainder of the mice in the freezer compartment of the little fridge tucked away in a corner of the room and placed the locusts secure in their jar by the bedside table. I was a little concerned about his food staying fresh on such a long journey and was contemplating what could go amiss when my thoughts were interrupted by a knock at the door. It was Andrew coming to tell me that we were needed on the runway for a couple of photo shots and to meet some people. I picked up Nigel who was now quietly nodding off and followed Andrew downstairs where we were met by a Corporal Johnson. He escorted us out of Gateway House along a maze of roads eventually passing through a couple of gigantic and very noisy aircraft hangars.

The noise was deafening as engineers busily worked on an assortment of aircraft from VC10's to fighter jets. I was a little concerned as to how Nigel would react to all the commotion but he seemed fine and once again took it all in his stride. After dodging around aircraft and personnel, we passed through two enormous doors leading out onto a complex of runways. Everywhere was buzzing with activity with trucks, jeeps, army and RAF personnel dashing here there and everywhere. A very large military aircraft was coming in to land whilst another was preparing to take off, it was all hustle and bustle and very, very noisy.

"We're going over to this one," shouted the Corporal over the din as he led us to a parked VC 10.

The corporal introduced us to Flt. Sgt Jill Corner, the aircraft's loadmaster and Nigel's carer and stewardess for the long flight to Belize. We were shortly joined by an RAF photographer who was there to take a few pictures for the Royal Air Force News along with Kevin Holt the Daily Mail photographer. Nigel, myself and Jill Corner posed for numerous photographs taken both inside the aircraft and on the runway with the VC 10 in the background. They took a nice one of Jill in the cockpit with Nigel sat contentedly in the palm of her hand. He took all this attention totally in his stride and showed not the slightest hint of being perturbed, if anything he seemed to be enjoying his moment of fame. The way he reacted to captivity and handling amazed me, anyone not aware of his circumstances could be forgiven for assuming that he was a tame bird fully accustomed to people and being handled which of course he wasn't. He was a totally wild bird, never having been in captivity or handled by people until his unceremonious crash landing in a flower bed on the Wirral.

Finally, with rapidly fading light the photographers called it a day leaving me free to instruct Jill on feeding Nigel and hand over a list of instructions on caring for his food and feeding schedule. We also decided that she should give him his next feed whilst I was there to watch over her. She was a natural and took to it like a duck to water. After the feed she gave me a tour of the aircraft and showed me where she would be sitting during the flight explaining that the seat next to hers was reserved for Nigel! She had thought of everything, making sure that any noise and vibration would be kept to an absolute minimum by putting foam padding around his box. It was dark when we descended from the aircraft and it took a second or two for my eyes to acclimatize to the strong arc lights that now illuminated the scene.

As we walked back along the tarmac, I could make out the dark shapes of aircraft silhouetted against the night sky, the lights of the runways flickering bright and fading away into the distance. I felt much more at ease and fully confident in Jill's ability to care for Nigel on his long journey to freedom. The corporal escorted us back to Gateway House where I popped Nigel back into the room before retiring to the officer's mess for a long overdue meal washed down by a couple of beers. Feeling more relaxed and with the pangs of hunger satisfied, I returned to give Nigel one last feed before finally collapsing into bed at around 11.30 pm and was out like a light as soon as my head touched the pillow! I could have sworn that I had only been in bed a couple of hours before I was rudely awakened by the alarm clocks incessant ringing - it was 5.30 am. Bleary eyed and half asleep I stumbled out of bed had a quick shower and at 6 am fed Nigel for the last time. I felt a twinge of sadness knowing that in a short while we would be parting company for the very last time. At 6.30 am I made my way down to the officer's mess for breakfast.

Andrew was already there and, looking as bleary eyed as me, greeted me with, "Morning, sleep well?"

"Fine thanks."

"How's Nigel?"

"He's fine he's just had his breakfast."

I sat myself down as the aroma of fresh coffee and the sound of sizzling egg and bacon began to awaken my senses. Not being a breakfast person, I wasn't particularly hungry but my caffeine levels were in dire need of replenishment and I craved for a coffee. Andrew got up and wandered over to the breakfast table to help himself to orange juice and a bowl of cornflakes. I settled for toast and a large cup of that delicious smelling coffee. Once happily seated with my toast and caffeine fix I began to take in my surroundings.

The walls were adorned with an assortment of RAF shields and framed prints depicting various types of aircraft from Lancaster Bombers and Spitfires to modern day jet fighters. The room was empty apart from Andrew, myself and a lady accompanied by two children who were noisily devouring a couple of bowls of Sugar Puffs. I guessed that she must have been an officer's wife flying out with her children to accompany her husband and probably on Nigel's flight destined for Belize. Two RAF stewards were hovering around ready to serve up their culinary delights in the form of freshly cooked eggs, bacon and sausages and to replenish our cups with that delicious freshly ground hot coffee.

Over breakfast, Andrew explained that we had to be on the runway by 7.30 am at the very latest in order to settle Nigel down and to check on any last minute details, the flight was scheduled for take-off at 8.30 am. I glanced at my watch, it was 6.55 am - just enough time for another cup of coffee before the off. Andrew had already downed a glass of orange juice, a bowl of cereal, two fried eggs sunny side up with three rashers of bacon and was now tucking into toast and marmalade washed down with coffee. I have never really been a breakfast sort of person; two cups of coffee have usually been my only requirements to kick start my brain and body into some resemblance of normality, but Andrew was a journalist and as such required a greater amount of sustenance to oil the wheels of that journalistic brain of his. At least that was his excuse!

At 7.10 am, I left him devouring the remains of his toast and marmalade and made my back to the room to collect Nigel and his food. I glanced in his box and those two big black shiny eyes stared back at me, he was fine and probably still digesting his breakfast of mice and locusts. I checked on the food again for the umpteenth time, the mice were still frozen and the locusts alive and kicking. I told myself that I was becoming paranoid! With butterflies in my stomach and pangs of trepidation, I tucked Nigel under my arm picked up the box of food and made my way down the flight of stairs to the main door. Andrew, having demolished his toast and marmalade was chatting to the Corporal who once again was to be our escort onto the runway.

"Morning," he greeted cheerfully; "follow me please

gentlemen, the Captain is waiting to meet you."

We walked briskly away from Gateway House and passed once again through the hustle and bustle of the aircraft hangers to emerge onto the runway.

We were met by Flt. Sgt Jill Corner who, upon wishing us good morning, shook our hands and said, "Hope you had a comfortable night, how's Nigel?"

Andrew and I answered in unison, "Yes, very comfortable thank you and Nigel's just fine and raring to go."

"Good, if you will follow me I will take you on board and introduce you to the Captain."

It only seemed like an hour ago that Nigel and I were walking away from this scene then all illuminated by the powerful arc lights. Now here we were again on this chilly fine October morning with the early morning mist still hanging low over the runway but this time it was for real, we were to board the aircraft once more but this time only one of us was getting off, and it wasn't Nigel! It had been mentioned originally that I might be going with him but apparently the problem was that the return flight wasn't until the following Wednesday. I did try to convince them that I wouldn't mind in the slightest to be twiddling my thumbs in the tropics for a week but it wasn't to be! The VC10 was parked on the runway and was a hive of activity with luggage being stowed in the hold; ground crew walked around kicking the tyres and making other last minute external checks.

Jill said, "Follow me," as she climbed the boarding steps and entered the aircraft and what a difference from yesterday!

The atmosphere was hot and noisy with military personnel and their families jostling up and down the aisle looking for their seats and stowing away their hand luggage. Yesterday it looked so large and roomy; today it looked quite small and claustrophobic!

Eventually Jill's voice jolted me out of my momentary lapse of concentration as she said, "Come on Malcolm this way to the flight deck."

We squeezed our way along the narrow aisle to enter the inner sanctum of the Captain's cabin whereupon Jill introduced Andrew and myself to Flight Lieutenant Stan Black who was to pilot the aircraft out to Belize. After shaking our hands, he asked if he could have a quick peep at his VIP guest. I opened Nigel's box for him to have a peek inside but time was catching up with us and Jill decided that it was time to get him settled down for take-off.

As we left the flight deck, Flt. Lieut. Black said reassuringly, "Don't worry we'll give him a safe flight."

I thanked him and shook his hand once again before following Jill back into the hustle and bustle of the main passenger deck. The atmosphere was much more subdued with the majority of passengers now in their seats and preparing for take-off, some in army or RAF uniform and others in civvies. One or two were still stuffing their hand luggage into the overhead lockers whilst others read newspapers or a book; some were gazing out of the small oval windows that were now beginning to mist over with condensation from the heat generated within the aircraft intermingling with the cold damp morning air coming from the open doors. Some smiled as I passed whilst a few stopped me for a chat, curious about this fellow passenger called Nigel. Sat at the very back was the lady from the breakfast room with her two children, she looked a little nervous and pensive whilst the children busily rubbed the condensation from the windows in an attempt get a better view of the outside world.

"Here we are" said Jill, "this is where I sit and this one is for Nigel, the locust box will fit under the seat and I'll keep the mice in the freezer box, here is a list of his feeding times what do you think?"

"Great, you've thought of everything."

Suddenly I became aware of a sound other than the intermingling chatter of the passengers; the aircraft's engines were beginning to rev up, eventually the roar drowned out all normal conversation and then it subsided into a low rhythmic throb. I glanced at my watch it was 8.20 am, time to get off.

"Ten minutes to take off, time to go." said Jill.

I glanced at Nigel for the last time and as I lifted the lid of his box those two shiny enormous black eyes stared back at me, I wished him luck and closed the box for the last time.

"He'll be fine," Jill assured me as she escorted me off the aircraft.

We bade our farewells on the tarmac, Jill promising to let me know how he got on. She paused for a second as she climbed the steps to give a final wave before vanishing into the aircraft sliding the door tightly shut behind her. Andrew and I moved away towards the hangars as the VC10 revved its engines once again and began to taxi towards the runway. At 8.30 am precisely it was given the all clear for take-off and with a deafening roar of the four powerful Rolls-Royce Conway Turbo engines it sped down the runway. I stood and watched as it slowly lifted off the tarmac, the landing gear disappearing back into the fuselage as it climbed higher and higher finally disappearing into the clouds.

Nigel was now up in the clouds, but I was suddenly brought back down to earth with Andrew saying, "I'll just make a quick call to the office and let them know he's on his way, and then we'll grab a coffee."

We made our way back to Gateway House and whilst Andrew wandered off to make his call, I made my way to the officer's mess to be met once again by the now familiar aroma of freshly brewed coffee.

I poured myself a cup and sat down to reflect over the past few days, the steward wandered over enquiring, "Has he gone?"

"Yes, he's on his way at last."

"Are you staying long?"

"No, we'll soon be on our way as well."

At that point Andrew returned saying, "The office is pleased with the result," as he poured himself a coffee,

"Should make a nice story, I'll down this and we'll be on our way what do you think?"

"Yes, fine, I suppose the quicker we get home the better."

Coffees over, we thanked the steward for his hospitality and went off to collect our bits and pieces from Gateway House. Fifteen minutes later and the BMW was packed and ready for the off. All that was left was to say a few goodbyes and make our way back to the Wirral and by 10.30 am we were on the road and heading for home. We stopped off briefly for a pub lunch at a quaint little Cotswold village hostelry and over a pint and a ploughman's we chatted about the story and hopefully, the follow up from Belize.

Mr. W. Craig, Executive Director of the Belize Audubon Society had promised to keep me informed of Nigel's progress from landing to the final release and send me any press cuttings. Apparently, the Belize newspapers had picked up on the story and wanted to take a few photographs of Nigel's arrival and release.

The journey home was uneventful but my thoughts were still with Nigel and the long journey he had in front of him, but my own journey was coming to an end and within a few short hours we were back on the Wirral and home.

As we shook hands and bade our farewells Andrew thanked me saying, "That was a good trip, I'll give you a ring in a day or two, and hopefully we may have some news."

For the first couple of days I heard nothing and then at long last he called to say that he had just received a call from the RAF. They established that after fifteen and a half hours and 4,840 miles after leaving Brize Norton, Nigel had finally touched down in Belize at 16.30 hours. Dusk was falling when Jill took Nigel off the VC10 and handed him over to RAF Corporal Paul Triggs, who was accompanied by a couple of representatives from the Belize Audubon Society. They immediately took him to Belize Zoo where he was given a check over by the zoo's vet. Dr. Sheila

Schmeliny and allowed to rest for the night prior to release early evening the following day. On the 4th November, I received a letter from Paul stating the following:

Dear Malcolm,

I must say the bird was certainly big news out here!!

I spent most of the flight time running around trying to sort things out, the flight was delayed by about half an hour and arrived at approx. 16.30 hours. The bird was very active and indeed very perky as 16.30 hours is in the twilight of the day out here.

It was decided to bed him down at the zoo overnight to allow him to recover from the turmoil of the long flight. On Thursday evening he was released in the grounds of the zoo and was last seen disappearing at a great speed of knots and so hopefully will make its journeys end.

Yours Sincerely

Paul Triggs.

Andrew eventually received a letter from the Belize Deputy High Commissioner giving details of the release. On the

12th December, I received a letter from the Executive Director of the Belize Audubon Society enclosing various photos and press cuttings from two Belize newspapers the 'Reporter' and the 'Amandala.' The Daily Mail ran the final story of Nigel's release and a few weeks later, he even made it into the December issue of Cheshire Life. The Daily Mails list of credits read as follows:

Care and Rehabilitation by Malcolm J. Ingham.

String pulling by Robin Barret, Ministry of Defence.

Flt. Lieut. Strachan, RAF Brize Norton.

Export Licence by Jennie Howland, Dept. of the Environment.

Diplomatic wheels oiled by David Hallet, Foreign Office.

U.S. clearance by Larry Larochelle, Federal U.S. Wildlife Permit Office.

Paths smoothed by John Crosby, British High Commissioner in Belize.

VC 10 piloted by Flt. Lieut. Stan Black.

In-flight catering by Flight Sergeant Jill Corner, and last but not least, after care by ornithologist Corporal Paul Triggs, RAF Belize.

A lot of water has passed under the bridge since the day Nigel finally flew to his freedom in Belize. He was fit and healthy and identifiable as our Nigel by his British Trust for Ornithology ring and that was the last I ever heard of him with not even a postcard! As far as I know, he was never picked up again and his rehabilitation was a total success.

I like to think that he made it and lived a long life making many successful migrations to finally spend his dotage telling his grandchildren of his great adventure way back in 1985 and of how, on his first migration south, he battled against a great storm that blew him across the oceans to a strange land. Of how he was found, weak and exhausted but cared for and nurtured back to health until eventually he was able to return on one of man's great iron birds amidst much pomp and ceremony and of how his story was told across the world.

It would be nice to think that he concluded by telling that, once in Belize, he flew even farther south over many strange lands to spend his first winter in South America, returning once again in spring to the plains of the North where he met Mrs. Nigel and together they raised a family before embarking on the perilous journey South once more.

Chapter Five
Deer Hunting in Birkenhead, Barn Owls in a Bell Tower and a Weasel in the Bathroom

Early April 1986 and finally, winter was releasing its icy grip; it had been a long, hard, cold winter with prolonged periods of sub-zero temperatures. At last, the days were getting warmer, the daffodils were in full bloom and the birds were busy preparing for the coming breeding season.

The 'Wildlife Rehabilitation Unit,' as the ever growing collection of pens, aviaries and treatment shed was now known as was literally bursting at the seams with various creatures all suffering from the freezing temperatures. At least we now had a proper treatment room supplied by the council in the form of a second hand shed from the Parks and Gardens Dept. They even equipped it with hot and cold running water, electricity and hospital cages. It was an enormous improvement on the tiny old garden shed that we had been using.

Birds in particular suffered terribly and not a day went by without something turning up at the door. We found ourselves caring for numerous waders, gulls, a great crested grebe, heron, moorhen, coot and even a water rail, plus numerous blackbirds, thrushes, robins, wrens and a tiny goldcrest.

One Wednesday morning, 19th February 1986 to be precise, I was called out to a heron that had been spotted by a couple of walkers. When I arrived at the location it was standing in a shallow stream hunched up and appeared very weak. It looked a sorry sight standing there knee deep in freezing water, feathers all fluffed trying to conserve vital energy. Its eyes were half closed and it was wobbling precariously. The stream was at the bottom of a steep bank, which, despite the long awaited thaw, was still very slippery with ice making the going a bit precarious to say the least.

After slithering down to the water's edge and just about managing to stop before joining the heron in the freezing stream, I was able to get a better look at it. It was totally exhausted and didn't attempt to move as I waded in and quietly popped a catching net over it. The next hurdle was to slip and slide my way back up the bank, not an easy task whilst cradling a sick heron at the same time!

Once back at the wildlife unit I put it into a heated hospital cage to rest and warm up a little. After a few hours, it began to look a little brighter but it was painfully thin with a sharp protruding breastbone. Despite its extreme weakness, it was critical that I got some nourishment into it otherwise I feared it wouldn't last the night and so set about blending a concoction of glucose and fish into a smelly liquid and began tube feeding. This is something I didn't readily resort to as it's very stressful for the bird and can, on occasions, be the final straw that tips them beyond the point of no return. Also you have to ensure that the liquid doesn't enter the lungs and cause even more problems, but this was a do or die situation. Fortunately, and much to my surprise and relief, the bird was still alive the following morning and endured another day of tube feeding. This went on for three days until at last I began notice an improvement; it was now looking brighter and stronger, though still very weak with wobbly legs, but now at least it wasn't using its wings and beak to stop itself from falling over.

On the fourth day, I decided to try it on solid food and popped a slippery herring down its long slender neck fully expecting it to be honked back up again as soon as my back was turned but thankfully it stayed down. After this initial success, we progressed to three herrings or mackerel a day and within a few days, the change was remarkable. It was now looking quite perky and active but it was still refusing to feed itself with feeding times turning into a battle of wills. My once weak, placid heron had now gone through a metamorphosis and turned into a writhing beak-stabbing monster. It was very adept at using that lethal weapon of a beak with such dexterity that it could easily have auditioned for the part of a swashbuckling swordsman in some Errol Flynn movie. It appeared to be totally oblivious to the fact that had it not been for my intervention it would have popped its clogs ages ago!

It was during one of these feeds, when I had just wrestled the heron to the ground and had the squirming, grey, long legged monster firmly wedged between my knees. I was in the middle of prying its beak open with one hand whilst struggling to come to grips with a slippery herring with the other when, of all the inopportune moments the blasted phone began to ring loudly and incessantly!! The herring slipped from my hand to go sliding across the floor followed by the heron as it wriggled free from my vice like grip.

I snatched at the receiver impatiently barking, "Hello, who's this, I'm busy!"

A rather startled voice said, "Oh, hello Malcolm, Simon here RSPCA, sorry to bother you but can you give us a lift to catch a deer?"

"Catch a what?"

"A deer."

"Where," I asked?

"In Birkenhead," he replied.

"Listen mate, I'm very busy and I don't have time for your wind-ups at the moment, now bugger off."

But he wasn't to be put off and with a tone of urgency in his voice came back with, "I'm serious, we've had a call from a member of the public that there's a deer roaming around a large garden in Oxton, Birkenhead, can you help or not?"

I was well aware that there was no shortage of wildlife in Birkenhead but it consisted mainly of the two-legged variety! I was still haunted by the memory of being called out to a so-called rampant badger trapped in a dark, junk littered garage and arrived to be met by a very strange gentleman wrapped in bandages from ankle to thigh after supposedly being savaged by the black and white devil.

The gentleman in question had rung me to say that he

had a badger trapped in his garage and could I get it out. I suspected something was amiss by his rather abrupt attitude and reluctance to divulge too much information. Anyway, me being the obliging soul that I am immediately set off to the address on my mission of mercy arriving some 20 minutes later. As I pulled up outside the small bungalow, I sensed that something wasn't quite right. The first indication being that despite it being early afternoon the curtains were tightly drawn but as I walked up the drive, the living room curtains began to be drawn back very slightly as someone peeked out. Anyway despite my reservations and armed with my catcher I proceeded to the front door and rang the bell. The curtains fell still as the person peeking from behind made their way to the door and as it opened, I was met by a rather large man bandaged from ankle to thigh resembling someone who had just been disturbed whilst in the process of embalmment in preparation for being confined to an Egyptian sarcophagus.

"Good afternoon, I understand you have a badger trapped in your garage."

He began to twitch uncontrollably, his face taking on the appearance of someone who had just come face to face with the devil himself.

"Badger, Bloody Badger!!!" He retorted! "Look what the beast has done!" pointing to his heavily bandaged lower half. "I only went in for a paint brush and it leapt out at me, not going back in there until you get it out! At which point he slammed the door and vanished.

I thought 'this guy's off his rocker, but better humour him.' I slowly raised the up and over garage door just enough for me to enter and closed it behind me. It was quite dark with only a few shadowy rays of light filtering through a cobwebbed encrusted window. As my eyes adjusted to the semi-darkness, I could just make out items of discarded furniture with boxes stacked upon and around them. Old rusty paint cans littered the floor and shelves and an ancient Qualcast lawnmower stood idly in a corner. I fumbled for the light switch, click: nothing!

'Great,' I thought. 'Can't open the door in case whatever is supposed to be in here makes a run for it. Suppose I'll just have to fumble my way around.'

At which point a sound came from the back of the garage before falling silent again. I made my way towards it stumbling over various bits of junk and paint cans as I went. I stopped and listened, nothing, and then I heard a low croaky growl coming from behind an old sideboard. Once again, I cautiously made my way forward, grasper at the ready. I was certain that whatever was in there it wasn't a badger, but what could it be? What on earth had supposedly inflicted so much damage on the bandaged nutter?

There it was again! A low croaky growl. Whatever it was it appeared to have a case of laryngitis! I crept ever closer to the sideboard and was just about to peer over the top when the biggest badger in creation suddenly leapt up screaming like a demented banshee! I shot back with grasper held high ready to give the monster from hell an almighty whack on the head when it suddenly collapsed in a heap on the floor rolling about in fits of uncontrollable laughter. I had been well and truly set up!! The screaming badger turned out to be a copper by the name of Simon Vaughan dressed in a giant badger suit with the heavily bandaged householder being another copper with an equally warped sense of humour. He and his wife Michele were friends of ours who thought it would be great fun to play an April fool's joke on me!

Before we return to the story in hand, I must stress that revenge was sweet!!! I tied the Vaughan's side and front door house handles together making the only available exit via a window. Simon only discovered this when attempting to report for duty at the local nick and, after almost ripping the only two external doors off their hinges, had to make a quick exit through the living room window!

I apologise for digressing but thought it worth explaining my reservations when asked to go chasing deer in Birkenhead! Now back to the deer.

Reasonably convinced that this was indeed a genuine

plea for help, I returned one very smug looking heron back to its pen before jumping into the Land Rover. Twenty minutes later, I turned into a tree-lined avenue made up of large Victorian semi-detached houses with long narrow gardens to the front and rear. Within a couple of minutes I spotted Simon's white van with its distinct blue and white RSPCA signs emblazoned on the side parked outside number 24 and pulled up behind it. He was propped against the garden wall puffing away on a cigarette and proceeded to inform me that the deer was last seen bounding wildly around the back garden. He explained that he was waiting for his colleague Fred and a vet from Chester Zoo to arrive.

"What are we going to do with it if we catch it?" I enquired.

Simon, with his usual dry wit answered, "The Zoo said they will take it, they reckon it will come in handy as a titbit for the lions!"

Finally, the team was assembled and we were invited into the house to take a peek at our intended quarry.

"This way gentleman, follow me please," instructed the householder. "You should be able to see it from in here."

We were escorted into the dining room where the French windows overlooked a patio leading onto a long narrow garden made up mainly of lawn with a scattering of fruit trees dotted here and there and herbaceous borders running along the length of a solid six-foot high boundary fence that enclosed the garden. We peered through the windows but couldn't see a thing except for the occasional blackbird flitting across the lawn emitting their distinctive 'Chack-ack-ack-ack' alarm calls and obviously taking umbrage at the strange intruder invading their territory.

"Can't see it, are you sure it's there?" said Simon.

Taking affront at the suggestion that he may have been hallucinating, the house owner impatiently elbowed his way to the front frantically waving a finger in the general direction of a large bush.

"There it is over there, look, over there, surely you can see it?" he retorted impatiently.

Eventually we spotted a brown bundle curled up under a bush in a far distant corner of the garden. It was a small Chinese muntjac deer!

Simon looked at me with a self-satisfied grin saying, "Didn't believe me did you?"

Fred chipped in with, "But where in the world could it have come from?"

The vet, obviously being a little more au fait on the history of muntjac deer went on to explain that in the early 20th century, Chinese muntjac, also known as Reeves's muntjac, were introduced into the Duke of Bedford's estate at Woburn Park in Bedfordshire and others into Whipsnade Park and inevitably some escaped into the countryside. They thrived to such an extent that they are now pretty well established particularly in the southern counties but also recorded in Cheshire and other northern counties and spreading. He went on to explain that they are very shy, secretive and mainly solitary animals much preferring the seclusion of dense shrubbery and woodland rather than the suburbs of Birkenhead even though there have been reports of them living in some urban areas of central London.

Bringing the lesson to an abrupt end, he said, "Right, now we need a plan of action, I've got a long net, a carrying crate and a sedative in the van and propose that we quietly bring everything into the garden. Malcolm and Simon, you two take hold of either end of the net and slowly move towards him, Fred, you be ready with the box, once we've got him I'll jab him, everybody clear? Good, let's get cracking."

With all the gear secreted from the vet's van, Simon and myself stretched out the long net which was about a metre high by some three metres long and began to stealthily approach our quarry that, by now, had slunk even deeper into the bush watching every move with deep suspicion. It surveyed the garden nervously and began stomping the ground with its foot as it prepared to scarper at any moment. Fred and the vet approached from another angle, the vet armed with his syringe of tranquiliser and Fred with his brand new large animal catching net. We crept stealthily forward trying to anticipate its next move when suddenly it shot out of the shrubbery like a bullet from a gun. Simon and I ran towards it in a futile attempt at capture, whereupon it swerved to avoid us with the speed and skill of a professional rugby player. Fred, on the other hand, had it well and truly in his sights with net at the ready, it headed straight for him, its eyes darting from side to side frantically looking for a means of escape when suddenly it made a last ditch attempt to swerve around him, but Fred with a lightening swoop of the net, had it!

The deer was in, or so we thought! I don't think it even stopped to take a breath, it was in, and then it was out, leaving poor Fred's net shredded. It shot across the garden and bounced off the fence as it attempted to clear it. Undeterred it then ran like the clappers across to the other side, and, with one almighty leap cleared the fence and vanished into next doors garden! Our intrepid team of hunters shot off in all directions with our carefully thought out plan now resembling Fred's net, in tatters! Simon and I made for the road scaling a high wall topped by an even higher rickety wooden fence that looked down into a garden about seven houses down.

Simon yelled, "I've spotted it!"

Unfortunately, it had also spotted Simon and once again was off leaping over fences in a manner that would have given Red Rum a run for his money. Our main worry was that if it got on to the road it could easily make its way into the centre of Birkenhead. The consequences of a deer running amok and dodging traffic in Birkenhead town centre didn't bear thinking about. Finally, it came to rest a few of gardens down. Simon and I sneaked into the garden from a side gate and crept as close as we dare. We were pondering over our next course of action when all of a sudden Fred appeared as if from nowhere armed with a second net. He had apparently scaled a six-foot fence and dropped down into the garden.

The deer, with ears twitching, stared nervously first at

Fred, then at Simon and me, and deciding that Fred looked the easier of the two options and made a mad dash towards him. Fred stood his ground, and as the deer bolted towards him, he did a nifty sidestep and with a lightening swoop of his trusty net had our determined little deer once more in his grasp. At this point, everyone seemed to appear from every orifice all helping to restrain one squealing, thrashing muntjac as Fred's second net was quickly beginning to succumb once again to sharp wildly thrashing hooves. The vet quickly administered a sedative and it was soon on its way to Chester Zoo and a comfortable straw filled stable. I was assured that it didn't end its days as a lion's breakfast but was instead given a permanent home at a wildlife park. When asked how he managed to scale the high fence so rapidly Fred modestly stated that his agility was more than a match for any deer but according to the vet he was given the required impetus by an almighty push up the backside!!

On Wednesday 13th February 1991, a member of the public came into the Visitor Centre cradling a dead heron and as he placed it down on the counter said, "I know it's dead but it's got a ring on one of its legs and I thought you might be interested."

It was a British Trust for Ornithology ring bearing the number BTO 1090961 and upon checking my records discovered that it was the very same Errol Flynn swashbuckling beak stabbing heron that I had rescued starving from the stream, nursed back to health, and released on the ponds in the Country Park at Thurstaston on Saturday 15th March 1986. The winter of 1991 had once again been severe with prolonged freezing conditions. It had been found dead in a field having starved to death almost five years to the day of its release in 1986! It was a classic example of the value of ringing birds prior to their release in order to determine the success of avian rehabilitation.

Another example was a herring gull recovered not dead, but alive and well during a BTO netting exercise of seabirds. Once caught, the ringers examine the birds to determine their condition, weight, sex, age etc. and also to check for rings or tags indicating that the bird has been captured previously or rung as a nestling. This will give them vital information as to when and where the bird was originally rung, at what age and how far it has travelled. These exercises provide vital information regarding migratory routes etc. Any bird without a ring is given one and the details recorded. Once armed with the BTO ring number my records told me that the herring gull arrived at the Unit very close to death suffering from Botulism and after many weeks of careful nursing made a full recovery. It was released on the beach at Thurstaston and caught some six years later fit and well during the netting exercise 15 miles up the coast. Magic!

Another was a peregrine falcon that I had nursed back to health after it had been found with a broken wing and taken to a local vet. It had taken me many months of careful nursing and training to build up its muscle and stamina until I was able to release it on the Dee Estuary marshes at Parkgate. I chose the location because it had an abundance of natural prey in the form of waders, ducks and the odd feral pigeon. Twelve months later, I received notification from the BTO that it had been recovered in North Wales after being hit by a car. Luckily it had suffered only mild concussion and was kept overnight at a veterinary practice and released the following day, and as with the heron, almost a year to the day after its initial release on the marshes. Proof that correct rehabilitation works doesn't get much better than that!

Over the years many creatures passed through the Wildlife Rehabilitation Unit's doors with the vast majority of them being successfully rehabilitated back into the wild, but with the best will in the world it's inevitable that not all will make it for one reason or another. Some succumb to their injuries whilst others will never be fit or strong enough to cope with the demands of a life in the wild again. In such cases, you have to weigh up the many pros and cons with regards to the animals future. If a life of permanent captivity is to be considered, the most important factor is quality of life, without that, there is no point at all in keeping a wild creature in captivity; the animal has to be totally free of stress and content with its lot. Over the years, a number of creatures did end up living with us permanently, William the razorbill being a typical example. There were always extenuating circumstances that brought this about and all lived a happy, contented life whilst with us, but I never intended the wildlife unit to be a sanctuary in the true sense of the word; the emphasis was always on successful rehabilitation if at all possible. There's a very fine line between the two and it's all too easy for your passion for wildlife to allow sentiment to creep in and cloud your better judgment, often to the detriment of the creatures you're trying to help in the first place.

Unfortunately, and all too often, I would be asked to take in captive bred barn owls. They breed readily in captivity and as such, young owls are frequently offered for sale in various bird fancier journals and often end up being bought by someone with no knowledge whatsoever of caring for a barn owl. Sadly, a great number of these birds either escape or are released into the wild only to starve to death.

In the early 1980's, to see a truly wild barn owl on the Wirral was a very rare sight indeed and yet from what I was told; in the 1960s and 1970s they were a familiar sight. I was intrigued to know what had caused the bird to become such a rarity. It was true that over the years a fair amount of prime habitat had been lost to development but there was still good habitat out there, particularly around the Country Parks and Nature Reserves, which held a decent population of small mammals, the main prey item of the species and yet no barn owls! I spent a lot of time pondering over this and finally decided to attempt to discover if a captive breeding and reintroduction scheme could be a feasible solution to bringing this iconic bird back as a breeding species on Wirral. Pretty soon, I set myself the task of determining just how much decent barn owl habitat was still out there along with their small mammal populations, coupled with what was available in the terms of roost and nest sites.

I contacted the Hawk and Owl Trust who, at the time, had just completed a national barn owl survey and asked for their findings on the Wirral. I was told that we had a breeding pair under a flyover of the M53 motorway at Bidston in Birkenhead and a second pair in an old sandstone Bell Tower at Royden Park, a few short miles up the road from Thurstaston. Due to my own observations, I was able to tell them that the M53 pair had long since departed and for the past few years only tawny owls had bred in the Bell Tower at Royden Park meaning, to all intents and purposes, Wirral had completely lost the barn owl as a breeding species.

Twelve months later at the end of my survey, I could find no reason at all as to why barn owls should not be around and doing well, the habitat and the food source were there so theoretically we should have barn owls! Most of the local farms still had barns or other outbuildings suitable as barn owl roost and breeding sites.

Indeed when asked, the vast majority of farmers said, "Haven't seen a barn owl for years, used to breed every year in that barn but not anymore."

Now of the opinion that Wirral did indeed still have all the necessary requirements to sustain breeding barn owls I, along with the cooperation of farmers and landowners, began to install nest boxes in suitable buildings. An artificial owl loft was built in the roof space of the estate yard garages at Wirral Country Park complete with an entrance hole in the gable end and a nest box in the form of a converted tea chest. All we needed now were the owls!

I had already made a few enquiries and was eventually contacted by a vet in Bristol who offered me two pairs of wild disabled barn owls and after a few questions regarding their disabilities etc., arrangements were made to send them up to Wirral. A few days later the birds arrived via British Rail from Bristol to Liverpool Lime Street Station and after collection were soon settled into their respective aviaries.

With luck they would soon provide me with chicks for

my reintroduction scheme. We didn't have too long to wait and within a few months both pairs were feeding six tiny barn owl chicks. The plan was that they would stay with their parents until around five or six weeks old. At this age, the chicks are capable of picking food up and swallowing it whole rather than the parent bird having to feed it. At this point, I would separate them from the parents and provide them with food in the form of dead day old chicks and mice purchased from suppliers to zoos and falconry centres etc. Once satisfied that they were feeding well they were given a BTO ring and placed in a nest box in a farm building surrounded by prime small mammal habitat.

At this stage, they were still covered in fine white feathery down and totally incapable of flight. They made a comical sight as they pounced around the box trying to catch some invisible prey or a bit of fluffy down that would go floating off as they attempted to grasp it. Every evening I would climb up to the respective nest box and leave food for them, the principle was that the chicks would fledge naturally and when fully feathered, take short exploratory flights during the hours of late evening and nighttime but return to the box to sleep the day away. As time went on and they became more familiar with the outside world, they would begin to explore farther afield and may even begin to roost away in another box close by. Food was always left in the release box for as long as it was being taken and this proved to be an excellent way of determining their comings and goings. I would also collect and dissect any regurgitated pellets looking for signs of natural prey within their diet.

Young barn owls are taught virtually nothing by their parents and once fully-fledged have to rely totally on their natural hunting instincts in order to survive. The mortality rate for young barn owls, particularly during their first winter, is very high. It only takes a few days of inclement weather making hunting difficult to put them on the slippery slope to starvation and so, by providing food to supplement their natural diet, we were giving them a head start and giving them time to hone their hunting skills and reduce the risk of starvation. It worked well; very well in fact, all six chicks survived their first winter.

A few day old chicks were still being taken as food but not on a nightly basis as they were now quite adept at catching natural prey. I would often find the odd dead vole or mouse stashed away in a corner of a nest box along with their regurgitated pellets containing the tiny bones of mice and voles.

The reintroduction programme was now in its second year with the emphasis not on captive breeding but on monitoring what was already out there, in particular two unrelated chicks that had been placed in the tea chest nest box in the artificial loft in the garage of the rangers estate yard. All six of the original chicks were still accounted for with the two in the estate yard garage loft now tending to roost away but would, on occasions, still return for food.

I continued to pop a couple of the bright yellow dead day old chicks in the box on a nightly basis and removing any untouched ones from the previous night. More often than not, the chicks wouldn't be taken but I knew if an owl had returned due to finding fresh regurgitated pellets full of natural prey remains by the box platform or on the floor. Then suddenly things changed dramatically!

The distinct yellow day old chicks began to be taken on a nightly basis and I increased the number being left from two to four and all were taken! Then six, and once again all taken! One night I put ten chicks out with the same result, all taken! Something was going on, but what? The most obvious answer was that the pair had bred, were feeding young and coming back to the loft umpteen times a night to collect my offerings in order to supplement their natural diet and ease the burden of having to be constantly hunting to feed a hungry family. I knew that they couldn't be too far away because of the constant comings and goings and so I carried out a thorough search of the probable sites and came up blank.

A possible solution in how to solve the mystery came from a friend who happened to be a keen wildlife photographer and a wizard at knocking up discreet motion triggered cameras out of various bits and pieces. One evening he offered to 'knock something up' as he put it that just might help solve my problem. True to his word, a couple of weeks later he turned up at the door with a plastic carrier bag.

"This should do the trick, he said."

I peeked in and at first glance saw what appeared to be a conglomeration of wires, bits of plastic, a small wooden box and half a dozen AA batteries. I invited him into the house whereupon he tipped the contents of the bag onto the floor and began to give me an in depth account as to what went where and what it was supposed to do. He completely lost me in the first few seconds, all I managed to grasp was that it was some device that would allow the owl to clock himself in and out of the loft on a piece of paper and also photograph himself doing it. It worked a treat!

At long last we had pictures of the mystery owl, it was the male and you could clearly see the BTO ring on his leg and, more importantly, we now had a time scale for him from entering the loft to collect the food to leaving and then returning for more. An average of around 15 minutes! This obviously meant that his nest site wasn't too far away and greatly narrowed down the search area. But still no luck! A week later, I had some great pictures of him but was certainly no nearer to discovering his nest site! Then one day I received a frantic phone call from a local BTO bird ringer who, for the past five years, had climbed up to the Bell Tower at Royden Park (the same Bell Tower that the Hawk and Owl Trust had down as a barn owl nest site) to ring tawny owl chicks.

Upon picking up the receiver I heard an excited voice saying, "Malcolm is that you?"

"Yes it is."

Get yourself to Royden Park ASAP; there's something you need to see."

I jumped into the Land Rover and drove the three miles or so to the Bell Tower to be met by one very excited bird ringer and pointing to the highest point of the tower stating, "Get yourself up there and tell me what you see."

I opened the creaky steel door at the foot of the tower and proceeded to climb the first section of the vertical wooden ladder. I squeezed myself through the narrow trap door which led onto a platform and the second section of the climb, whilst trying to avoid the cobwebs and falling clouds of dust along with the remains of the odd dead pigeon. Eventually I reached the third and last section of the climb and was just about to scale the last few rungs of the ladder leading me to the final trapdoor when I heard the distinctive snoring and hissing sound of barn owl chicks when they think that a parent bird is returning with food.

Barn Owl eggs & a newly hatched chick under the Tower bell in Royden Park

I slowly climbed the last few remaining rungs leading to the final trapdoor. It creaked as I pushed it open and, protecting my eyes from the falling dust, I stuck my head up into the bell chamber to be met by the strong pungent smell of bird poo and the ever increasing sound of hissing barn owl chicks. It was a small space, around one and a half metres square and just under two metres high with louvered sides giving just enough space for an owl to enter. The old cast iron bell, which hadn't tolled for many a year, was in the centre hanging about six inches from the floor and huddled together directly underneath it were six fluffy white wild barn owl chicks, the first to have bred on the Wirral for many a year!

As I climbed into the small space, they shuffled up close to each other hissing loudly and snoring. The floor was littered with piles of regurgitated pellets containing the indigestible remains of mice and voles. Then I spotted the conclusive proof I was looking for, three bright yellow day old poultry chicks that the adults had brought in from the loft at Thurstaston! I was ecstatic! I had found their nest site at long last. Not only had they produced six healthy chicks, but they had ousted a pair of tawny owls in the process to reclaim what had been, for many years previous, a traditional barn owl breeding site. It couldn't get any better!!

I made the long dusty climb back down the ladder to be met by, "Well, what do you reckon?"

Excitedly I retorted, "We've found it at last! We've now officially got a breeding pair of wild barn owls on the Wirral."

The ringer climbed back up to the tower to place BTO rings on the chicks whilst I drove home to get my camera to record the historic event on film. The Bell Tower became a permanent roost and nest site with the pair producing young the following year plus three more breeding pairs at other locations. The captive breeding and release programme on Wirral lasted only a couple of years. Once I had achieved the intended goal of establishing a wild breeding population it would have been pointless and counter-productive to continue.

The priority now was to monitor the owls in the wild and to ensure that their roosts, nest sites and habitats were recorded and secure, combined with erecting more nest and roost boxes. Despite ending the reintroduction of barn owls on Wirral, the captive breeding and release scheme continued with reintroduction programmes in North Wales with the Forestry Commission around the areas of

Clocaenog Forest and even as far away as Lancashire and Yorkshire.

The years went by and the Bell Tower became quiet once more until a second pair took up residence and the cycle began once again. The loft at Thurstaston became a permanent roost and breeding site, even now as I write; some twenty odd years later, barn owls are still roosting and breeding there.

In an effort to give some form of continuity and future to the conservation of this beautiful silent predator as a breeding species on Wirral I contemplated with the idea of forming a Wirral Barn Owl Group to continue with and expand upon my work of the past few years. I passed the idea around a little, resulting in myself, Colin Wells the RSPB manager for the Burton Marsh reserve and a few other interested individuals meeting in a local pub. We decided to place an article in the local paper asking for anyone interested in forming a Barn Owl Group to attend a meeting at the Wirral Country Park Visitor Centre.

The idea was that Colin and I would give a slide presentation about the plight of the barn owl nationwide and its present situation on Wirral and what we hoped to achieve from such a group. The attendance exceeded our expectations culminating in what is now known as, 'The Wirral Barn Owl Trust'. Many years have passed since that inaugural meeting, with the Trust developing into a well-established group of dedicated people who, through their programme of education and practical conservation, strive to ensure a secure and long lasting future for Wirral's barn owls.

Another day and the arrival of yet another cardboard box containing some animal or other in need of care, the exact date and circumstances lost in the realms of time but the creature itself difficult to forget for its endearing, playful and mischievous nature lingers on. It was a weasel, which on arrival weighed no more than a few grams, was totally blind and almost hairless apart from a very fine pinkish down. It bore more resemblance to a little fat pink worm than anything else.

Both Ann and I took one look at it and said, "How on earth can we hand rear that?"

But like many other creatures before, we gave it a go. First and foremost it was warmth and quickly! If its body temperature were to drop below 10 or 12 degrees centigrade, it would go into a coma and die. To give it immediate heat, Ann held it cupped in the palm of her hands whilst I rigged up a heat lamp in the wildlife unit. By the time I had finished and got back to the house it was beginning to warm up a little and was squirming around in her hand, its tiny mouth opening and closing in a futile attempt at finding its mothers teats. It was hungry and needed sustenance pretty quickly, but what? We decided to see if it would take some rehydrating fluid in the form of a glucose solution fed from a tiny pipette and with a bit of perseverance Ann finally succeeded.

We then put it inside a woollen glove placed in a small cardboard box under a heat lamp. At this stage we had no idea as to whether it would live or die but if we were to have placed bets the latter would have been odds on favourite. All we could do was try our best and after a few more feeds of glucose we checked on it one last time before retiring to bed fully expecting it to have faded away by the morning. We were up at first light and hesitantly peeked into the glove and much to our surprise it was still alive.

From here on it was a routine of constantly checking to ensure it was warm, followed by more weighing and feeding. On day two we decided to try it on Cimicat kitten replacer milk using a 1 ml syringe. We'd reared tiny hedgehogs on this formula without any problems, so why not a weasel! The days went by and much to our surprise; it appeared to be doing well. After about a week the eyes opened and slowly but surely our little pink worm began to turn into something resembling a tiny female weasel. Her teeth erupted next, putting her at around two to three weeks old, followed by her pink downy skin growing hair, firstly along the neck and then and as it spread along her body she began to transform into a real miniaturized version of her species.

At this stage, we began to offer her tiny pieces of meat. (Weasels are weaned on meat about three to four weeks of age and capable of killing prey at eight weeks.) Before long, she was completely on solid food, which she devoured with great enthusiasm. She was now weighing in at a healthy 45 grams, very hyperactive and inquisitive, meaning that her hospital cage was now just not big enough and decided that for the time being at least, we would transfer her to a small rabbit hutch and confine her to the bathroom. Yes, the bathroom! Not the ideal place to keep a rabbit hutch I grant you, but it was nice and warm and we could keep an eye on her without constantly having to pop outside to the wildlife unit.

From the very beginning, Ann had taken on the role of surrogate mum and as such our little weasel, now known as 'Whizz,' was devoted to her. Whizz would emit high pitched excited cries of delight when she saw Ann, whilst I, on the other hand, generally got a short screaming bark or chirp meaning that she wasn't over enthralled by my presence, much preferring that of her surrogate mum! Weasels are members of the *mustelidae* family, which includes polecats, stoats, pine martins, ferrets, otters and badgers etc. all of which, particularly when youngsters, have a terrific sense of fun and can have you in fits of laughter at their crazy antics and our little Whizz was no exception.

I find it amazing that some in the animal scientific world are of the opinion that animals don't play or have a sense of fun. At least not in the way that we perceive, but that they are merely acting upon instinctive behaviour that allows them to perfect their hunting or fighting skills in preparation for adult life and determine the hierarchy within a social group. Or, even worse – that animals are not sentient beings unable to perceive or feel things! Yes, play does serve that purpose, but I refuse to believe that animals don't also have a sense of fun or play. If the purists of the scientific animal world are right in their assumption then all I can say is that I have met quite a few animals that appear to have no knowledge of that fact and have shown every conceivable indication of having a sense of fun and mischief!

Whizz would take great delight in hiding in Ann's coat pockets or sitting on her shoulder emitting loud purrs of satisfaction, she would play for hours with anything that she could pounce on and drag around the floor and would have us in hysterics with her crazy playful antics.

The downside, for me at least, was going for a bath and forgetting that I had a weasel loose in the bathroom! On more than one occasion, I would alight from the bath one minute feeling totally refreshed and relaxed only to be hopping around the floor with a weasel attached to my big toe the next! She would lie in wait; hiding behind some piece of furniture or other just waiting for her opportunity to make her attack and attach herself to whatever part of my anatomy happened to be the most convenient. Ouch!!

If I was lucky, I would catch a glimpse of her from the corner of my eye as a thin brown streak came dashing across the floor like grease lightening in full attack mode. I would make a feeble attempt at evasive action but more often than not too late and end up emitting ear-piercing cries of pain as she latched herself onto my body. This of course gave Ann a great deal of amusement, she was of the opinion that her little Whizz could do no wrong and that I must have done something to provoke the attack. At long last and much to my relief, the time came for her to be evicted from the bathroom and be given the freedom of a natural outside enclosure. The reason for this was twofold, firstly she was ready for the transition and secondly I was developing a nervous twitch due my never knowing when or where she would launch her next attack.

I had converted a small aviary into an escape-proof weasel habitat with log piles, rock piles, old clay pipes and a network of tunnels and chambers for her to explore. When all was ready, I carried the hutch from the bathroom to her new enclosure and placed it on the floor. Up to this point she had been hiding away in her sleeping compartment but quickly emerged as I opened the hutch door, taking the not to be missed opportunity to nip my finger before dashing out to explore this strange new world. The plan was to allow her time to adapt to her new surroundings before embarking on a gradual soft release from her enclosure back into the wild, but unfortunately, fate had other ideas.

Some months earlier, we had booked a long overdue three week holiday in the Gambia. It had been arranged that Ann's mum Elsie would house sit and look after the dogs and goats whilst a ranger would turn up twice a day to feed the various assortment of wild creatures in the wildlife unit. Sadly upon our return we were met with the news that little Whizz had been found dead in her enclosure a few days prior our return. She'd enjoyed a good life, albeit a captive one and had brought a lot of laughter to the Ingham household. Thankfully they had kept her body for me to examine and she appeared to be in good bodily condition with no obvious signs as to why she should have died.

A few years later, we would once again have the pleasure of caring for another member of the *mustelidae* family this time in the form of a baby stoat that proved to be just as inquisitive, mischievous and as endearing as Whizz! Mustelids are a fascinating group of animals all with very similar endearing traits. Little did we know at the time that in the not too distant future, we would be hand rearing other members of that captivating family leading us into many nocturnal adventures.

We had been on the Wirral for four years now; I was responsible for my own patch of the Wirral Way plus the reserve. I was no longer subject to Wilf's morning roll calls and task designations thus allowing me a fair bit of freedom and flexibility within my working day.

The Rehabilitation Unit was not officially part of my job even though I did snatch the odd hour or two here and there but it virtually dominated evenings and weekends with everyday life having to revolve around it. The powers that be within Wirral Council fully supported and even encouraged my rehabilitation work, not particularly through any real interest in wildlife rehabilitation but due to the fact that it was generating a fair bit of media attention from both local and national newspapers plus radio and television. They perceived it as an excellent public relations venture and so long as the authority looked good, they were quite happy for it to continue. At one point Granada Television even ended their nightly regional news spots with a shot of a barn owl hunting over Thurstaston!

But I was getting itchy feet: I had been invited to attend an interview in Ashdown Forest but after weighing up the pros and cons with Ann, who was by now working as a veterinary nurse after completing a three year course at Mabel Fletcher College in Liverpool, we decided to give it another couple of years. Those two years were now almost gone and we felt that now the time was right to start looking for a post elsewhere, but once again this thing called destiny or fate, whatever you want to call it, had other plans for me.

Due to reorganisation, Wirral Ranger Service now had two Head Rangers. Wilf Watson, my boss, in charge at Wirral Country Park and a second Head Ranger managing all the other parks and countryside areas i.e. Eastham Country Park, Dibbinsdale Local Nature Reserve, Royden Park, Heswall Dales, the North Wirral Coastal Park, Bidston Hill and last but not least Hilbre Island in the Dee Estuary.

This second post had just become vacant due to the Head Ranger having taken up the offer of a job with the National Trust in the Lake District. The post was to be advertised nationally and as with all of these jobs was expected to attract a few hundred applicants, particularly for a senior post as they are very few and far between. All existing full-time rangers within the authority were invited to apply with the guarantee of an interview.

Ranger jobs are difficult to acquire at the best of times, but promotion to senior or Head Ranger level can be equally as difficult if not more so. The post was advertised nationally attracting the usual deluge of applicants. Gossip amongst my fellow rangers was rife as to who may or may not apply internally, with two in particular being regarded as fancying themselves as Head Ranger material.

One day a couple of colleagues and I were speculating on who would apply when one said, "You going for it Malcolm?"

"Don't think so, not really up my street."

Up to that point, I hadn't even considered it, my intention was to move on and then I thought, 'Why not? You have nothing to lose.' The following day I submitted my application, albeit a little tongue in cheek. I was interviewed the following week after which, I was ushered into another room whilst the panel deliberated over my performance. Thirty minutes later I was called back into the interview room and to my utter amazement was offered the job! They also stressed that if I accepted the post they would want me to continue with my work at the Wildlife Rehabilitation Unit and even offered me a small annual budget to help with the ever increasing food bills. What could I say? Promotion plus a Unit budget thrown in for good measure!! This was the second time Wirral Council had offered me a post, but now there was no doubt in my mind. Head Ranger experience would stand me in good stead for when I eventually decide to move on and in the meantime the Unit's new found wealth would come in very handy.

And so it came to pass that I made a gigantic leap forward from countryside ranger with only my patch and the Unit to worry about to Head Ranger responsible for a large number of parks and nature reserves. Most daunting of all was that I was also responsible for a dozen or more ranger staff that could, on occasions, be far more belligerent than any wildlife and to make the transition even more unnerving two of my newly acquired staff had just been pipped at the post!

Two days later and not without a little trepidation, I walked into Wilf Watsons office, not this time to discuss site management issues with my boss, but on an equal footing and to occupy the desk opposite! The very same office that, four short years earlier, I had nervously walked into for the very first time to begin my life as a countryside ranger.

He shook my hand and congratulated me, but rather like my first week at Limmer & Trinidad all those years before when I was told by my wagon loading partner, "I'll pull you through for a week, then you're on your own," Wilf, if not in so many words, implied the same!

Almost overnight my daily work load increased tremendously, my flexibility became less flexible and I had many more demands on my ranger time. The council had not only promoted me but they had also made an investment in the Wildlife Unit and they would want a return in the form of more PR.

The expectations from me seemed overwhelming. I had to manage, promote and improve my own large section of the Ranger Service whilst at the same time carrying out a similar task at the Wildlife Rehabilitation Unit, which of course now had the council's official stamp of approval. The difference in the two being that the Head Ranger's job was mainly five days a week whilst the Wildlife Unit was seven. Needless to say, I had jumped in at the deep end; I had to learn to swim and swim fast and to become an expert at juggling time whilst wearing two hats. I have always liked to think that if faced with a challenge head on in a sink or swim situation, I much prefer the swimming option if at all possible.

Little did I realise that within the week two little orphan badger cubs would arrive on our doorstep that would put my time juggling capabilities to the test and present both Ann and I with even more challenges. Challenges that would, over the coming months, present us with a conglomeration of emotions from laughter, sadness and trepidation coupled with an experience that we would never, ever forget.

Chapter Six
Toby, Pickles, Cassie, Millie and Kippy -
Five Badgers that took over our lives

It was Sunday morning 23rd March 1986 and I had just finished my routine feeding around the Wildlife Unit. With nothing else immediately demanding my time, I was looking forward to spending the rest of my Sunday doing as little as possible when the phone rang. It was Michele Vaughan, a friend and member of the Wirral and Cheshire Badger Group. She was the one who set me up in the rampaging badger in the garage saga and wife of the copper in the giant suit. Who needs friends?!!!

She explained that she had received a telephone call from a farmer on the outskirts of Crewe in Cheshire saying he had just rescued two tiny badger cubs and could we take them? Apparently a road building scheme was underway that was going directly through a field close to a badger sett. He had been walking the field early the previous evening and decided to check on the sett and as he got close, spotted a badger running off. It soon became obvious that a JCB digger had damaged the sett and two tiny badger cubs were blindly crawling around above ground. Being in a quandary as to what to do and assuming that the badger he saw running off was the mother, he decided to cover them over as best he could with grass etc. in the hope that she would return. The following morning he was up bright and early to check on them only to discover that they were still there and very cold and hungry. He took them back to the farm and placed them under a heat lamp before contacting the Wirral and Cheshire Badger Group who, in turn, collected and delivered them to the Wildlife Unit wrapped snugly in a blanket. We took them into the house and carefully unfolded the blanket to reveal two wriggling and squirming little male (boar) badger cubs emitting pitiful whickering sounds. Their eyes were tightly closed and the umbilical cord was still attached but now dry and shrivelled. We estimated them to be around three weeks old. One was the typical black and white colour whilst the second a ginger and white one known as Erythristic. We immediately checked them over and apart from having a few parasitic sheep ticks they seemed uninjured. The next task was to weigh them with the ginger one topping the scales at 1lb. 10oz. and his sibling at 1lb.12oz.

With warmth being the next priority we wrapped them in a warm blanket placed on a hot water bottle and put them in a box by the radiator in the living room. Priority number two was nourishment but not having hand-reared tiny badger cubs before we were at a bit of a quandary as to what to use as a milk substitute. We knew that cow's milk was out of the question due to the fact that it could cause a reaction in the form of hair loss and other skin problems. All we had immediately to hand was a tin of Welpi puppy replacer milk and based on their weights, mixed the formula and attempted their first bottle feed. The black and white one took to it surprisingly quickly and was soon sucking on the teat and paddling away with his front paws as he would have done at his mum's tummy whereas his sibling wriggled and squirmed. During that first day and with ticks removed they took a total of three feeds; whereupon we would then gently massage their lower abdomen with cotton wool in order to induce them to empty their bowels and bladder. Their mother would have licked them as a cat does with kittens or a dog with puppies in order to achieve the same result.

It was just turned midnight when we checked them for the last time before retiring to bed - they were warm and sleeping contentedly but what would morning bring, would they still be alive? Even though snug and warm and sleeping peacefully with full bellies they were on a diet that their digestive system could possibly react to and potentially bring about its own set of problems in the form of diarrhoea which, in such a young animal, could very quickly bring about dehydration and death.

The following morning, Monday 24th March, we were up

at first light and with bated breath we went downstairs to check on our two little orphans hoping that they had survived the night. We slowly lifted the blanket and to our great relief they were alive and blindly crawling around constantly chattering. Ann mixed their bottles whilst I weighed them, to our relief their weight was stable, and they were soon suckling away. At this point we decided to give them names with the ginger one being Pickles and his brother Toby. The days went by and the cubs were slowly but surely gaining weight. Pickles still needed a little persuasion to suckle, but not Toby - sometimes he sucked so hard on the teat he almost sucked the bottle in as well!

Toby & Pickles as tiny cubs

Not only were we now ensuring that they peed and pooed, but also popped them over our shoulder and burped them. Toby in particular took in so much air whilst sucking so vigorously on the teat that he became quite bloated hence needing a belch or two! On day four, we noticed that Toby seemed a little lethargic and began to show all the classic hair loss and dry skin symptoms relating to suffering from a milk allergy. Obviously the Welpi wasn't agreeing with him and we needed to find a more suitable milk substitute and decided to ring Jane Ratcliffe.

Jane was a wildlife campaigner, naturalist, author and a much respected expert in all matters relating to caring for and rehabilitating wildlife and having successfully raised and rehabilitated badgers herself, was the obvious person to turn to for advice. Jane and her husband Teddy were friends of ours with Ann and me occasionally visiting them in their delightful home overlooking Lake Windermere in the Lake District. She would take great pride in giving us a guided tour of her wildlife garden with its endless variety of visiting species from red squirrels to badgers and last but not least, her pride and joy, her compost heap with its resident grass snakes. She was more than willing to help, explaining that she had successfully reared cubs on Complan, a vitamin, mineral and protein drink and as luck would have it, she had a few boxes that we could have. The following day we were soon on our way up the M6 to the Lakes returning with the magic formula, albeit raspberry flavoured! Toby took to it immediately and within a few days we began to see an improvement. Thankfully Pickles seemed not to have been affected and continued to do well on Welpi.

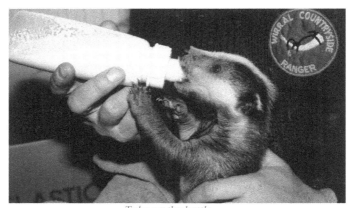

Toby on the bottle

One day Granada Television rang to ask if they could come along and feature them on Granada Reports. We gave it some thought and decided that it would do no harm and highlight badgers in general. The wheels were put in motion and it was arranged that Granada would arrive around 1 pm to film them as they were being bottle fed along with an interview on how they came into our care etc. They were not the least perturbed by their five minutes of fame, and continued to suckle away to their hearts content, and even managed the odd burp or two for the camera!

They were now on two hourly feeds with the first around 7 am and the last around midnight and with pee, poo and burp over, we settled them down in their box by the radiator and crept off to bed. They were weighed in the morning before their first feed and again after the last with weights recorded to give us an indication as to their daily progress. Toby now weighed in at 1lb.14oz. and Pickles 1lb.12oz. They had only gained a few ounces but it was progress! Despite their young age, it soon became apparent that they had their own individual characters with Toby being the more confident of the two whilst Pickles seemed a little insecure and if left alone would constantly chatter away until Toby was returned or he was picked up. Good Friday 28th March, day five and Toby was now fully recovered and loving his raspberry flavoured Complan. He now weighed 2lb.4oz with Pickles at 2lb.2oz. By the 31st Toby had gained another 4oz. whilst his sibling Pickles remained at 2lb.2oz.

On Tuesday the 8th April I recorded that we were approaching week three with eyes now fully open – both very active and playful with lots of excited whickering and chattering. Now on three hourly feeds of Farley's rusk baby food blended with Lactol. They no longer required stimulus to pee and poo, using a cat litter tray as a latrine. Toby was now weighing in at 3lb. and Pickles 2lb.8oz.

On Tuesday 15th April Granada TV arrived again to film a follow up of their progress with the cubs once again taking fame in their stride albeit now much more aware of their surroundings and a little more boisterous.

Very soon, Toby was topping the scales at 3lb.14oz. and Pickles at 3lb.7oz. with their daily feeds now down to every four hours. Pickles was still lagging behind his sibling in weight but other than that seemed fine and full of life. It was difficult to believe those two little cold and hungry close to death badger cubs that arrived on our doorstep a few weeks ago were now two bundles of mischief and taking over our lives!

I was very busy in my new job as Head Ranger and despite the demands of the cubs still had other sick or injured wildlife needing my attention including a sick gannet and a sparrowhawk, but we were coping and the cub's mischievous antics were guaranteed to bring a smile to your face even after the most stressful of days. Little did we know that things were just about to get much busier!

On Friday 18th April, I received a telephone call from RSPCA Inspector Barry Williams down in Shropshire explaining that he had been called out to a sickly badger cub discovered in a field lying by a dead sheep and could we take her. Presumably, something had happened to her mother and the only security she could find was to curl up by a dead sheep. Needless to say we said yes and within a couple of hours we found ourselves with cub number three. It was a sow (female) around two or three weeks older than Toby and Pickles and a fair bit bigger but weighing much less. The two boys were almost topping the scales at the 4lb mark now but she weighed a mere 2lb.14oz. and infested with lice and fleas. The first job was to get some sustenance into her and luckily when offered a dish of water and Lactol she drank the lot as if there was no tomorrow.

The next job was to get rid of the lice and fleas and gave her good dusting of delousing powder. This wasn't the easiest of tasks as being older than the other two she had spent more time in the sett with her mum and as such didn't take too kindly to being handled responding with a great deal of wriggling, growling and biting. She was a feisty little beast despite her condition and it was probably this gutsy fighting spirit that had kept her alive. Finally, with mission accomplished we put her in a warm straw bed in one of the Unit's hospital cages and offered her a dish of dog meat, which she ate with relish plus downing a second bowl of a water and Lactol. By Sunday 20th April she was looking much brighter and feeding well and topping the scales at 3lb.4oz. The idea was to introduce her to Toby and

Pickles but this could only happen when we were certain she was wasn't carrying anything that could be transmitted.

By Monday 21st April, Toby and Pickles were coming on in leaps and bounds with Toby at 4lb.6oz. and Pickles at 4lb.2oz. The little Shropshire sow now christened 'Cassie' was also doing well and weighing 3lb.6oz. She even seemed a little friendlier and not biting quite so hard!

By Thursday 24th April, Toby had topped the 5lb mark with Pickles at 4lb.10oz. and feisty little Cassie at 4lb. She had shown no signs of illness other than starvation and infestations so we decided the time had come to take her out of isolation and introduce her to Toby and Pickles. We put her in a fairly large box next to Toby and Pickles in the living room with the idea of them becoming familiar with one another's scent before actually meeting face to face. By midnight, all three had taken their final feed of the day and were tucked up in their respective boxes. We followed suit and wearily climbed the stairs to bed.

We were awoken at around 6 am to the sounds of excited whickering and thumping coming from downstairs. Creeping down to investigate we discovered all three cubs had climbed out of their boxes and were excitedly chasing each other around the living room giving off their playful whickering calls. The thumping sounds we heard were their heads banging under the sideboard as they chased underneath it. They were having a whale of a time! Toby interrupted his game of 'catch me if you can' to come romping over to have his little fat tummy tickled. This induced even more excited whickering at which point Pickles and Cassie decided that they would also like a bit of human attention and came bounding over all fluffed up and bouncing around stiff legged resembling bottle brushes on legs with Pickles jumping around our feet and pouncing on Toby. Cassie at this point suddenly remembered that she was the aloof one and regaining control of her emotions turned and trotted off to watch the antics of the other two from under the security of the sideboard and from that moment on all three shared the same box.

By Friday 25th April, Toby was at 5lb, Pickles, 4lb.10oz. and Cassie 4lb.3oz. Toby and Pickles were now around eight weeks old and still on four hourly bottle feeds of a mixture of Lactol, bone meal and Farley's Rusk plus a sprinkling of vitamin supplement totalling approximately 16 oz. each per feed. Thankfully, we never had the need to bottle feed Cassie due to her age and her willingness to drink and eat readily from a dish. If the need had arisen, it would undoubtedly have been a battle of wits with some growling and a few nipped fingers! On Tuesday 29th April, Toby weighed in at 6lb with Pickles at 5lb.8oz. and Cassie 5lb.3oz. Bodily she was bigger than the other two but still below their bodyweight and still had some catching up to do.

On Friday 2nd May, Granada television returned to film the cubs again for the programme 'The Week in View' followed a few hours later by the BBC for 'Look North West.' By the 4th May, their respective weights were Toby at 7lb.1oz, Pickles at 6lb.4oz. with Cassie at 5lb.9oz. which meant that they were rapidly outgrowing their box by the radiator and urgently required something much bigger and more secure. Being very playful and mischievous they were constantly scrambling out of the box to wrestle and chase around the living room floor whickering with delight. The only time they were quiet for any length of time was when they were sleeping and even then, they snored! We had nothing big enough in the Unit and apart from that, they still needed constant attention.

We solved the problem by investing in a large collapsible puppy playpen placed on the tiled floor of the dining room. Not the ideal thing to have in your dining room but at least it would confine them and give them much more room. They could still have their daily romps around the living room but at our discretion, not just when they felt like it. We lined the pen floor with layers of newspaper, provided them with a large cardboard box to sleep in and a cat litter tray for their toilet. At the opposite end to the litter tray, we made an area for food and water dishes.

Toby and Pickles were almost weaned by now and were feeding happily from feeding bowls and Cassie of course had been on solids since arriving. With the new pen ready, we transferred the three delinquents to their new quarters and they loved it! In no time at all they were shredding newspaper, wrestling on top of their sleeping box almost causing it to collapse and generally causing mayhem, but at least it was controlled mayhem! By the 8th May, Toby was topping the scales at a massive 8lb. with Pickles at 7lb.3oz. and Cassie at 6lb.4oz., they were growing fast!

They had been in their new pen four days now and at long last we had our living room back. We could watch television in peace without the constant 'thud, thud, thud' of heads banging under the furniture or feet being pounced upon and toes playfully nipped. The latest game now was who could shred the newspaper into the tiniest possible pieces or just generally turn the interior of their pen into something resembling a mini war zone! They still had their nightly romps around the living room but now we were in charge and would dictate when they could, and could not, have the freedom of the house. Or so we thought! We had underestimated the power of reasoning and sheer determination of our three delinquents!

One evening we were so engrossed in watching the television we hadn't noticed that the now familiar sounds coming from the dining room of newspaper being shredded coupled with whickering and squeals as they wrestled and played had suddenly been replaced by the sound of claws on wire! The first we realised something was afoot was when we heard a dull thud followed by two more dull thuds followed the sound of claws on tiles. Then it happened! There was a sudden realisation that we had been lulled into a false sense of security as our devious, scheming little band of juvenile delinquents came charging round the corner, claws scraping on the tiles.

They skidded to come gleefully bounding into the living room all fluffed up and stiff legged huffing and puffing and now resembling three hairy balloons on legs. They gave off cries of sheer delight as they bounced around in mock battles; snorting and puffing away until eventually deciding that we and our two whippets, Sally and Tigger would make much more interesting playmates and became the main focus of their attention. Tigger, despite being totally accustomed to sharing his living space with strange furry creatures sneaked off to find refuge in his bean bag on the upstairs landing whilst poor old Sally, with a pathetic forlorn expression, pleaded with us to restore at least some sense of sanity back to the Ingham household.

Badgers are nocturnal creatures and that at least gave us some respite in that they tended to sleep for most of the day but come evening chaos reigned as they became a three-cub demolition squad! We were now turning nocturnal ourselves, bedtime would be around midnight if we were lucky, but more often than not more like one or two in the morning, whereupon we would drag ourselves off to bed in the hope that the trio would be exhausted enough to stay in their pen. The slightest noise coming from downstairs would have us up and about to investigate that they weren't creating mayhem once again in the living room. Something had to be done! As charming and endearing as they were, they had outstayed their welcome in the house and so I began to convert what had originally been our very first treatment shed into outdoor accommodation for them. It was much larger than their puppy playpen and had a solid stable door, the top of which I replaced with strong galvanised wire so that we could leave the top portion open to allow in ample light and fresh air.

Their sleeping quarters were two wooden boxes lined with straw and entered through a section of ten-inch drainage pipe. The floor was covered with copious amounts of straw, their litter tray was tucked away in a far corner and we provided logs and other paraphernalia for them to climb around and play on. The door opened out onto the garden and the idea was to allow them supervised access to it. But before that could happen I needed to replace the old rickety wooden boundary fence and so set about replacing it with a five foot high wire fence incorporating an overhang half way up which would, theoretically at least, stop them from climbing to the top and vanishing into the park.

Toby, Pickles, Cassie and Kippy in their shed

By the 12th May, Toby and Pickles were ten weeks old and totally weaned. Their new quarters were ready and the garden fenced, so that afternoon we carried all three of them from the house and introduced them to their new home. They were in seventh heaven as they scrambled over logs, vanished down the pipe to explore their box and just generally having a whale of a time. They were now on one evening meal a day consisting of all in one dog food mixed with raw minced beef, cereals, peanuts, honey and chopped apple plus a sprinkling of vitamin powder and bone meal. They were also given raw eggs; worms and the occasional road kill in the form of birds and small mammals. Despite having been raised on an alien diet, when presented with natural food they showed not the slightest hesitation in devouring it with relish.

At long last we had the house to ourselves! We could watch TV in peace and the dogs could slumber away the hours in front of the fire without constantly being pounced upon. But, any illusions we may have had about them being less of a commitment quickly evaporated as they still demanded constant attention. The plan was to return them back to the wild but that was going to take a lot of hard work. Little did we know then just how much!

Their nightly routine now was rather than romps around the living room they had supervised romps around the garden. The duration of these nightly bouts of freedom very much depended on just how long we could stay awake, often finding ourselves enticing them back to their quarters in the early hours with the promise of some tasty morsel. This was their nightly routine regardless of the weather and as dusk descended you would hear the banging and general commotion coming from their quarters as they became active. As soon as we opened their door, out they shot into the garden - three bouncing, whickering excited young badgers. God help us if we were late! Then they would attempt to batter the door down or scramble up to the upper wire section of the door to peer out in eager anticipation of our arrival. More than once, I had this vision of three little badgers shoulder charging the door in an attempt to dislodge it from its hinges.

On the 10th June, Toby and Pickles were around 14 weeks old and Cassie around 16 or 17. She was still the smallest of the three with Pickles, despite his slow start, now the largest. He looked very handsome with his beautiful ginger coat. In fact, all three were a picture of health and very much full of mischief and a pleasure to be around. Their amusing antics and individual characters more than made up for all the hard work and constant commitment. Little did we realise that, once more, things were about to change with the arrival of two more cubs about to join our little group.

On the 12th June, I received a telephone call from a Department of the Environment Inspector in Leicestershire, explaining that in January he and his wife had taken in two tiny badger cubs about three or four days old and weighing a mere four ounces. Apparently, they had been taken from the sett by a terrier dog and were very close to death with one of them having to be revived by gently blowing down its nostrils and massaging its chest. By some miracle, they did survive and were hand reared on Welpi and eventually weaned on to cat food - and of all things, spam! They were both females coming up to six months old and named Millie and Kippy. Kippy was the one that had been close to death, but now both were fit, healthy and very boisterous and could we possibly take them? Despite the constant commitment with the other three over of the past couple of months, we agreed with the rationality of 'what difference would another two make?'

It was arranged that they would travel up from Leicestershire on Sunday 15th June and so we set about preparing temporary accommodation for them in a shed next door to the main Wildlife Unit's hospital cabin. They arrived at around 3 pm. Our first reaction on seeing them was surprise as we hadn't realised just how much bigger they were to our own three, with Millie in particular being built like a tank. She had been lightly sedated for the journey due to her having strained a leg muscle the previous day and had apparently been limping quite badly. Both were a little subdued on arrival and we quickly settled them down in their quarters leaving them to recover from the long journey. The idea was that we would gradually introduce them to our own three delinquents until they could live together as a family group.

That evening I sneaked off for a pint whilst Ann supervised Toby, Pickles and Cassie in the garden. Upon returning home I discovered Ann in the shed sitting on a bale of straw with the new arrivals and with big Millie, now fully recovered from her sedation, bouncing all over her with not the slightest hint of a limp and Kippy sitting on her knee scratching her tummy. Her own, not Ann's!

When I asked how they were doing, she replied in a rather exasperated voice. "My God they are a lively pair!!"

They were bigger and stronger than our other three and hoped that they would not be too big and powerful for our little trio to cope with! By the 18th June, they had settled in well, were extremely tame and unlike our own three, had not the slightest idea about natural food. Our three tucked readily into worms and carrion but not these two! Show them a worm and they looked at you in utter disgust as if to say 'What am I supposed to do with that?' but at least they were now tucking into the same diet and hopefully once all together would get a better idea as to what natural food was.

We put some of Millie and Kippy's bedding in with the other three and vice versa in order that they would become accustomed to each other's scent. We also carried Millie and Kippy into the garden allowing them to run around, play and scent mark before carrying them back to their shed prior to letting Toby, Pickles and Cassie into the garden. As mentioned before badgers can be territorial and even though they were only cubs, we weren't quite sure what to expect, hence the gradual introduction through scent familiarity.

On the evening of 20th June we decided to take things a step further and to split the garden into two sections with a temporary wire fence, this would allow all five to be in the garden together but with Millie and Kippy partitioned by the fence. They would be able to see and sniff each other without actually making bodily contact. With the fence in place, we carried Millie and Kippy into the garden placing them on one side of the fence where they proceeded to do their usual playing, exploring and scent marking. Before long, the other three were becoming impatient doing their usual shoulder charging and scrambling up the door and as such, we decided to bite the bullet and let them out.

All three tumbled out falling over each other in their eagerness to greet us and sit on our wellies. Badgers greet each other and strengthen individual bonds within the social group by sitting on each other and leaving a tiny secretion of musk from the subcaudal scent gland at the base of the tail. We were afforded the same accolade because as far as they were concerned we were part and parcel of their little social group. With formalities over, it was then a race to see who could reach the garden first. They made a comical sight as they shot off around the corner as fast as their little stubby legs could carry them. No sooner had they rounded the corner and reached the lawn before they stopped dead in their tracks as they spotted the makeshift fence. They looked totally bewildered wondering what this unfamiliar thing was that had suddenly appeared in their garden.

Cautiously they moved towards it all puffed up with hair stood on end ready to make a mad dash back to the security of their little shed at the first sign of danger. By now, Millie and Kippy had picked up their scent and with an equal mix of curiosity and trepidation crept closer. Toby, Pickles and Cassie bounced around huffing and puffing on the other side. With curiosity beginning to overtake apprehension they slowly but surely crept closer, with noses pressed tightly up to the wire they gave each other a good sniffing. This went on for ten minutes or so and seemed to be going well with no sign of animosity from either side.

Gradually they became more relaxed with the body language giving way to 'come over here and play' rather than 'I'm not sure about you.' With everything looking good, we decided to allow them one by one to meet face to face. First to go was Toby. We lifted him over the fence and popped him down next to an inquisitive Millie and Kippy; they sniffed him all over for a minute or so before unceremoniously plonking their bottoms on him to scent mark him before chasing around the garden in a state of absolute bliss with lots of excited whickering and play fighting. Pickles was next, followed by Cassie and within minutes all five were getting on like a house on fire and the fence came down.

We just sat there on the garden bench and watched mesmerized as five badgers romped and played to their hearts content. Occasionally one would break off from their games to come running over to check that we were still there followed by a quick musk on the welly before dashing off again to join in the fun. From that night on, they became one big happy family living together in the shed and enjoying their nightly forays into the garden. Cassie, though still small for her age, was no push over; she could stand her ground with the best of them and was rapidly proving to be the comedian of the group.

She gave the impression of being aloof but in reality was just the opposite. She would charge around the garden like a demented imp. If the other four were in a heap play fighting she would bounce around them in circles resembling a child in a school playground encouraging a punch up and if there was any mischief to be had you could guarantee that she would be at the front of the queue. Pickles, although still enjoying the rough and tumbles in the garden was beginning to devote more of his time to other pastimes such grubbing for worms or dissecting a rotten log for grubs. Toby was just Toby, a very pleasant well-adjusted soul who loved playing, eating and us, but not necessarily in that order.

One of his favourite tricks, particularly if he thought he wasn't getting the attention he deserved, was to run to the garden fence, climb up to the overhang and with the cunning of an escapee from Colditz, managed to traverse it and continue his climb to the top. This was where his escape mission came to a halt, once at the top there he would hang wobbling precariously whilst looking around to see who was watching knowing full well that Ann or I would go dashing over to rescue him. We would place our hands on his rump whereupon he would twist himself round, let go of the fence and drape himself over your shoulder, content in the knowledge that he had once again achieved his mission of becoming the centre of attention.

Big Millie loved nothing more than to play and wrestle with us. She was a very pleasant individual who, on occasions, particularly during boisterous play, tended to forget that human skin is not quite as tough as that of her own kind. Even her sibling Kippy, though much smaller could be equally as rough. It was obvious that the pair had been spoilt something rotten unlike like our own three who had been brought up to respect their peers. At least most of the time anyway!

Kippy in the garden pond

By July they were now mainly truly nocturnal sleeping away the day and wanting the freedom of the garden from dusk to the early hours. Play was still a very important part of their lives but they were now becoming real badgers with even Millie and Kippy spending more time foraging for worms and doing real badger things. The downside to all this was that what was once my carefully nurtured garden now resembled a scene from the Somme, with craters here, there and everywhere, flower beds were flattened and my small but serviceable wildlife pond now more akin to a large muddy puddle. They absolutely loved to play in water, particularly during the summer months when they would spend hours just sitting in the pond splashing water all around themselves. Being lively inquisitive creatures meant that they soon became bored and were constantly on the lookout for new things to explore.

One such opportunity arose one evening when Ann forgot to take a sheet off the rotary washing line, which was very quickly spotted by Cassie. She ambled over to investigate and grabbing hold of the sheet proceeded to worry it with great gusto then, with the sheet firmly gripped in her teeth, began to twist around and around as fast as her little legs could go. Once she considered it to be twisted tight enough she would lift her back legs off the floor to spin around and around as the sheet unwound eventually letting go to fall to the ground and wobble around the garden in a dizzy haze. Once the effects had worn off, she would return to repeat the performance.

As mentioned before, I will never believe the assumption by some that animals don't possess a sense of fun, and dare I say it, even humour! Cassie certainly had both in abundance! One of her favourite tricks was to wait until Ann was sat on the garden bench engrossed in a book and totally lulled into a false sense of security, whereupon Cassie would sneak up behind her, nip her ankles and run off like some demented imp to hide in the bushes. Once the cussing and cursing had ceased and Ann was once again engrossed in her book, Cassie would again sneak under the bench for another ankle nip.

At one point, Ann had to go into hospital for a minor operation which left me in sole charge of the nightly garden romps for a couple of nights and boy did Cassie take full advantage! One night in particular is firmly embedded in my mind as she decided to climb the wire of one of the aviaries bordering the garden. I watched as she very nonchalantly wandered over to the aviary, peered through the wire as if to see what was in there. Then with the agility and speed of a chimpanzee she shot up the wire and on to the roof where she began the taunting game of peering down at me as if to say, 'now what are you going to do?'

Now it was my turn to curse and swear! My main concern was that she could climb down the other side and be gone into the darkness of the park never to be seen again. I tried coaxing her with kind words and when that didn't work; I tried enticing her with her favourite tit bit but all to no avail. It soon became apparent that there was no alternative but to get up there myself and as such ran into the house for a pair of stepladders. I returned a few minutes later relieved to see that she was still there and peering down at me with a quizzical expression, obviously wondering what I was going to do next. I placed the stepladders sideways on to the aviary and proceeded to climb to the top.

Unfortunately, both they and I weren't quite tall enough and to complicate matters the little imp began to move farther away from the edge until I lost sight of her. I stretched as far as I dared on my tiptoes in an attempt to peer onto the roof and in between wobbles I could see that she had wandered over to the very far edge and was looking at me with a bemused expression on her face. I whispered sweet nothings in the hope of enticing her to me. She crept just a little closer - I stretched a little further - the stepladders wobbled unsteadily and I made a grab at the wire to stop myself from falling backwards. At this point, she decided to wander over for a closer look but still just out of reach. Once again, I whispered sweet tones of endearment and she came closer still.

"Come on Cassie, there's a good girl," I whispered as she crept even closer.

I was at the very top of the stepladders, still precariously hanging on to the roof. She came to the very edge and sniffed my hand and I remember thinking, 'it's now or never' and made a grab for her. She wriggled, the steps wobbled and I, tightly clutching Cassie by the scruff, suddenly felt myself becoming airborne as the stepladders toppled sideways. I landed with an almighty thud on the ground with Cassie sat on my chest! I lay there dazed and winded as she gave me a quick sniff before casually ambling off to see what the others were up to. I suppose I should count myself lucky she didn't sit on my face and scent mark me!

Another episode that's guaranteed to get Ann sniggering like a demented schoolgirl was one particular night when, once again, sweet little Cassie got the better of me. We were in the garden as usual, the badgers were engrossed in playing and foraging for worms when the heavens opened and I mean opened! It came down in bucket loads sending Toby, Pickles, Millie and Kippy all scampering back to the shelter of their shed - but not Cassie! She had other ideas and obviously thought what a load of wimps dashing off to bed at the first sign of rain and carried on mooching around the garden resisting all attempts at trying to coax her back inside.

The rain showed no signs of abating and was obviously in for the night: we were getting wetter and wetter as the rain got harder and harder until pretty soon we resembled two very soggy drowned rats. Time was getting on and there was no way we could leave her out all night, somehow we had to get her back to the shed, we attempted to grab her, we tried rugby tackling her but all to no avail!

She evaded all our efforts of capture with the dexterity of a rugby player running for a try, and as a last desperate attempt, I decided that I had no alternative but to net her. It's not something I would have contemplated under normal circumstances but we were at the end of our tether and had to do something pretty quickly. At least with the net I could creep up without getting too close and with a lightning swoop have her gathered up and off to the shed in no time. With net poised, I stealthily crept towards her, at least as stealthily as I could.

My jacket was by now reduced to a soggy mess with the sleeves so wet and heavy that they were virtually dragging along the ground and my boots oozed water at every step. I squelched my way forward with net poised - she gave me a sideways glance, I was close, very close - it was now or never and with one lightning swoop of the net I missed as she triumphantly scampered off once more into the darkness as I cursed and cussed. After a few moments she reappeared, taunting me to have another go - I moved forward once again staring her directly in the eye, I quickened my pace, she stood her ground, I leapt forward and with one almighty sweep of the net, missed again! She shot off around the garden only pausing momentarily to tease me into another attempt. I took the bait and shot off after her.

By this time, the rain was torrential – my jacket sleeves were now so long that I was beginning to resemble some form of ancient humanoid in the early stages of evolution from walking on four to two limbs. Ann, being the helpful considerate soul she is just stood there with her hands over her mouth trying desperately to suppress uncontrollable fits of laughter. Eventually after much slipping, sliding and more cursing I finally succeeded in getting the impish little devil into the net and back to the shed. That night whilst soaking up the warmth and comfort of my bed I had visions of Cassie in the shed sat smugly on a log relating the tale to the other four as they all rolled about in fits of uncontrollable hilarity.

After all we had been through with the cubs it's impossible not to form a bond and become attached, but they were not pets, they were wild animals and as such the ultimate aim was to reintroduce them back into the wild. We had been checking out potential release sites for many months but for one reason or another all turned out to be unsuitable. Our plan was to release them as an established family group into a disused natural badger sett in ideal badger habitat with foraging pasture and easy access to water all within close proximity and if possible, on private land.

Another equally important factor was having no badger activity in the immediate vicinity or active sett within a two or three mile radius. We would also require the full and long-term co-operation of the landowner in giving us complete freedom to come and go at will whatever the time of day or night for possibly many months whilst we monitored their progress. We were well aware that the chances of finding such a site would equate to looking for a needle in a haystack. If and when we were fortunate enough to find such a site then we would have to delve into the history of both the area and the sett to determine that if it's so good, what happened to the previous occupants and why is there no present badger activity within the area? Only once those questions had been answered satisfactorily could we seriously consider it suitable. But if we were going to give our five bundles of mischief the best possible chance of living a natural life in the wild we would have to find it.

We had no illusions regarding how daunting a task we had set ourselves. The reintroduction would be very time consuming and potentially fraught with difficulty. All we could do was to at least try to envisage some of the potential problems that could occur and hopefully be prepared to deal with them. Despite having been brought up in captivity, they were a well-adjusted little group with their own established hierarchy. Human contact other than Ann and me had been kept to a minimum and in their eyes; we weren't just human foster parents, but an integral part of their social group with Ann and me being the pinnacle of their social standing. Although I strongly suspect that Cassie may have thought otherwise! This trusted position that we held within the group was to play a vital role in their eventual rehabilitation. Little did we visualise at the time just how crucial a role our trusted standing in the group was to be, but all that was yet to come. We were to face more challenges and dramas before that day arrived!

On the 24th July Kippy, suddenly and for no apparent reason became very subdued and lost her appetite, but thankfully after a couple of days of close monitoring in isolation and an injection of broad spectrum antibiotic was soon back to her normal self. On the 3rd August, Pickles began to show similar symptoms, becoming very lethargic and obviously unwell and, as with Kippy, he was placed in isolation and given antibiotics but he showed no signs of improvement. We racked our brains for an answer as to what the problem could be but all we could do was to wait in the hope that, like Kippy, he would recover.

On the 5th August he seemed much brighter and he wasn't at all happy at being separated from the others so we decided to put him back with the group. We checked him every hour or so throughout the day, he was a little quiet but other than that he seemed fine. That evening we opened the shed door to let them into the garden; they came bounding out as usual with the exception of Pickles. Ann discovered him dead in his sleeping box.

To say that we were heartbroken is an understatement

but what of the other four? Kippy had already shown signs of being unwell and God forbid anything should happen to the rest. We needed to know what Pickles had died of and fast! The following day I took him to Leahurst, the Liverpool University Veterinary Hospital in Cheshire for a post-mortem. They discovered that he'd died from a Clostridia bacterium which can be found in soil, water and the gastrointestinal tract of animals and humans. It was alarming just how rapid his decline had been from first showing signs of something being not quite right to his death. We were told that it was common in sheep, which are routinely vaccinated against it, we were also told that the only thing we could have done was to administer a penicillin type of antibiotic, something we had done with both Kippy and Pickles. Thankfully it worked for Kippy but unfortunately not for Pickles. Due to the fact that he was unusual in respect of him being Erythristic, his body was given over to the Liverpool Museum Natural History Dept. whereupon he was recorded for posterity. He was sadly missed! Thankfully Kippy made a full recovery with the others showing no signs of illness and all continuing to thrive.

Time moved on and we were now approaching September and still looking for a release site. Eventually Michele, who originally brought Toby and Pickles, put us in touch with a landowner in North Wales who apparently owned a small estate with woodland and a disused badger sett. We lost no time in making contact and upon explaining our quest confirmed that yes, she did own a small private estate and woodland with an old natural disused badger sett and asked if we would like to see it?

As you can imagine, the reply was a resounding "Yes please, where is it and when can we come?"

She explained that it was in Denbighshire, North Wales and about a 45 minute drive from the Wirral. We eagerly scribbled down the directions and arranged to meet the following weekend. Saturday finally arrived and we made the journey over to North Wales, eventually leaving the flatness of Wirral and the busy A494 behind us to enter the more rural and undulating countryside of the counties of Flintshire and Denbighshire. As our little Peugeot 205 green ranger van climbed the steep hilly roads heading towards the historic town of Ruthin, our minds were full of unanswered questions. Was the site really as good as we were led to believe? Had we finally found a new home for our four delinquents? It seemed too good to be true!

As we left the ancient little market town of Ruthin behind with its hilly narrow streets and historic buildings, we headed south eventually climbing through the Nant y Garth Pass with its steep wooded banks. We continued climbing the winding road eventually taking a right turn onto a track which climbed and twisted even more steeply bringing us to a very tight, steep right hand turn followed by another short climb to reveal a thirties style detached house set amongst woodland. Our first impressions were good; it looked and felt right.

The owner was there to greet us and over a cup of tea explained that she had known the old sett since her childhood and that badgers had not lived in the wood for many a year also that it was quiet and very private. Over tea, we told her all about our little band of orphans, how five were now four and the criteria we were looking for in a release site.

She listened with interest and with tea finished said, "Well we had better let you have a look then hadn't we," whereupon she marched down the long oak panelled corridor to the front porch to pull on her wellington boots.

Once we were also suitably attired with the appropriate footwear we followed her down a narrow twisting path leading into the wood as she explained a little of the estates history. At one point, just before entering the wood, she stopped by a little area tucked away in its own little niche. It had the appearance of a semi-wild secret garden with what looked like small gravestones dotted around it. She explained that they were indeed gravestones due to the fact that a few long past family members were buried there. We followed the narrow winding path a little further until at last we entered the woodland. It looked perfect!

Situated on a steep hillside it had a mix of Scots Pine, Oak and Ash leading steeply down to a large rocky pool fed by a stream, which eventually left the pool to cascade over a waterfall to meander its way down a steeply sided wooded valley. The pool had a strange prehistoric air about it with damp limestone moss and lichen encrusted rocks forming its precipitous slippery banks - long fallen ancient trees lay slowly decaying, shrouded in large damp ferns - their greenness contrasting sharply with the dark, almost black decaying trunks. There was definitely a strange atmosphere to the place - nothing sinister, just a deep sensation of nature mingled with a hint of secrets and mystery.

The top western section of the wood, in contrast to the lower eastern section, led onto seemingly never ending hilly pasture. It was obvious that the wood had been completely untouched for many years with trees decaying where they fell whilst others, their tumbling halted as they rested against another, their branches encrusted in lichen and green damp moss whilst ivy clung and weaved its way up the leaning decaying trunk. Finally we arrived at the sett and had we not been guided would almost certainly have missed it as it was now virtually hidden from view by ferns and other woodland flora. It was immediately obvious that at some point in its life it had been an active badger sett and from what we could see consisted of four or five holes their entrances now blocked by old mouldy and decomposing leaf litter, intricately woven spiders webs stretched across the entrances.

Old spoil heaps lay below the holes where years ago the previous occupants had excavated the sett throwing out earth and stones but now forming a base for fern and foxglove. Even though it was obvious the holes hadn't been occupied for a long time we still examined the spoil for badger hair but none was to be found. With no obvious sign of badger either around the sett, the wood or beyond in the form of paths, hair under fences or latrines we concluded that that sett was, as our host initially explained, totally devoid of badgers.

The next stage was to carry out more field and survey work plus contacting the Clwyd Badger Group in an effort to determine where the nearest active sett may be and an idea as to the occupant's home / territorial range. Over the next few weeks, we returned on a regular basis scouring every inch until we were confident that we were very familiar with not only the wood but also the surrounding area. Finally, we decided that at long last we had found our badger utopia and as such began to prepare for the reintroduction. The plan was to place bedding from their sleeping boxes in and around the sett with the idea that familiar smells would help them to settle more quickly. It was also decided to mark them individually by shaving off a little hair and marking with a purple spray. Not perfect or long term, but in the early stages at least it could prove useful. Once everything was in place we would transfer the cubs from their quarters to the release site where they would be given time to recover from the journey.

At this stage, the actual form of transportation hadn't been decided upon. Once fully recovered, a couple of hours before dusk, we would then walk them through the wood to the sett on the assumption that they would willingly follow us. (This in reality proved to be a very naïve assumption!) Upon reaching the sett, they would then busy themselves smelling familiar smells in the form of their old bedding to eventually exploring the sett and its immediate surroundings. The plan was that we would virtually live in the wood until we were confident that they had indeed accepted the sett as their new home and were becoming familiar with the surrounding area.

In their eyes not a lot would have changed other than the fact that their sleeping accommodation was now a natural sett and the garden wild woodland. Ann and I would still be there to continue the routine of feeding, walking and monitoring with the idea being that after a week they would be sleeping away the day in the depths of the sett only being active after dusk allowing us to be at home or work during the day returning just before dusk ready for their re-emergence. Our presence would gradually diminish over a period of weeks, possibly even months depending on the circumstances.

We hadn't raised these four delinquents just to be abandoned in a few holes in a wood on the assumption that they would survive – on the contrary, we were acutely aware that if this was to be completely successful we had to be in it for the long-term. We both had full-time jobs and it was going to be one heck of a commitment but we would do it, we weren't quite sure how, but we would do it.

Chapter Seven
The Trials & Tribulations of a Badger Release

At long last, it seemed that we had found our release site and could finally begin to put plans into place for the reintroduction. It was vital that once the cubs had accepted the sett as their home Ann and I were still around in order to feed them and walk with them on their initial explorative jaunts around the wood whilst monitoring and recording all that happened. We concluded that ideally we would need to be at the release site for much of the day and practically all night for around two weeks. This would, of course, very much depend on how things progressed. If it went well from the start and they accepted their new surroundings quickly, then rather than spending just about every hour in the wood we would be there from early evening to the early hours of the morning with our involvement tapering off over a period of months depending on how well they adjusted to their new life.

But we had a problem! I didn't have enough leave left to be able to spend all night and every night in the wood for a couple of weeks and Ann was in the same predicament with her job at the vets. The only way it would have been possible was by the pair of us spending our nights there and our days at work and realistically that was impossible, we would have been dead on our feet! The only other alternative was that we arrived on site as soon as possible after work and stayed as late as possible, but even that wasn't really workable. It was a ninety minute drive there and back and as a consequence we would have no sooner got home and snatched a couple of hours sleep before it would have been time to get ready for work and I also had the Wildlife Unit to manage as well as my full-time job.

It was quickly becoming apparent that to devote the time we had considered necessary for the release wasn't realistically possible. Anything could happen during our absence and we just couldn't risk it, but they needed to go back into the wild and we felt that we were the only ones that could make it work due to the close relationship we had built up with them over the past months. There appeared to be no easy solution. Whichever route we chose, it was going to involve serious sleep deprivation for ourselves with possible detrimental consequences for the cubs plus other creatures needing our attention at the Unit. If it was going to be done, it had to be done right! Thankfully the problem was soon to be resolved!

One day whilst visiting Heswall Dales Local Nature Reserve, one of the areas under my wing as Head Ranger, I happened to mention our dilemma to the site ranger Mike Jackson who immediately and without hesitation said, "I've got a couple of weeks leave outstanding, I'll live in the wood and watch over them!"

Mike was, and still is, a very good naturalist with a keen interest in badgers and being a bachelor at that particular time seemed to be the ideal candidate. I knew that I could trust him implicitly and that he would put his heart and soul into the task. Little did he know at the time just what he had signed up for otherwise he may have had second thoughts! Ann and I talked it over and it was agreed that Mike was the ideal solution to our predicament. We would still be living a semi-nocturnal existence for a while in having to travel out to the wood after work and staying quite late, but Mike would be there in our absence watching over them and recording all that happened. It was agreed that he should begin to spend time with the cubs in order for them to become familiar with him and likewise for Mike to get to know them and their individual characters.

From that moment on, he began to spend his evenings in the garden and was quickly accepted into the gang; quite soon, they afforded him the accolade of sitting on his wellie and scent marking him. Even Toby, who had built up a special relationship with me, accepted him into our little world without hesitation. As Mike was now going to be playing a vital role in the reintroduction he was of course included in all of the planning and preparation. We had agreed that they were to be individually marked in order to recognise them more easily in the field and decided on the following - Cassie was to be marked with Gentian Violet on her tail and the white area between her ears. Toby was to have a small area of hair clipped from his neck and rump. Millie was to have an area of hair clipped from her left shoulder whilst her sibling Kippy was to have an area of hair clipped from her right shoulder. We decided against clipping hair off Cassie due to her tendency to squirm, growl and nip when handled – we could easily have ended up with a very patchy badger! Mind you, we could just as easily have ended up with a purple one!!

It was now confirmed that the transportation was to be in the form of a small horsebox provided by a friend who also offered to tow it there with her Daihatsu jeep. The floor of the horsebox was to have a good thick layer of straw spread around with straw bales at the back and sides. The badgers would be lightly sedated and transported loose in the box with Ann travelling in there also to keep them company. Once at the release site, the box was to be parked at the woodland edge by a small clearing where Mike was to construct the makeshift camp that would be his home for possibly the next two weeks.

The plan was to allow them to recover from the journey for a short while before allowing them out of the horsebox to be walked up through the wood to the sett early that evening. The idea was that once let out of the horsebox, they would do as they always did at home on being let out of their shed, eagerly run around us jostling for who would be the first to sit on our wellies and musk us. Then, without the slightest hesitation, they would follow us up through the wood to the sett. Once there, they would pick up the familiar reassuring scent from the bedding taken from their sleeping boxes, then settle down to explore the sett and, hopefully, accept it as home. To be honest we just didn't know what would happen; we were hoping that by knowing the cubs as well as we did, we could at least predict as much as possible how they would react and, if everything went according to plan, by the following morning they would be snoring their heads off in the sett.

At least that was the theory; in reality, it could be so very different! It was very much a case of suck it and see and hopefully be in full control if it all went pear shaped! We also decided that the release should take place around late October, the reason being with a bit of luck the weather would still be fairly mild and even though the clocks would be going back we should still have a reasonable amount of evening light. Another factor was that for badgers in the wild, October is a month of concentrating on putting on the pounds for the coming winter with a little bit of hanky panky thrown in for good measure, but by late October and into November activity levels begin to drop off and by December they tend to sleep longer and deeper. This would be to the cubs' advantage by giving them plenty of time to become established before any chance encounters with other badgers. It was inevitable that at some point, possibly around March onwards of the following year they would indeed come face to face with others of their kind and that the encounter, in all probability, would not necessarily be a friendly one, particularly for Toby.

Badgers live in tightly knit social clans and can be fiercely territorial. Boars in particular will patrol and defend their territories / home ranges and do battle with any boar from another clan that has had the audacity to venture into his patch, sometimes resulting in serious injury or even death. To hear the sound of badgers in a serious fight is not pleasant and is guaranteed to send shivers down your spine and make the hairs at the back of your neck stand on end! We hoped that when it happened, which it inevitably would at some point, Toby would be strong and fit enough to give a good account of himself and come away relatively unscathed and all the wiser for the experience. It's an important part of the learning process for any young badger, particularly a boar…but not just yet!

Finally, after much work all the necessary arrangements were made with transport organised and everything planned down to the finest detail, with Monday 20th October 1986 being chosen as the big day. It was decided to have them loaded up and ready for the off by around 4.45 pm, arriving at the release site by around 5.30 pm. Mike was to be on site a couple of hours earlier to set up his camp and to place their familiar smelling bedding down the sett entrances and around the general area. A military operation couldn't have been better thought out, or at least that's what we hoped! But that was a week away and in the meantime they continued to enjoy their evening romps around the garden totally oblivious to the fact that their lives were about to change beyond belief and that they were to experience events that even we could not have imagined!

October 20th the day of reckoning arrived all too quickly; Mike had arranged to meet us at the wood and our four trusting and now not so little young badgers were feeling the effects of the sedative with eyelids becoming droopy. Cassie was the first in the box and confined to a carrying cage whilst the other three were to remain loose watched over by Ann who would be travelling in the horsebox with them. As we carried them one by one from their little shed we couldn't help but feel an overwhelming sense of trepidation. We were taking ourselves, and more importantly the badgers into the unknown. We had no idea what the next few days held for us: what if it turned out to be an absolute disaster and we were to lose them forever, never knowing what happened to them? It just didn't bear thinking about!

But we were committed to seeing it through and there was no going back. We knew that the transition from the horsebox to the sett was going to be a critical time followed by their first night in the wood. We also knew that if we still had all four badgers at the sett of their own free will on the second night, we would have crossed the first major hurdle. We were very soon to find out….the hard way!

The red Daihatsu jeep slowed almost to a stop as it took

the hard right hand turn into the track and began the slow twisting uphill journey to the wood. It wasn't finding the going easy, the gears crunched down from second to first, struggling to tow the horsebox along with Ann and our four badgers locked within up the steep winding track. Eventually it came to the very sharp and thankfully last hairpin bend followed by the more gradual climb to the clearing on the edge of the wood. We had reached our destination! Mike was already there and had been busy setting up his camp. He'd made himself a shelter out of a tarpaulin hung on timber poles containing a makeshift bed and other luxuries such as candles, torch, kettle, mug, spade and loo rolls etc. plus a small fire area with a log table and a couple of log seats. We uncoupled the horsebox and bade farewell to the driver as she explained that she would return to collect it in a few days.

Despite the sedation there was a fair amount of activity coming from inside the box and Ann, who had by now released Cassie from her travelling cage, was struggling to squeeze herself out of the little side door of the horsebox whilst at the same time pushing four inquisitive badgers back in. Even though they were active, we felt that the sedative hadn't fully worn off and as such decided to keep them contained in the box overnight.

Despite still being a little wobbly, they were surprisingly active with Toby and Cassie climbing up the vertical tail ramp forcing us to block the top opening with straw bales, lengths of wood and bailing twine. Millie then decided that Cassie and Toby's escape plans were futile and evolved her own ideas by playing with the internal handle of the side door until it opened, whereupon she tumbled out and with drooping eyelids ambled sleepily under the horsebox. Despite her wobbly state her brain and jaws were far from sleepy as Ann found out when she picked her up only to collect her second set of teeth marks of the day. Cassie had also nipped her when being caged ready for the journey. Even though she had been bitten by both Millie and Cassie neither one had intended a serious bite; if they had she would have had something far worse than a few slight teeth indentations!

Finally things quietened down and Ann and I went into the box to feed them and tuck them in for the night before departing for home and work the following morning, comforted in the knowledge that they were safe under Mike's watchful eyes. It was around 12.30 am as we began our journey home, winding our way down the track now bathed in moonlight filtering through the trees. We tumbled into bed exhausted but sleep didn't come easy with our thoughts constantly drifting back to the wood and what lay ahead. But at least we slept, unlike Mike who wasn't afforded such luxury!

The following extracts are taken from his notes:

Day Two – Tuesday 21st October. 86

1.00am

Malcolm and Ann now departed.

Lots of whickering, grunts and scratching persists from the horsebox, whilst crows and jackdaws called as they flew over the woodland.

Maybe the bright moonlight is making them restless?

2.40am

Silence prevails, following a hectic hour or so.

At last the scratching, grunts and squeals have subsided.

3.58am

Lots of activity.....noises as earlier.

5.28am

Very loud banging noises issuing from the horsebox, sounds like feeding bowls being hammered against the metal sides.

7.00am

Peace again!

9.00am

Still peaceful except for the occasional snuffle, grunt and rustle.

10.00am

All remaining quiet.

Managed to follow the big track for a short ramble into the woodlands and observed Great Spotted Woodpecker, Raven, Redwing, Chaffinch, Wren, Robin and a small flock of mixed tits.

We both finished work early and returned to the wood around 4.30 pm. Despite the clear early morning sky and bright moon, thick cloud had descended by midday bringing heavy rain and a cold damp chill to the air. Mike was sat on a log by his little camp having a brew of tea; he looked bleary eyed and cold and this was only the beginning! We sat ourselves down on a log and over a brew of steaming hot tea he filled us in on the previous night's events.

Before long we were interrupted by the occasional thump and bang emanating from the horsebox. They were confused by their confinement and the quicker we got them out of there the better. We stuck to the plan of attempting to walk them up to the sett as originally planned. We were reasonably happy in the assumption that they would be only too willing to follow us; we knew that they would stop occasionally to sniff around and possibly wander off the path a little but would soon return when called and continue following us…How wrong we were!!

At 5.30 pm we slowly dropped the tail ramp of the box to see four black and white faces staring curiously back at us. We spoke to them and stroked them as they sniffed the cold damp air and cautiously wandered onto the ramp stopping briefly to smell the air once more and then out they came. As their feet touched the softness of the damp soil they paused for a minute or two, noses held high catching all the exciting new smells. We encouraged them to follow us but to no avail.

Even the traditional wellie scent marking went through the window as Toby and Millie quickly wandered off along a narrow track into the wood stopping every few yards or so to sniff the ground and scent mark. They ignored all our efforts to call them back as they quickly ambled off in the wrong direction, completely preoccupied with all the new exciting smells of fern, decaying timber and damp earth. We needed to get them back and quickly! Leaving Mike to try and keep an eye on Kippy and Cassie, Ann and I chased after Mille and Toby, finally catching them up and attempted to entice them to turn around and follow us, but they were having none of it. They were far too engrossed in their new surroundings and on scent marking everywhere and everything. We had obviously greatly and naively underestimated their interest in their new surroundings to the extent that we were now no longer their main focus of interest.

We decided that there was no alternative but to carry them back and, with two very indignant badgers slung over our shoulders, made our way back to the horsebox. By the time we re-appeared and secured our two wriggling charges back in the horsebox Mike was frantically attempting to stay in contact with Cassie and Kippy who, it seemed, had by now completely vanished and to make matters worse it was now getting dark! Suddenly we heard a sound coming from out of the blackness as Cassie appeared nose to the ground sniffing everything around her, stopping every now and again to scent mark her path, but Cassie being Cassie wouldn't let us get close enough to catch her. It was decided that with Toby and Millie secured in the horsebox and the fact that Cassie appeared to be coming and going at regular intervals we should now concentrate our efforts on finding Kippy.

The following are extracts taken from Mike's notes:

With Toby and Millie back inside the horsebox and the re-assurance that Cassie was continually returning, we set off into the darkness to locate Kippy.

Quite a time had elapsed with no sign of her, feelings became anxious. Eventually Ann also vanished into the darkness, but it appeared that Malcolm's feelings were more committed towards Kippy's absence than his wife's!!!

However, sometime later a puffing sound could be heard coming from the enveloping blackness of the damp woodland, Ann had returned and having located Kippy was carrying her back.

We all settled a little more easily now in the knowledge that we had at least three badgers once more secure in the horsebox.

It was now just a matter of awaiting the return of Cassie, who had, up to that point, been periodically returning of her own accord. And so we waited, and we waited, but no sign of Cassie and decided once again to set out into the woodland to look for her.

Several hours later we abandoned the search in the hope that she would return when tired of exploring or became hungry. We secured Toby, Millie and Kippy in the horsebox with food and water once again for yet another night of confinement.

The rest of the evening was not unlike a scene from Shakespeare's 'Macbeth' with three muffled and huddled creatures sat around a candle set on a large log in a woodland clearing.

Shadows flickered, sounds of the night issued from the depths of the wood, but still no Cassie.

It was midnight when plan two was agreed upon.

Instead of attempting to walk the animals to the old sett we would carry them as all the new smells and temptation of exploring were proving too strong an urge for them to ignore.

As Mike recorded in his notes we had now decided that the following day we would carry the badgers through the wood to the sett - something we should have done in the first place! Before departing for home, we left food and water under the horsebox in case Cassie returned and with a heavy heart bade farewell to Mike.

We drove slowly down the winding and by now, very dark track illuminated only by the beam of our headlights, our eyes searching for any sign of movement that might have been Cassie. Suddenly the heavens opened and the rain came pouring down adding to our already feelings of doom and gloom. The journey home seemed to take forever, the wipers were struggling to cope with the deluge, the headlights dazzled as they bounced back off the wet road and our minds were full of uncertainty. Had we made an enormous mistake and totally underestimated the complications of our task? Only time would tell!

After our departure, Mike made the following notes in his diary:

Day Three - Wednesday 22nd October. 86

12.30am

All quiet, apart from minor rustlings and grunts but no sign or sound that Cassie may be around. Persistent heavy rain seems to be easing a little.

2.00am

Loud noises from horsebox, inmates have woken up.

Food left for Cassie untouched.

3.30am

Badgers active in box, food for Cassie still untouched.

Walked adjacent tracks and pathways searching for Cassie but heavy rain and strong winds made it impossible.

3.49am

Demolition of the horsebox now evident if

the sounds are anything to go by!

(It was later discovered that they had ripped off the box's side padding and shredded it.)

Cassie's food still untouched but disturbed some small, very fast moving creature nearby.

Inspected the track and pathways again for signs but the heavy rain is making things very difficult.

Now feeling cold, damp, hungry and almost miserable!!

4.15am

Prepared food and a hot drink but can't seem able to warm up.

6.00am

Squeals, grunts and banging coming from the box.

6.30am

Quietness prevails, just the sound of heavy rain.

Cassie's food still not touched.

The very cold, damp atmosphere creeping into everything!

9.30am

Still raining heavily.

11.00am

Visited the pool at the end of the lower track, grey wagtail present plus crows, raven and great spotted woodpecker.

12.30pm

Food left for Cassie been disturbed.

Ann and I returned to the wood around 2.30 pm and it was still raining! We'd checked the long range weather forecast before the release and it said mainly fine with a few showers. Just how wrong can they be! The weather had been atrocious since day one with heavy rain and gale force winds. It was certainly a test of Mike's determination to complete his mission! Little did he know what was to come; if he had he may have gone home there and then!

Once again, we sat around the log table sipping our tea, with candles flickering and damp embers spitting from the fire we went over the plan to carry Toby, Millie and Kippy up to the sett and the likelihood of Cassie turning up again. We all agreed that this was just like her, it was her nature to be independent and do her own thing and yes, Cassie being Cassie could quite easily and nonchalantly turn up again, or at least that's what we hoped! One thing we were all agreed upon was that there was no way the badgers could spend another night in the horsebox and today really was make or break time. If this failed we would be left with no alternative but to abort the release and return them to the Wildlife Unit but we also had to consider Cassie, we couldn't just abandon her – failure is one thing but to leave one behind was unthinkable!

We began to prepare for their transition from the horsebox to the sett by stuffing bedding from their quarters at home down the sett entrances and scattered around the general area of the sett. We decided that this time, rather than lower the box's ramp Ann would go in through the side door and pass the badgers out one by one with Mike taking

Kippy, me Toby and Ann drawing the short straw taking big Millie. It must have made a strange sight; the three of us trudging up the steep, soggy woodland path each with a squirming badger draped over our shoulder! We huffed and puffed our way up until at last we arrived at the sett thankfully without dropping a squirming badger on route.

They may have been youngsters but they were now almost fully grown and heavy! By the time we arrived at the sett they were wriggling and squirming in their eagerness to be put down again and with more than a hint of trepidation we put them down one by one. First Toby followed by Millie and then Kippy. They immediately began to sniff and scratch at the straw bedding and explore the setts various holes. It wasn't long before their enthusiasm completely took over with straw being dragged here there and everywhere, long defunct holes were being explored and enlarged with soil flying in all directions.

Occasionally they would pause from their labours to have a short wander but never going far or out of our sight before returning to resume the exploration of their new home. The difference in them was amazing! We were now back on the agenda for greetings with them ambling over to Ann and me to check that we were still there and once satisfied, would scent mark our wellies before ambling off again.

At one point gunshots were heard in the distance and we guessed that it was probably a farmer out shooting rabbits but Toby, who at the time was busy enlarging one of the sett entrances suddenly stopped his excavations and began to trot off down through the woodland in the direction of the horsebox. I eventually caught up with him and after a few consoling words he turned around and walked at my feet back to the sett whereupon amid much snorting and grunting began to resume his explorations. Soil and rocks that had barred the entrance of a long defunct hole were now unceremoniously thrown about in all directions. Millie and Kippy also began to get down to some serious digging and very soon what had been a dormant badger sett for many years was now beginning to look very active indeed with fresh spoil piling up all over the place.

Occasionally a large stone, after being unceremoniously ejected from one of the holes, would go rolling down through the woodland at which point Millie would pause from her labours and turn to watch it go tumbling and crashing through the undergrowth. Toby would occasionally disappear into the depths of the sett to reappear again a little while later from an adjacent hole higher up the banking whereupon he would pause briefly to shake himself vigorously sending particles of soil flying in all directions and then vanish underground once more. Occasionally they would work in pairs with one badger in the sett throwing soil and stones part of the way up a tunnel whilst a second would then gather it up to bring it to the surface and scatter it. Toby and Kippy were by far the most industrious with Millie appearing content to let them do all the work until she spotted a long since disused hole that the others hadn't got around to excavating, then she too got down to some serious digging until she also vanished into the depths.

Within an hour, what had been for many years an abandoned badger sett now looked quite the opposite. Once our industrious little clan were satisfied that their new home was to their satisfaction they began to gather up mounds of straw bedding between their front legs and, once tucked tightly under their chest, would shuffle backwards with it into their newly excavated chambers. As time went by and with most of the bedding gathered up and taken underground we began to see less and less of them as they remained in the sett for longer periods.

This was everything we had hoped for. Why on earth didn't we carry them to the sett in in the first place? They say hindsight is a great thing! At this point, we took it in turns to return to camp for a warm and a hot drink, always ensuring that at least one of us was by the sett. Eventually darkness began to envelope the wood once more and one by one, the badgers began to emerge once more and with their food prepared, enjoyed a hearty meal by the sett. Once fed and with full bellies they began to explore the immediate area of the woodland but returned at regular intervals to vanish into the sett once again.

At one point, whilst they were underground we crept a little farther up the slope and sat by a large old Scots Pine tree. We still had a good view of the sett and thought it would be interesting to watch their reaction when they emerged to discover that we were no longer there. We didn't have long to wait as one by one out they came. Toby was the first and after looking around for a second or two sniffed the air and immediately picked up our scent and came ambling up the slope to greet us, shortly followed by Millie and Kippy. After the reassurance that we were still there they wandered back down to resume their explorations, returning periodically to check on us. At one point, Ann and I returned to the camp for a hot drink leaving Mike above the sett by the big Scots Pine.

I shall let Mike relate what happened next:

Whilst Malcolm and Ann returned briefly to the horsebox/camp area leaving myself at the base of the large scots pine, I was visited by Toby who, presumably grumpy at not finding Malcolm, promptly sniffed up the sleeve of Malcolm's jacket that was lying close by then scent marked on both his jacket and tea mug.

My own mug was sniffed at and pushed around followed by him sniffing my leg. I bent down to stroke him but, either through grumpiness or playfulness, he made a grab at my hand, teeth snapping shut just as I moved my fingers away.

He then jumped and grabbed me hard by

the right arm, teeth pinching through my waterproof jacket and two jumpers. Next he grabbed me hard on my right leg.

This I decided, was enough and leapt for the safety of the large pine.

Toby being Toby wasn't going to be put off and grabbed my left leg. I was, by this time pulling hard on a branch overhead, but clearing the ground wasn't enough as Toby was suspended from my left leg and swinging freely with teeth firmly locked through my trousers and into my thick wellington boot. The weakest soon gave way, as my trouser leg ripped, returning Toby to earth with a thump but, not to be defeated, he attempted to climb up after me. As he reached the first large bough, I pushed at him with my foot and he swung beneath the bough, his body swinging freely as his forearms hugged the bough. Soon he once more landed on the ground and though he made several half-hearted attempts to re-climb the tree he soon tired and wandered away towards the area of the sett whilst I remained half way to heaven until Malcolm and Ann returned.

We returned to the sett to find Mike half way up the big Scots Pine looking rather shocked and stunned. With the two of us now back on the scene and no badgers in the immediate vicinity he cautiously climbed down to relate the tale of how Toby had attacked him and proceeded to show us his ripped trousers and the teeth indentations in his wellies.

We couldn't believe it, surely not Toby! I had, over the months, built up a very special relationship with him and found it difficult to believe that he could have behaved in such a way. He knew Mike; he had even played with him in the garden! Surely he must be exaggerating? My Toby would never do such a thing; he was a badger not a grizzly bear! Anyhow whilst sat at the base of the Scots Pine listening to Mike's tale I must admit to a little scepticism, despite the state of Mike's trousers and wellies I wasn't totally convinced and came to the conclusion that Toby was merely indulging in a bit of light hearted play albeit combined with a little over exuberance. With Toby having taken himself back to the sett Millie is next to appear on the scene.

Toby chases Mike up the old Scots Pine tree

I will let Mike relate the jottings from his notes:

Millie ambles up the bank from the sett and decides on the siting of the toilet and having excavated the dung pit makes full use of it immediately beside where Malcolm and Ann are sitting.

Was this an honour, or merely a hint for us to move away?

We waited until such a time that all the badgers were below ground or otherwise engaged and headed for the horsebox encampment.

Whilst the three of us walked back to camp I couldn't help but reflect on Mike's tale of events. I still found it hard to believe! Perhaps he was mistaken and wrongly interpreted Toby's childish playfulness for aggression? We couldn't help but notice that he wasn't quite his normal self of late. (Mike not Toby!) He was developing a distinct dishevelled look and his eyes had that fixed faraway stare of a lost soul. There was even a hint of wildness creeping into him and he was beginning to take on the appearance of 'The Wild Man of the Woods.' We couldn't help but worry a little that one day when we arrived he would run off to hide and talk to the trees! Yes that must be it! Living alone in the wood coupled with the appalling weather he'd had to contend with was getting to him and he was now hallucinating. But little did we know, worse was to come!!!!

The biting winds and rain were with us again and as we sheltered under the flapping tarpaulin, having just stoked the fire to boil the kettle, we heard the sound of footsteps coming along the track by the house above. We knew the house was empty only being used as a weekend retreat but a little further on there was a wooden bunkhouse that was the permanent home of a gentleman who lived alone and went by the name of Roger. Mike had briefly spoken of Roger on a couple of occasions who had, apparently knowing that Mike was down there on his own, wandered down and offered him some warmth and comfort by his living room fire whilst enjoying the treat of a decent mug of tea and biscuits. Now Mike, being a suspicious sort of character, was sceptical about Roger's intentions and decided to decline the kind offer. Anyway as the footsteps got closer and we peered into the darkness through the haze of wood smoke and driving rain and wind a hooded figure began to emerge.

We couldn't help but notice that Mike was looking a little nervous. Had he encountered this hooded spectre before? If so, perhaps it explains a little of his strange behaviour?! But as the figure got closer a hand went up to slide away the hood to reveal the smiling face of Roger. He had braved the weather to wander down and kindly invite us back to his humble abode for warmth and refreshments. This was our first meeting with him and as he seemed a decent enough chap and, much to Mike's horror, we accepted. Roger led the way, with the dim light of his torch struggling to illuminate the path as we trudged through the darkness with the wind and rain stinging our faces, to the bunkhouse whereupon he warmly invited us in. We entered a small wooden porch where we discarded our wellies and waterproofs and followed Roger into a tiny but very cosy and warm living room whereupon he invited us to take a seat whilst he went into the kitchen to make tea.

He returned some five minutes or so later with a tray containing four mugs of hot steaming tea and a plate of delicious looking chocolate biscuits. Now, you would have thought that Mike, given his present circumstances, would have gulped down his tea as if it was a brew sent from heaven whilst stuffing his mouth with as many chocolate biscuits as he could possibly fit in. On the contrary, he was looking distinctly uncomfortable, constantly squirming in his chair and giving us furtive glances indicating that we should really be going. The final straw came when Roger asked him if he took sugar and I replied that he was sweet enough! That was it; he downed his tea, stuffed a couple of biscuits in his mouth and headed for the door. Ann and I quickly made our apologies and explained that we really should be going and followed Mike into the porch who was, by now, bending down to pull his thick yellow industrial waterproof trousers on when I whispered that Roger was coming up behind him.

He shot bolt upright with such speed that his waterproof trousers practically split at the gusset and with a spluttering of tea and crumbs was gone! Ann and I rather embarrassingly thanked Roger for his hospitality and hurried after Mike through the darkness back to the cold, damp, and candlelit little camp with its soggy, flapping tarpaulin roof. It was now almost midnight and time for Ann and me to be heading for home leaving Mike once more to spend another cold, miserable night in the wood.

The badgers were now spending more time in the sett than out of it and at long last we felt confident that they wouldn't wander too far and would spend the following day secure in their new home. All we needed now was for Cassie to turn up safe and well, that would really put the icing on the cake and put us on the road to success. We said our goodbyes to Mike, arranging to be back the following day as soon as work and other commitments would allow. The fact that he was still sticking with us was a credit to him. He could cope with living rough for a while but the conditions were totally against him. I think he'd forgotten what sleep was, apart from a word that was locked away somewhere in the distant memories of his mind plus the fact that he hadn't had a decent hot meal in days, but I'm sure Roger would have cooked him one if only he'd had the courage to ask!

Everything seemed to be going fine at last and all three badgers appeared to have well and truly taken over the sett but things were about to take an unforeseen and for Mike at least, a rather disconcerting twist that would put a premature end to his involvement in the release.

The following events are taken directly from Mike's notes:

Day Four: Thursday 23rd October. 86

The weather wet, cold and windy as usual!

1.19am.

Bumping sounds coming from under the horsebox where food has been continually left in case Cassie returned.

2.25am

Bumping sounds continuing, did not investigate fully, as no wish to disturb Cassie if she had returned.

Would check thoroughly first light.

4.45am

After giving in to exhaustion, I awoke from a sleep of sorts still lying on the large log beneath the tarpaulin shelter almost too cold to do anything.....Why do I enjoy punishing myself like this!!?

5.00am

Inspected the horsebox, some of the food has gone.

Wanting to sleep now becoming a habit, after acquiring some inner warmth from a mug of tea, I lay on my log gaining some warmth from a lighted candle wishing that I may be allowed to die or, at the very least, get some sleep!!

8.00am

Owing to the fact that my eyelids were just about open, I decided that I hadn't died after all! Anyway, I reckon the place reserved for me when that time does eventually arrive, is reputed to be very hot and I was far from even warm. I was too cold to remain inactive and so crawled off my log to attack yet another wet and windy day.

After a mug of hot tea I wandered off deep into the woodland carrying spade and toilet roll.

8.25am

Quietly visited the sett area, all quiet.

Set two twigs across the nearest entrance hole. If anyone were to emerge in my absence I would know due to them being moved.

Was about to do the same across the next hole when suddenly and without warning I was forcibly grabbed by the right leg. Sure enough, Toby had me in his grasp once more but released his hold when I made my usual rush for the pine tree, which, by this time, I was getting to know very well, every knot and branch!

He chased me as far as the tree, which he made a half-hearted attempt to climb, then returned to the sett and disappeared down one of the holes. I was satisfied at least that Toby and presumably Millie and Kippy had also returned to the sett after their night of exploring the wood to spend the day in the sett on the slope beneath the pine.

3.15pm

Visited sett again, added more bedding, food and water.

4.12pm

I was at the encampment once again with a large mug of tea in the wind and rain when a thought struck me, why should I sleep on a log beneath a leaky tarpaulin when I could find comfort and luxury within the now empty horsebox?

I could create a shelf bed high off the straw floor so that I could view any nocturnal visitors. I'd be dry, maybe warm even! But sod's law struck again as I was condemned to sleep once again on my log as I watched a little jeep vanishing down the track towing the object of my dreams back to Wirral!

6.00pm

Headed for the sett and another long evening vigil.

After many false starts through forgetting items of comfort i.e. Thermos flask, mug, mittens and camera etc. I was eventually seated on my usual perch on the pine bough above the sett.

6.40pm

Rooks and jackdaws numbering many hundreds twisted and dived as they flew over the woodland to their favourite roosting trees across the valley. The sett was as I had left it earlier, food and water bowls still full and untouched plus a great mound of straw for their bedding.

8.10pm

Toby was the first to appear; he looked at the huge pile of straw and immediately took up the challenge to remove it all by himself spending the next half hour bundling it up beneath his belly and front and rear legs, whilst shuffling backwards feeling his way by extending his right hind leg.

I felt that if even Toby couldn't actually see me, I felt sure that he knew I was there. He continually sniffed the air and wandered up the slope towards the base of my pine tree locating my scent where I had climbed on two previous occasions when he had chased me.

This time he was content to rear up on his hind legs as though exacting my location. Soon he retraced his route back to the sett in his own wobbly amble whereupon he snuffled at the food bowls. He either decided he wasn't hungry or that the removal of all the straw bedding was paramount whereupon he proceeded to drag it all below the surface. Millie soon appeared and snuffled around the remaining straw pile then moved on over to the food bowls sampling a little but didn't appear hungry either and set to work on the straw except that as Toby worked hard to take all below, Millie worked in reverse and brought it all out again! And so it went on for ages.

Much later Kippy appeared from one of the holes and wandered around the general area apparently too tired to be bothered with mundane tasks such as bedding preparations. She also didn't appear to be hungry completely ignoring the food.

Eventually Millie wandered up the slope to the big pine and sniffed up towards where I sat on the bough above. I descended a little for her to sniff and snuffle my boot and once satisfied at knowing where I was she visited her toilet taking her time and squatting comfortably over one of the many scrapes which she had prepared the previous evening.

All three animals were observed making use of the latrines during the period from 8.10pm to 9.15pm.

Eventually torches were observed in the distance flashing from the area of the encampment. Muffled voices could be heard in the distance, too far away to be identified and all three badgers headed for the sett with Millie and Kippy disappearing below ground leaving Toby keeping guard.

Ann was the first to arrive on the scene and by this time Toby had melted away into the darkness.

After a short while with Ann calling to the badgers by their names they began to appear above ground. Millie was the first who ran up to greet Ann, followed by Kippy who with Ann, now sat on the ground, decided to make full use of her legs to lie across whilst enjoying tickles and cuddles! Toby, now more relaxed, reappeared briefly but soon vanished again just as quickly.

Within a short time Malcolm arrived and was also greeted by both Millie and Kippy.

Eventually sometime later Toby reappeared and eagerly greeted Malcolm and Ann.

10.00pm.

After having been sitting up on high amongst the pine boughs for some three and a half hours and feeling somewhat cold and in need of a hot drink only to discover now that after all the false starts I'd had before through forgetting various items, I'd also forgotten the essential things -tea bags!

I'd only brought hot water! Anyway, another problem quickly arose. I urgently needed the use of a loo!

Upon descending to the woodland floor I was greeted by Toby!!! He approached with his friendly wobbly amble rather than the direct charge to kill attitude of the previous evening.

I decided to give him the benefit of the doubt and even blamed myself for what I received for not playing with him when he grabbed my wellie dismissing his boisterousness as just his rough way of playing; maybe it was just his idea of encouraging me to play? He reached my legs sniffed and snuffled at my feet and I stood my ground. I even spoke kindly (to the swine!) at one stage I was even tempted to bend down and roll him about (with a well gloved hand of course!) but then his mind and ideas overtook mine and he made a hard grab at my leg.

My legs thought far more rapidly than my brain at that moment as without hesitation, my legs were propelling my body towards the big pine again and the safety of its large outstretched arms but however fast my legs moved Toby's jaws and legs moved faster as they snapped shut with a loud clump firmly into the upper part of my left leg (midway twixt crutch and knee!)

'Hell Fire!!' I thought 'How that hurt.' It may sound funny, but it resembled more of a burning sensation. The next bit may be of interest to anyone not experienced in the art of climbing trees in the darkness

with a two stone badger fastened firmly by its teeth into your left thigh.

Upon reaching the tree my arms, assessing the situation, stretched out frantically for the comforting branches of 'Mother Tree,' arms and one leg struggling to get a grip on the roughness of the thick bark, when I felt Toby fall away (probably lost his toothy grip when he laughed at my desperate efforts to escape him!)

In reality escape came when the weak parts gave way and my clothing ripped. The sudden weightlessness enabled me to gain height and I continued my upwards assent

I don't remember how high I actually reached but I do remember seeing and hearing Toby hit the ground with a dull thud and a muffled grunt or was he merely spitting out bits of my leg?

In the next instant he was once more up the tree after me and not only did he pass the large overhanging bough but was digging his claws deep into the bark.

I can only assume that he'd spent the previous evening practicing for an event such as this as his past efforts had merely enabled him to reach the first bough before he fell to earth again. Urgent grunts, snuffles and the desperate sound of bark tearing claws were imprinted in my ears. Then suddenly Toby was close, too close for comfort when I heard that other now familiar sound, a loud clump followed by a pinching sensation in my right ankle. Sure enough Toby had me again, but this time we were halfway up a large pine tree!! I shook my heavily laden leg in a futile effort to dislodge him and with fingers clawing at the tree one painful leg and foot kicking into darkness for a foothold which would hopefully project me higher and away from this striped monster, but again he held on. This was, after all, what the devil had been practicing for. Toby's Olympic gold medal was waiting to be claimed!

I can't remember just what Malcolm and Ann were doing during all this; to me it felt as if it lasted hours.

I remember seeing Ann approach the tree and make a grab for Toby as he swung freely on the end of my leg well above the ground. Ann grabbed and pulled downwards whilst I pulled up and eventually the weakness showed, wellie and trousers ripped yet again! Jaws snapped several times in a frantic frenzy to regain a grip on my leg having stretched far beyond its normal limits, retracted upwards, towards my bottom from whence it was attached, taking it out of reach of Toby's jaws.

I was free again at last!!

As Ann held Toby firmly after my release, I swear I saw a smile slide over his jaws. I'm sure he thought, and hoped, that Ann was actually assisting him to climb up the tree to the next bough in order for him to reattach his jaws onto my person.

I also swear that his smile changed dramatically when he was put back onto the woodland floor. He looked terribly disappointed and ambled back to the sett in a very disgruntled manner, probably to lie and sulk over what might and indeed could have been achieved had Ann not intervened! Toby's motto must now surely be 'up and at em!!'

Eventually with Toby now out of the immediate area, at least hopefully, but one could never be quite certain where he might turn up in the darkness of that wood.

I climbed down the tree and crawled, limped and swore my way back to the camp area where the sight of that mucky tarpaulin felt very welcome indeed!

Once Mike was out of the tree and Toby with Ann, I escorted him safely out of the wood back to the camp area. Mike continues:

There I attempted to assess the damage. One pair of thick waterproof leggings badly ripped in two places i.e. left thigh area and right ankle. A pair of green ranger uniform cord trousers and a pair of jeans worn underneath, both with a hole torn into the left thigh, corresponding to holes in leggings. One leg with two deep puncture holes, plus broken skin and bruising, all corresponding to holes in leggings, cords, and jeans plus a large chunk of black rubber torn out of the ankle part of my wellie boot!

I lowered the waist of my trousers to show Malcolm proof of the damage when I heard a light scuffling noise from the rear of my tarpaulin home. I directed my torch beam, which was now fading fast, but not so faded to prevent me from identifying that clipped patch of fur on a badger's neck and for the second time that night my legs moved more rapidly than my brain. My feet strove madly to grip the wet and leafy bonnet of my vehicle whilst my left hand still clutched hold of my unfastened trousers in a tenacious grip while my right hand held the dim torch.

Unknowingly to Malcolm, Toby had followed him back at a discreet distance in the darkness. Had he merely followed Malcolm as a friend or was he using him as a means of tracking me down in readiness for the next conflict?

Mike omitted to record the next chain of events so I will tell the tale for him. By this point Mike had leapt onto the bonnet of his car in order to escape once more from Toby who, having succeeded in tracking down his quarry was jumping up at the bonnet trying to reach him. Mike on the other hand was doing something resembling an Irish Jig in order to retain his balance on the wet slippery bonnet whilst at the same time trying stop his trousers from entirely falling down to his ankles.

Now remember Roger from the Bunkhouse who, according to Mike, had ulterior motives in offering him tea and biscuits? Well picture the scenario! Mike's doing a jig on the bonnet of his car, his feet slipping and sliding on the wet smooth surface with his trousers which are, by now, practically around his ankles whilst Toby is trying desperately to join him to complete his mission. Suddenly headlights appear out of the darkness coming up the track.

At first shining skywards illuminating the treetops and then from around the sharp bend comes Roger in his little Fiat Panda slowly chugging up the track and catching Mike full beam in his headlights. Mike's face was a picture as he desperately tried to work out who was the worst of the two evils, Roger or Toby!

The little Fiat Panda paused momentarily, presumably for Roger to capture this picture of wonderment illuminated for posterity in his mind for evermore! Time froze for those few seconds as I took in this bizarre scene and I swear that even Toby thought that this was far more than he could ever have wished for! Eventually Roger drove slowly by and with one last lingering gaze the headlights vanished once more into the night leaving Mike illuminated with nothing more than his rapidly dimming torch.

At this point Mike notes in his diary that by sheer tenacity and a bit of skilful slipping and sliding he managed to retain his foothold and not slide off the bonnet into the jaws of Toby. Eventually Toby, considering his mission well and truly accomplished, ambled over, sat on my wellie and scent marked me and looked up as if to say, 'didn't I do well!' With Toby by my side, we made our way back to the sett allowing Mike to compose and dress himself.

Mike takes up the story once more:

After Malcolm had finished laughing he walked back into the woodland towards the sett and thankfully Toby followed by his side. With Malcolm and Toby now gone, I fastened my clothes, replaced the batteries in my torch, put on a warm, dry jacket and made a mug of tea whilst awaiting Malcolm's return.

After his return, we chatted and laughed over what had just taken place and I was persuaded to return to the sett area though keeping a discreet distance away and preferably at the base of a climbable tree. A few hours later the three of us returned to the encampment and yet more tea. The time was now around midnight with the three of us sitting around the large log table with the flame of the candle flickering away in its glass. Suddenly in the soft glow of the candlelight I spotted a striped head and two shining black eyes appearing from the woodland, unrepeatable words came flowing from my mouth, followed by is it Toby?

Thankfully it turned out to be Millie!

She ambled about idly snuffling around our camp and then wandered off along the lower track and vanished once more into the dark, damp woodland.

Very soon yet another pair of eyes was spotted staring into the illuminated circle from the upper path, thankfully this turned out to be Kippy who also snuffled around the camp for a while before she too followed the lower path and could be seen meeting Millie coming from the opposite direction. They paused to greet each other before we watched Kippy's wobbly backside grow ever smaller as she travelled deeper into the woodland.

Millie wandered once more into our camp and snuffled each of us in turn as though

bidding us goodnight, then she ambled off
toward the sett.

The fact that Toby now appeared to be totally incensed by Mike's presence complicated matters enormously and was completely unexpected. The release itself couldn't be going any better, the badgers had by now completely taken over the sett and were becoming very familiar with the woodland and considered it their territory and unfortunately, that's where the problem with Mike and Toby stemmed from!

In Toby's eyes, I was still very much an integral part of the group and even though Toby had been fine with Mike in the garden, in the wood it was a different matter altogether! He was now making the rules and as such considered Mike to be too low a ranking male within the group's social standing to be tolerated. Had Mike been a male badger in the same situation he would have been driven out of the group never to be seen again, except upon the threat of a severe thrashing!

I was to experience a similar situation myself in the coming years that would have more serious consequences where I would be subject to a full blown, no holds barred attack from a hand reared boar badger that, after reaching sexual maturity, challenged me for dominance and needless to say he won on a knockout! But I digress!

Back to Mike who, although still living in the wood, was avoiding, if at all possible, any direct contact with the badgers, particularly Toby and attempting to monitor from a safe distance. Friday 24th October 1986, day five came and there was still no sign of Cassie. Mike noted in his diary:

4.27am

Food left for Cassie still untouched.

Everywhere still feels damp and cold.

This is strange woodland! Crows, rooks

and jackdaws appear to call and fly throughout the hours of darkness, it's a little eerie!

5.10am

Still feel cold, all been quiet with no sign of badgers, Cassie or otherwise.

6.30am

All peaceful but still that deep, cold, penetrating dampness.

7.38am

Visited water tap farther up the woodland slope by the house. I left this task until daylight as further attacks from Toby are more likely during the dark hours.

1.50pm

Walked the sett area, noticed that a quantity of food left the previous night had gone.

8.00pm

Very wet and windy. Millie, Kippy and Toby observed at the sett area. Malcolm and Ann now arrived. Removed encampment late evening and departed the area around midnight.

Mike had been living rough in the wood for four days in very cold wet and windy conditions, plus he had to contend with Toby's aggression towards him. He took it all in his usual quiet, good humoured matter of fact way but that was Mike and one of the reasons I had every faith in his ability to be able to do this but enough was enough. The badgers were now well and truly settled; the time had come for him to go home in the satisfaction that he had done a sterling job under difficult and sometimes intimidating and occasionally hilarious circumstances. It was certainly an experience none of us would ever forget.

With Mike back home and languishing in the luxury of a warm bed, decent food and the bonus of another week off before work, Ann and I continued to return to the wood every evening until very late, sometimes on a Friday or Saturday staying practically all night. Mike still retained his interest and often came along with us keen to follow the badger's progress and on Sat. 25th October he made the following notes:

8.30pm

Weather still very wet and windy.

Travelled out to the sett again with Ann and Malcolm.

A chance sighting of badger on middle path but not identified, Ann visited the immediate sett area, still food left from previous night.

A badger emerged from one of the holes and much to Ann's surprise and delight; it was Cassie!!!! Still with traces of the Gentian Violet used to mark her.

A few nights later Ann and I were at the sett when Cassie and Toby emerged but with no sign of Millie or Kippy. We weren't worried about their absence as in all probability they were either out foraging or snoring their heads off in the sett. By now we were much more confident in the knowledge that they were doing well and our spirits had been lifted tremendously with the sudden re-appearance of little Cassie.

Despite the initial hiccups and the shocking weather

conditions, the release was now going very well with all four badgers living in the sett and acting as though they had been there for years. The only possible reservations now related to Toby and his clinginess towards me. I had always enjoyed a close bond with him, but I fully expected that to diminish as he spent more time in the wild but he appeared to be doing the opposite. We decided, very reluctantly, that I as well as Mike would now have to back off a little and become less directly involved, but for entirely opposite reasons. Toby wasn't trying to attack me; he just wanted to be friends but he had to severe that bond and so I too was delegated to watching Ann with the badgers from a respectable distance. But inevitably he would pick up my scent and come looking for me.

On one occasion as he picked up my scent I even ran from the wood and sat in the van in the hope that he would give up, but he didn't, he followed me out of the wood and, standing upright with his front paws at the window, stared in at me wondering why I was suddenly ignoring him. I felt awful! He obviously couldn't understand why I was suddenly rebuffing him and it confused him, but it had to be done; it was for his own good, the quicker I began to fade from his memory the better. Eventually he slowly ambled off towards the woodland again stopping occasionally to look back at me. I felt like a father ostracizing his only son and not telling him why! It slowly began to have the desired effect to the extent that I was able to return to the sett and recommence my dealings with Millie, Kippy and Cassie once again and even Toby would amble over to greet and scent mark me but now thankfully without wanting to follow me everywhere. It was as though he'd suddenly got the message and I was glad to be able to have contact with him once more, I'd missed him! At long last everything was going well, very well in fact!

After the initial hiccups of them having to spend more nights than planned in the horsebox and of losing Cassie coupled with the awful unpredicted weather and to top it all, Mike and Toby's love hate relationship (mainly hate on

Toby's part) it was now going as planned. We knew from the start that it was never going to be easy and that we were all being thrust into the unknown but it was working. But things were about to change once again and more drama was about to descend upon our little group.

It was now the first week in November, the 5th to be precise, Bonfire night. Snow had been falling steadily for much of the day but nothing too drastic and Ann and I were in the wood once again. We scrambled up the slippery path to the sett, it was a clear bright night and we could hear the whizz and bang of fireworks going off in the distant valley and occasionally a rocket would shoot up into the sky and explode into a thousand brightly coloured stars above us. We wondered how the badgers would react to the noise but they had become accustomed to the sound of the occasional gunshots whilst a farmer was out rabbiting and took no notice. They were also becoming a little less active now as winter slowly crept into the woodland and one of the main reasons we chose late October for the reintroduction.

We were nearing the sett when we heard the very distinctive and unmistakable sounds of badgers fighting, not serious fighting as such, but fighting none the less! We thought it strange but dismissed it as possibly a domestic squabble but on approaching the sett we caught sight of a badger in the beam of our torches as it ran off. Was it one of ours? If it was, why run off instead of not just retreating back down the sett as they would normally do if unsure about something? As we got closer we called their names and one by one they all appeared from underground. That was all the conformation we needed to confirm that we had a stranger within our midst.

As mentioned before, badgers can be very territorial with boars not tolerating intruders in their area home range, particularly another boar. But we had done our homework; there shouldn't be any other badgers in the immediate area. However, obviously there was! We expected them to have contact with wild badgers but not this early on in the release! All we could do was to monitor the situation. They were well established by now and hopefully weren't going to relinquish their home to any Tom, Dick or Harry! Toby was the one most at risk; he was a boar and would attempt to defend his territory which could put his life at risk. He could be badly injured or driven away, possibly even both! The only positive outcome would be for him to give a good account of himself and be accepted.

The days went by and everything seemed normal with no signs of further trouble, until the 12th November. Once again we were at the sett and all four badgers came out to greet us but it soon became obvious that Toby was injured! He had deep bite wounds on his rump and shoulder and had obviously been fighting. The other three seemed fine with no visible signs of injury but it was obvious that we now had another boar in the area that was visiting the wood and harassing Toby. Having found no evidence of badger in the area other than our own, we could only assume that the boar had picked up Toby's scent trail and followed him back to the sett, which seemed to indicate that he was now beginning to wander much farther afield. We could only wait and see how it would eventually be resolved. Toby was now big and strong but was he strong enough to face a truly wild boar badger and did he have the courage to stand his ground and fight? If he turned and ran, that would be it! He would eventually be driven away never to return leaving Millie, Cassie and Kippy, either to be accepted into another group or be driven off also, only to wander aimlessly into a very precarious and uncertain future. Whether driven off or accepted into another social group we would lose contact with them and never know for sure what their fate had been. There was an awful lot resting on Toby's young shoulders, what happened next depended entirely on him and his determination to hang onto his new home. He might have been able to intimidate Mike, but another boar badger was in a different league entirely.

On Friday 14th November we had more snow showers and Ann and I were at the sett once again and due to the fact that they were now foraging well and not reliant on us for food any longer we had merely taken some treats along in the form of peanuts and honey.

As usual, all four badgers came out when called and began to nibble on the peanuts and dissect the butties in order to get at the honey. Whilst Toby was busy eating, we checked him over and noticed that his wounds were not looking too good and that he'd been fighting again, resulting in fresh wounds to his stomach and a few more to his face with one of the original wounds now abscessing and looking very sore. The bond we had with these animals was so strong and trusting that Toby allowed Ann to clean his wounds and give him an injection of a broad spectrum antibiotic. With his wounds treated and all the goodies now devoured all four retreated back into the sett and knowing that they would, in all probability, stay there we departed for home in the hope that when we returned the following night Toby wouldn't be suffering from even more battle scars.

We arrived at the sett the following evening at around 8 pm, but only saw Millie, Kippy and Cassie who all looked fine and ran around our feet scent marking us before tucking into more treats, but no Toby! Was he out foraging?

Considering his wounds, we thought it unlikely, but where was he? Hopefully he was sleeping soundly in the sett and not aware of our arrival. We didn't want to contemplate the other explanation which was that perhaps had he been in another fight and seriously injured, unable to make his way home or even worse he could be dead?! Before leaving we left food and more treats in the hope that he would find it. Once again, we drove home worrying about the absence of one of our badgers and what the following evening would bring. Sleep was again fraught with thoughts of Toby and the following day with work and other tasks finished we sped off back to the wood.

We arrived a little earlier than normal and with some trepidation made our way to the sett hoping that Toby would be there. Our hearts sank a little as we saw that the food from the previous night lay mainly untouched. We called out their names but nothing we called again, still nothing! No black and white faces eagerly emerging to greet us. This was worrying! Was it a sign that our worst fears had finally materialised? It was bad enough not seeing Toby, but for the other three to be missing also was beyond the depths of our worst fears! We walked around the wood for a while looking for anything that may have given us a hint as to what had happened, but nothing! Eventually we made our way back to the sett in the hope of seeing at least one of them, but no, all was quiet, far too quiet!

The following days were the same, we scoured the wood and beyond in daylight looking for clues but absolutely nothing! If it hadn't have been for the sett looking active it would have been as though they had never existed! Was this really conformation of our worst fears? We placed twigs across the sett holes so that anything coming in and out would have to push them aside but they hadn't been moved. The previous evening we had left more food, some of which had gone, but we couldn't be certain what had taken it. A passing fox, birds or whatever could have taken it, we just didn't know! There wasn't even a footprint to give us a clue!

The following two days 17th and 18th November were the same and we were now beginning to resign ourselves to the awful realisation that things could have gone horribly wrong.

On the 19th November, we trudged to the sett with a mixture of emotions from desolation to hope. It had been a full three days now since we had last seen Millie, Kippy and Cassie but on approaching we noticed that the twigs around the holes had been moved and some food had gone. Ann called out their names and with enormous relief one by one three black and white faces appeared! It was Millie, Kippy and Cassie and they looked absolutely fine, but still no Toby. We stayed with them for quite a while enjoying each other's company once again, but where was Toby?

There was now no doubt in our minds that they had now made contact with another group and far earlier than anticipated. Everything indicated that the three sows had been living elsewhere for the three days and in all probability, with another group. If that was the case then it could possibly mean that Toby had been accepted and our badgers were now commuting between two setts or it could mean that Toby had lost his battle but the three sows had been accepted? At this stage, we could only surmise as to what was happening and hope for a happy outcome!

The following evening 20th November and once again, we made our way to the sett hoping beyond hope that Toby would reappear. As we approached, we could see fresh signs of activity around the area and within minutes Kippy, Millie and Cassie appeared but alas no Toby! We hadn't seen him for four days now and were feeling pretty despondent by his absence. The three sows were busy scent marking us when we suddenly heard snuffling sounds and rustling followed by the occasional crack as a twig was trodden on and snapped. Something was coming up from the bottom of the wood. We watched and listened, the three badgers with their heads held high, noses twitching to pick up a scent from the direction of the sound and poised for a hasty retreat into the sett. The sound was getting closer and closer, our eyes searched through the dense woodland understory trying to determine what was heading towards us. A fern leaf would quiver as something passed underneath it, a rotting twig would snap. Then, a black and white stripy face appeared from the undergrowth.

It was Toby!! To say we were ecstatic would be the understatement of the year!! He was looking much better from when we had last set eyes on him, his wounds were healing nicely and apart from having lost a little weight he looked good and he was hungry! He was obviously pleased to see us and after much greeting and scent marking, proceeded to devour the food we had brought along as if there was no tomorrow. Over the passing week he quickly regained his weight and was soon back to his normal self but wherever he'd been and whatever happened whilst he was there, it had changed him. He seemed a more confident and stronger young badger. It was obvious by the events of the past week or so and the wounds he'd received that he'd been in a serious scrap or two but despite his injuries had been back for more. We can only assume that he must have given a good account of himself, otherwise he wouldn't have been back looking as good as he did! (That was my boy!)

The change in him was remarkable! From that moment on he began to frantically patrol the woodland boundary enforcing claim to his territory through latrines and scent marking. I could walk through the wood during the day and easily follow where he had been the previous night by following his now well-trodden paths around the perimeter of the woodland and beyond and every so often come across a latrine where he had marked the boundary of his territory.

Five days after his return, all four badgers were still at the sett with everything seemingly back to normal with peace having descended on our little group once more. It was looking as though we may have crossed a major hurdle and come out the other side with flying colours, but only time would tell!

1986 passed into 1987 with everything still going well, even the weather had been relatively kind but on the 12th January, winter came with a vengeance bringing with it a period of prolonged snow and blizzard conditions which made getting to the sett totally impossible. Thankfully, after a few days there was a brief respite where conditions improved slightly and we took the opportunity to attempt the journey and on the 15th January, armed with a shovel, plenty of warm clothing and thermos flasks we set off.

The drive was better than anticipated with the snow ploughs and gritters having done their job. It still took far longer than normal but we made it to the bottom of the long winding track. We had come prepared to abandon the van at this point but much to our surprise the little green Peugeot 205 Ranger van gripped the snow and slowly but surely, albeit with the occasional wheel spin, made it to Mike's old camp. That was the easy bit, getting to the sett itself proved to be much more of a challenge!

The wood looked magical, with the trees bending and creaking under the weight of frozen snow and glistening like jewels. Occasionally there would be a loud crack as a branch succumbed and came toppling to the ground amidst a cloud of falling snow and ice. The going was tough with the snow over three feet deep in places; at one point I heard a scream behind me as Ann suddenly sunk waist deep into the snow. Once I'd managed to stop laughing and regained some composure I eventually helped her out, but not before recording the scene for posterity on film.

We struggled on to finally arrive at the sett. Dusk was now falling but we could clearly see badger tracks in the snow coming from the sett and heading upwards towards the pasture. Ann called their names and Millie and Kippy emerged from their underground home but with no sign of Toby or Cassie. We scattered a few peanuts around, some of which they ate but they weren't really bothered and after scent marking us vanished once again into the warmth of their underground home. We didn't want to hang around too long in case the snow came in again and so, satisfied that we had seen two at least and with the light rapidly fading, we slipped and stumbled our way back through the snow back to the van.

It was freezing hard by the time we reached the area of Mike's old camp with the van glistening and sparkling in its coating of thick frost. After scraping the ice from the windows and windscreen we sat there for a while with the engine running to get some heat circulating before making our way down the steep winding track which, by now, was becoming increasingly icy. Once defrosted I put the van into second gear and slowly began our decent down what was by now a very icy track. Going down was a little more perilous than going up, but also a little surreal with the only sounds being the hum of the engine, the warm air blowing from the heater and the crunching of frozen snow beneath the tyres. It was a magical fairyland sight as a full moon began to rise above the tree tops competing with the vans headlights in illuminating the snow and the frost covered trees now leaning heavily over the track resembling ghostly, silver glistening sentinels.

The snow and below freezing temperatures persisted for another week but we still managed to make regular visits to the sett and monitor the badgers as they experienced their first winter. One good thing about the snow was the fact that it was easy to keep tabs on them by following their unmistakable broad five-toed tracks coming from the sett and going off into the wood. Not they were going very far! They only tended to venture a little beyond the old Scots pine only to double back again and vanish back into the sett. As mentioned before we'd been cutting down on the food we had been providing and merely taking along treats but due to the bad weather had increased it again, but they certainly weren't starving and rarely touched it.

They had put on fat reserves for the winter and coupled with the fact that they were spending more time underground tended to leave most of it, but it certainly wasn't wasted and provided a very welcome feed during the harsh conditions to many other creatures.

Gradually the thaw set in and things became a little easier and the badgers a little more active. We continued with our regular visits but no longer on a nightly basis, we felt that the time had come to begin the gradual process of backing off a little and allowing them to become totally self-sufficient and truly wild badgers.

We arrived again on January 22nd after an absence of two or three days. It was a mild fine night for once and as we arrived at the sett, we were met by Toby and Kippy who immediately scent marked us and tucked into treats of peanuts and honey butties. They both looked fit and well and after about 30 minutes or so, we heard snuffling coming from one of the paths to see Millie and Cassie heading towards us, they ran up to greet us and then joined the other two in devouring the goodies. We were very relieved that Toby in particular was looking good and appeared not to be suffering from any more battle scars. He was still territory marking and we strongly suspected that he was still having contact with individuals from a neighbouring clan.

On the 26th January, we were at the sett and as usual had taken a few treats along plus a sack of fresh straw bedding and as I scattered the straw around Ann called down into the sett. Kippy was the first to emerge followed by a very cautious Toby, then Millie, but no Cassie. Again they all looked fit and healthy and Cassie could have been fast asleep and snoring her little head off down below in one of their cosy, straw filled chambers. They eventually began to sample the peanuts and honey butties followed by gathering up the straw and shuffling backwards with it down into the sett. We decided to leave them to it and after walking around the wood for a while heading for home.

On the 29th January, we arrived once again and all was well but Toby seemed a little preoccupied and after the formalities of scent marking us wandered off through the wood. As it wasn't quite dark I decided to follow him at a discreet distance. He seemed to have a definite purpose in mind and set off at a fair pace down towards the stream and woodland valley. Occasionally he would pause to look behind him as if to ensure that he wasn't being followed whereupon I would stop and, as he hadn't got my scent, would relax and continue on his mission content that he was alone.

Eventually he reached the very bottom woodland path and headed towards the pool with the stream on his right. He didn't pause to scent mark or investigate anything; his pace was quick and precise. Once he'd reached the small waterfall where the stream flowed out from the pool to continue down the valley he paused and looked across to the opposite bank looking up towards the high steep sided woodland slope. I stopped and watched, intrigued as to where he might be going with such intent. He then crossed the stream at a very narrow section where it flowed from the pool above the waterfall and proceeded to climb up the steep bank, higher and higher until he vanished from view over the ridge and into the rough pastures above. But gone where? I can only assume that the other badger clan's sett was over there somewhere and that's where he must have been heading. But for what purpose, had he another fight in mind or had he been accepted and was now commuting between the two setts?

On the 5th February we arrived at the sett to discover a newly excavated hole but no badgers, we walked around the woodland for about an hour before returning to the sett, but all was quiet. The following visit was the same, with us seeing very little of any of them and then on the 12th February, Kippy came out to greet us and we noticed that she was limping on her left hind leg but nothing serious.

We were back again on the 15th February when both Millie and Kippy appeared with Kippy's limp much better and Millie in a very playful mood wanting to romp all over us and have her tummy rubbed but no sign of Toby or Cassie! On the 19th February we noticed that Kippy had been in the wars with bites to her face, rump and leg. She ate a few treats but wasn't really interested and soon disappeared back into the sett. This time there was no sign of Toby, Millie or Cassie.

Nothing changed over the next few days with only Kippy seen at the sett but on the 22nd February we had no sooner arrived at around 5 pm when Kippy emerged and began to scent mark us, then Toby appeared at the entrance. It was the first time we'd seen him since I had followed him on the 29th January! At first, he seemed a little wary, but once he got our scent, he relaxed and came out to greet us followed by Millie.

Then we noticed that she too was limping there was nothing to see, no wounds or anything obvious and thought that perhaps she may have strained it whilst romping around with one of the others. Ann gave both Millie and Kippy a quick check up and just to be on the safe side gave them both an injection of broad spectrum antibiotic. By this time Toby had gone back down the sett and whilst Ann was checking Millie and Kippy a face appeared very briefly at one of the entrances but vanished back down again very quickly. We thought that it may have been Cassie but couldn't be sure.

On the 28th February we arrived quite late, 11 pm in fact and within minutes Kippy emerged and her battle scars were healing well. She ate a few peanuts and a couple of honey butties before vanishing into the sett once again. We stayed around for a while but there was no sign of Toby, Millie or Cassie. After walking around the wood we returned to the sett again whereupon Kippy reappeared and was obviously in a playful mood bouncing around all stiff legged with her hair stuck out like a scrubbing brush, rolling onto her back to have her tummy rubbed and we noticed that she smelled strongly of wild garlic. Wild garlic or ramsoms was prolific in the wood and though not yet in flower, the emerging leaves still gave off their pungent aroma. We left at 2 am, still with no sign of the other three.

On the 1st March, we arrived at the sett around 5 pm and all was quiet. Kippy eventually emerged at around 6.45 pm, followed by Millie. Both in a very playful mood and after a bit of rough and tumble and eating a few treats, ambled off into the wood but no sign of Cassie or Toby! By this time we suspected that Toby, Cassie and Millie were commuting between the release sett and the wild clan sett hidden away somewhere way up beyond the wooded valley. They could be missing for days only to suddenly re-appear again with Kippy seeming to be the only one being at home fairly consistently. We knew that she was having contact with other badgers but she didn't appear to be as nomadic as the other three, seemingly more content with her lot in the release sett.

On the 4th March we arrived quite late again and as we walked along the woodland path to the sett we suddenly heard a crashing coming from the undergrowth as Kippy came bouncing out onto the path to greet us having picked up our scent. She was in a very playful mood and as we continued towards the sett persisted in walking between our legs and grabbing our ankles in mock attacks almost tripping us up. On arriving at the sett, she tucked into honey butties whilst Ann and I just sat by her side and took in the night sounds of this dark mysterious woodland that we had come to know so well and once again, there was no sign of Toby, Cassie or Millie.

On the 8th March, we had more snow but thankfully not as bad as in January. We arrived at the sett this time to see not only Kippy, but also Toby and Millie! Millie scent marked us followed by wanting a rough and tumble but Toby seemed wary of us and a little unsure how to react. Was this really the same badger that used to be draped over my shoulder as I walked around the garden and not too long ago was jumping up at the van window as I tried to distance myself from him?

On the 13th March only Kippy was there to greet us but on the 15th after heavy overnight snow, the woodland was again transformed into a winter wonderland with badger tracks clearly visible coming and going from the sett but never going too far before returning. This time both Kippy and Millie appeared, Millie in particular being in a very playful mood and bouncing around our feet. Eventually Toby emerged; he seemed hungry and began to fill himself with honey butties and peanuts before disappearing back into the sett without even so much as a 'hello, nice to see you!'

We returned on the 19th March to see both Kippy and Toby but on our return again on the 22nd arriving around 10 pm, there was not a soul to be seen. We called into the sett but no response. We walked through the wood but again everything was quiet apart from the occasional call of a tawny owl in some far distant tree.

Our next visit was on the 29th March. It was quite poignant for us as Toby and Pickles had arrived on our doorstep on the 28th March 1986 and here we were on the 29th March 1987 visiting Toby in the wild a year later! And what a year it had been!! A real concoction of laughter, sadness, trepidation and achievement, but it wasn't over yet, the story wasn't quite finished.

As we arrived at the sett we were met by Kippy and

Toby, Kippy was her usual self but Toby was a maturing adult boar, albeit still only just over a year old, but now a sexually mature boar and with a few scraps under his belt. He was much more aloof towards us now and more independent. My boy was growing up!

As I watched him I couldn't help but reminisce about the long hours spent bottle feeding him, playing in the garden with him, walking around with him contentedly draped over my shoulder. About how he persistently chased Mike up the big pine tree and how awful I felt when I had to rebuff him when he came looking for me in the van and now here he was, a big mature boar badger. I felt like a proud dad!!

But, like all parents at some point, a time comes when you have to accept the fact that they aren't kids anymore and they will go their own way. And so it was that night with Toby, we never saw him again. Cassie soon followed and even Millie soon began to drift away from us. They were, by now, travelling back and forth from our release sett to the wild clan's sett and becoming truly wild badgers. That is except for Kippy, so far as we know she never really left the release sett even though she was still having contact with Toby, Millie and Cassie and others of her kind she remained where she was.

On the 2nd April Kippy had once again been in a scrap, suffering a few minor wounds to her rump, Ann bent down to stroke her but received a low growl for her troubles so we left her in peace. We returned again on the 5th April and this time she allowed Ann to give her a jab of antibiotic just to ensure that her wounds, although not serious, didn't become infected.

Our next visit was on the 9th April and as she emerged from the sett she appeared to have a sore back foot, she was also very grumpy and attempted to bite when touched and soon went back underground. By the 19th April her foot was a lot better and she was in a much better mood. She was obviously having disagreements for whatever reason with other badgers and apart from sustaining a few minor wounds every now and again was looking fit and healthy.

On the 26th April we arrived at the sett but no Kippy, we walked around the wood for a while before deciding to head back to the van but on the way there she came ambling out of the woodland wanting a fuss and to play. We turned around and the three of us strolled through the wood back to the sett just enjoying each other's company for an hour or so.

We continued with our periodic visits all through May, June and July. On the 25th July, we noticed that she had a bite mark on her rump. She allowed Ann to check her over and apart from the superficial bite and the odd flea or two seemed fine. Ten months had passed since the release and apart from the early hiccups, it had gone well. The sett was now an active badger sett in every sense of the word with umpteen active holes with large spoil heaps and a large well used latrine area higher up the bank by the fence separating the wood from the pasture.

July moved into August and we hadn't seen Millie, Cassie or Toby for some months now, in fact the last time we saw Toby was the 29th March almost five months previous. The sett was still very active, far too active to be home to just one badger. We were sure that the other three were spending time there and so decided to have a badger watch in the hope that we may catch a glimpse of them. So one evening we arrived just before dusk keeping well away from the sett but positioning ourselves at a decent vantage point where we could see any badgers emerging and we waited.

Dusk eventually faded into night with the moonlight filtering through the trees casting eerie shadows, the only sounds being the ke-wick, ke-wick of a tawny owl or the rustle of leaves as some small creature scurried by. Still we waited but nothing, by now we were getting quite chilly as the damp cold night air began to seep into our bones. It was becoming more difficult to be still as we shuffled about trying to keep the blood flow circulating or trying to resist the urge to scratch our nose or cough.

We were on the brink of calling it a night when, in the

moonlight, we thought we could make out the distinctive black and white face of a badger poking its head out of one of the holes. Our eyes strained to focus, was it a badger or were the shadows playing tricks on us? There it was again, but this time there was no mistaking the distinctive black and white head of a badger, the white facial stripe almost shining in the darkness. It paused to sniff the air and then retreated once more only to re-emerge a few seconds later.

We hardly dare breathe, who was it, could it be Toby, Millie or Cassie perhaps? Would we still recognise them? The hair we clipped all those months ago to mark them had long since grown back. Then slowly but surely a badger emerged from the hole, once again sniffing the night air. We watched intently as it stood there on top of the spoil heap looking around catching the sounds and smells of the night. We held our breath, who was it, would it come a little closer?

Then, as if in sudden recognition, it looked straight towards us, sniffed the air once more and came bounding over to us. It was of course Kippy! She was delighted to see us and boisterously began to climb all over us sending my thermos flask rolling noisily down the steep woodland floor. She eventually climbed onto Ann's knee and settled down for a tummy tickle and joined us in a badger watch. Needless to say we saw nothing! Despite our best efforts she had picked up our scent, come bounding over and in her excitement made enough of a commotion to send any self-respecting badger scurrying back down the sett for miles! How many people can boast that they have badger watched with a badger? Not many I bet!

The months drifted by until once again, a second winter was upon us bringing more snow and ice. By this time we had curtailed our visits to perhaps only once or twice a month. Kippy, despite retaining her bond with us was totally self-sufficient other than enjoying the occasional treats whilst the other three had completely severed the bond with their human foster parents and even though we no longer saw them we knew they still visited the sett.

By early March spring was in the air, the once snow covered winding track would soon be resplendent with its verges a mass of yellow nodding daffodils. The woodland would once again come alive with bluebells and ransoms carpeting the woodland floor with the latter filling the air with their garlic scented aroma. This was also a time of new life in the badger world with sows suckling cubs deep in the sett soon to be frolicking above ground and following mum on her nightly foraging forays. We couldn't help but wonder how long before Millie and Cassie and Kippy had their own families and Toby a father?

It was now 15th March 1988 seventeen months had passed since the release and Ann and I were travelling out to see Kippy. The sett was still very active and she was doing well. We hadn't been back for a week or so and we'd brought a few treats along for her. It was mainly a silent journey,

I didn't feel right; I had an overwhelming feeling that something was wrong; I tried to put it to the back of my mind and said nothing to Ann. When we finally arrived and quietly walked to the sett we spotted Kippy, not bounding around for joy at our presence, but dead! It was as though she'd just been coming out of the sett and lay down to die. We were heartbroken; we had just lost a very dear friend. It was with a heavy heart that we carried her now lifeless body out of the wood to the van for the journey home. It was a long silent journey! The following day I took her for a post mortem, which read as follows:

Kippy, a female badger weighing 11.9 kg died of acute renal failure with massive leakage of protein into the renal tubules.

This is a relatively uncommon disease of which the cause has yet to be discovered. In every other respect she was in good condition, the normal spring weight for a female badger is around 12 kg, Kippy was 11.9 kg.

Ann revealed later that she too had felt the same

overwhelming feeling that something was wrong but, like me, didn't want to say anything and tried to dismiss it.

Toby, Millie, Cassie and Kippy had been a large part of our lives for a long time and we were privileged to have had the opportunity to get to know them so well. But whereas Toby, Millie and Cassie had completely reverted to being what they were meant to be, totally wild creatures, Kippy refused to severe the bond and, as such, allowed us a little more into her life. To quantify or put into words such a privilege is difficult, but hopefully I have attempted to at least give you some idea in the following paragraph:

To walk through a wood of a night to the sounds of the creatures of the darkness and to feel part of that world is a magic all of its own, but to have one of those creatures accept you as an equal and accompany you on your walk of its own free will and treat you as a friend is an honour too great for mere words.

Kippy could be a very moody creature. (But can't we all at times.) On some occasions, she would be content just to greet you by plonking her bum on your foot depositing a tiny droplet of her musk before vanishing once again into the night. Other times she would walk along with you through her woodland home weaving in and out of your legs in a playful attempt to trip you up, but what she loved most of all was to sit on Ann's knee and enjoy a really good tummy scratch or just to quietly sit and enjoy your company.

After Kippy's death we occasionally returned to the wood and the sett still remained active. But, as time went by, our visits eventually came to an end. I was busier than ever with my job as Head Ranger and of course we had other wildlife to constantly take up our time but we often thought back over those times and of the badgers that had such an impact on our lives.

Some ten years later, the owner of the woodland contacted me to say that the sett was still active. On the 10th December 2012, some 24 years later, Ann and I visited the woodland and the sett again. It felt very strange; it was like walking into a time warp, it still had that strange air of mystery about it. Everything was lush with thick green moss and lichen blanketing the rotting fallen trees - the large green ferns by the pool and waterfall seemed so big, almost prehistoric!

Then we began to look for the sett, we wandered over in the general direction of where we remembered it to be and very soon spotted Mike's refuge from Toby staring down at us, the big old Scots Pine. We scrambled up through the woodland towards it and there just below was the sett and still showing signs of activity all these years later. Not massively so, it was December after all, a time when setts can look fairly dormant but there was, without a shadow of doubt, signs of badger activity still after all this time. Before leaving I collected a few strands of badger hair from the spoil heaps. I like to think that they could possibly contain the DNA of Toby, Millie or Cassie! As we made our way out of the wood and looked back towards the sett we had a vision of four black and white faces looking down at us watching us leave as they had done all those years ago.

Chapter Eight
Barney & Podge, Spikes Attack & Basil from Bridgemere

In May 1987, the Wildlife Unit was its usual busy self with various species of wildlife coming in including an adult sow badger brought in by the RSPCA from Shropshire after being hit by a car. Thankfully, she made a rapid recovery and was soon released back from whence she came, hopefully to avoid any further encounters with cars! I was also busy organising the Ranger Services' main event of the year, Countryside Week. This was an annual week-long event consisting of ranger led guided walks and talks culminating in a weekend Countryside Fair held at Royden Park. A large field was set aside with a main arena for falconry displays and dog agility etc. Numerous stalls were dotted around selling everything from home-made cakes to homeopathic remedies whilst a couple of traction engines, manned by men in oily overalls clutching equally oily rags, chugged noisily away belching out clouds of black sooty smoke to drift away over the field.

One of the most popular events was when the rangers competed against each other in anything from barrel rolling to tug-of-war. Not only was it a lot of fun but also a good team building event and gave them an excuse to let off steam and swear and curse at each other - as if they needed one! The public would also get into the spirit of things with much cheering or booing depending on their loyalties! Apart from organising the event I was also booked to give an evening talk on the work of the Wildlife Unit and was home preparing my presentation when the phone rang. It was the RSPCA asking if I could take a badger cub and of course, the answer was yes, but admittedly with just a hint of trepidation.

We were still monitoring Toby, Millie, Cassie and Kippy and the thought of doing it all again so soon was a bit daunting to say the least. Anyway, the following day a little eight-week-old male badger cub arrived followed two days later by a second. We had learned a lot from our previous five little rapscallions and as such were a little more prepared. It wasn't too long before they were weaned and living in the shed with its pipes and sleeping boxes still heavy with the scent of its previous occupants and enjoying their nightly jaunts around the garden.

Once again, we found ourselves looking for the proverbial needle in a hay-stack, a suitable release site! The big difference here was that we had two boars and no sows which are, from a release point of view, a little more complicated to say the least. Being boars, it would only be a matter of time before they started to wander as Toby did but they wouldn't have the comfort of a ready-made family group to entice them back home. In the meantime however, they were totally oblivious to the fact that they had presented us with a bit of a challenge and continued to enjoy their nightly romps around the garden and sleeping away the day in the shed. We decided to christen them Barney and Podge with the latter being the mischievous one with his favourite pastime being to follow me around the garden whilst constantly nipping the back of my ankles. The more I jumped around and swore at him the more he did it. By this time, the media were always on the lookout for a nice story about the Unit and it wasn't long before the pair of them became a couple of celebrities featuring in the odd magazine article.

Barney even starred in a Border TV children's programme entitled 'Badger on the Barge' based on a children's book by Janni Howker. It tells the tale of Miss Brady, a solitary old lady living on a barge with a badger. She dislikes people, especially children but due to needing help in looking after the badger forms a friendship with schoolgirl Helen Fisher. The filming took place on a barge moored on Lancaster Canal with Barney playing the part of the badger; Miss Brady was played by the acclaimed Broadway actress Rosalie Crutchley with Helen Fisher played by Rachel Griffiths. Barney took it all in his stride and performed perfectly. He was only handled by Ann and me and when not on camera was usually to be found draped around Ann's shoulders.

Sometime later I got a call from the BBC explaining that they were shortly to begin filming a programme called 'The Animals Road Show' and they would like to include Barney and Podge in the series. The host was to be none other than Desmond Morris the well-known TV presenter, zoologist, ethologist, painter and author of numerous books including *The Naked Ape* and *The Human Zoo*. We agreed and on the 7th August around 9.30 pm, a very large BBC outside broadcast van arrived armed with a mind boggling array of cameras, lights and miles of cable and quickly proceeded to turn the garden and dining room into a television studio.

Some twenty minutes later, there was a knock at the door and Desmond Morris strolled in, introduced himself and warmly shook our hands. With introductions over he and the producer proceeded to talk me through what they hoped to capture on film. The general idea was that I would be in the garden with the badgers whilst they romped around as normal totally oblivious to the fact that they would be illuminated by umpteen lights and have a film crew following them around. I must confess to being a little concerned as to how they would deal with the intrusion. It was quite possible that once seeing and smelling all the strange paraphernalia and people they would bolt back to the security of their shed never to be seen again. I hoped that they would just accept the situation and go about their normal business of playing, grooming and foraging for worms and other goodies? But only time would tell

Eventually everything was in place with Desmond Morris sat by a monitor in the dining room ready to relay a commentary to the filming. The garden was lit up like Blackpool illuminations and the film crew were poised for action. All we needed now was for Barney and Podge to perform naturally. As I approached their shed I could hear them scrambling at the door as they sensed my presence and came tumbling out in excited anticipation of a few hours freedom of the garden. After a few minutes of bouncing around my legs and scent marking my wellies they set off at a gallop into the garden only to come to a dead stop as they rounded the corner into the full glare of the lights and strange smells. Much huffing and puffing followed as they fluffed themselves up and bounced around on stiff little legs shortly followed by a quick turnaround as they ran back to me for reassurance.

Thankfully after a few words of encouragement they tentatively followed me back into the garden and after giving everybody and everything the once over soon settled down to their routine of rough and tumbles followed by a worm hunt and digging the odd latrine or two. By around midnight the producer decided that they had ample footage and began to wind up for the night. Whilst the crew were busy packing up Desmond insisted upon being introduced to the two stars and spent a good half-hour just playing with them and enjoying their company. It was transmitted on BBC 1 on Sunday 3rd April 1988 and came across very well with Desmond talking about how the badgers found themselves in captivity, their planned future and general badger behaviour and psychology.

Despite their brushes with stardom both were eventually released into a small natural disused sett in a large forest in North Wales. The local Forestry Commission ranger assisted with the release, which was followed by a period of after release monitoring and recording. Eventually the sett was taken over as a permanent residence with the Clwyd Badger Group recording it as still active and much extended some eight years later. All the indications were that they found themselves a couple of unattached females, taken them back their humble abode and raised a family. They probably wooed their respective wives to be with tales of their days as TV stars.

Badgers have been a big part of our lives for many years and not only from a hand-rearing and rehabilitation perspective. I was also called out on numerous occasions to animals that had either been hit by cars or found themselves caught up in a snare that some mindless idiot had indiscriminately set for whatever poor creature happened to walk into it. I have been called out to badgers found in sheds, coalbunkers and even a drained swimming pool. One of the most amusing was that of a badger that, having been found completely comatose by a roadside and presumed to be dead, was collected and taken by Michele Vaughan of the Wirral & Cheshire Badger Group to a local vet surgery for further examination.

It's not unknown for badger diggers and baiters to discard a dead badger by the roadside to give the impression that it had been killed by a vehicle. Michele asked if it would be possible for me to meet her at the surgery and assist in removing the dead badger from the boot of her car. On arrival, the vet suggested that rather than take it through to the surgery he would examine it in the enclosed garden round the back and could we carry it through.

We did as requested, laying the rather large and heavy badger on the lawn and as the vet was just about to begin his examination the carcass twitched! Not only did it twitch but its eyes opened! We jumped back in astonishment and disbelief as it proceeded to stand up; albeit a little wobbly, but it was standing. We stared open mouthed at each other and then at the badger that by now was looking anything but dead!! It gave a vigorous shake, looked around at its surroundings, then at us. It emitted a low menacing growl then it charged!

Unfortunately the only available refuge was a solitary apple tree and we made a mad dash for it – the spectacle of a vet, a member of the Wirral and Cheshire Badger Group and a ranger all vying for the safety of a single and not very big apple tree must have been hilarious. Thankfully rather than go in for the kill it decided to take refuge in the shrubbery whereupon the vet, armed with a long-reach hypodermic syringe was able to sedate the beast. After a full examination it was concluded that it wasn't dead after all but merely unconscious and was released that evening close to where it was found.

Occasionally we would be asked to take in a badger that someone else had hand-reared. These can, depending on how they have been handled in the past, prove to be somewhat of a challenge. The badgers that we hand-reared and released back into the wild weren't tame animals in the true sense of the word. We had developed a relationship built on mutual trust and understanding that proved invaluable on many occasions during their progression from captivity to the wild as with Toby, Millie, Kippy and Cassie. But a young hand-reared boar badger in captivity upon reaching sexual maturity can become quite a challenge, even to the extent of becoming aggressive to the person or persons caring for it.

It's imperative that a bond of trust and respect is there on both sides and that you, as a human, are familiar with the boundaries that can and cannot be crossed. The scenario in the wood between Toby and Mike was due to the fact that Toby viewed Mike as another male badger but very low down within the group's social pecking order. In the garden, I was in charge and allowed Mike into my territory and Toby accepted that, but in the wood he was in charge and he didn't want Mike around hence trying to drive him away. As far as Toby was concerned, I was still regarded as having some standing within the social hierarchy, plus the fact that Toby and I had established a very special relationship. But before too long I was to experience an attack by a young boar badger that was to remain indelibly imprinted on my mind and in my flesh for ever more!

It all began when we were asked to take in three young but well grown badgers - a boar called Spike and two sows. All three had been hand-reared by someone who, for whatever reason, felt unable to put them through a release programme. By this time, we had built a very large badger enclosure measuring some 60 feet by 20 feet with a network of pipes and chambers that also gave them access to an area of land surrounded by badger proof fencing. This allowed them to live a relatively normal existence within the bounds of captivity and was also good preparation prior to them entering a release programme.

All went well at first, Spike was very friendly and sociable and as such, we devised various things within the enclosure to keep him occupied. His favourite one being to sit in a hammock that Ann had made out of an old sack. He would spend hours just sitting in it grooming. It was also a favourite place for all three to play in. One would dive into the hammock whilst the other two would also try to climb in. It would swing and sway from side to side until the uneven weight of three boisterous young badgers became too much and it tipped them out. They would pick themselves up and scramble straight back in again to repeat the process.

But, as friendly as they were, we hadn't hand-reared them and the bond that we had enjoyed with Toby, Millie, Kippy and Cassie just wasn't there, at least not to the same extent. Due to them being that much older on arrival than our previous cubs it wasn't long before we were once again looking for the proverbial needle in a haystack, a suitable release site. The criteria had to be the same as our previous release with a natural disused sett in good badger country but with no active sett within at least a two or three mile radius. Eventually the Wirral and Cheshire Badger Group told us of an area of woodland in Cheshire that, on the surface at least, appeared to meet our needs.

The wood was quite long and narrow with fields on either side and it had a disused badger sett, which, according to the badger group records, was well away from any known active sett and had been inactive for a long time. It certainly wasn't as good as our first release site with Toby and company but it was the best we had seen so far. After much deliberation, coupled with checking out the area, we decided that it would serve the purpose and once again began a plan of action. We decided to follow the same principles used during the release of our other four and that once transported to the site, Ann and I would spend the first week in the wood with them.

With a plan of action in place, we chose a day in October for the reintroduction; this time we ensured that we could take time off work, plus being able to return to the Wildlife Unit and home for a few hours every day. That would at least give us the opportunity to do whatever needed to be done at the Unit whilst also giving us the chance to grab a meal and a shower and with a bit of luck, a couple of hours sleep before heading off out again.

The date was almost upon us when Granada TV contacted me saying that having done a piece on the badgers a couple of months earlier they now wished to follow it up by filming the release. My first reaction was to decline – we needed to focus purely on the badgers without the added complications of having a film crew tagging on.

Their response was that they would merely film the badgers being loaded up for the journey followed by filming them being carried in their respective crates to the wood and nothing more. I relented and said yes on the understanding that the location was not made public and once we reached the sett they would leave.

The day of the release arrived and sods law it was pouring with rain! Not ideal conditions! Had Granada TV not been coming I would have delayed it until the weather improved but it was all arranged and postponement was out of the question. The film crew arrived around mid-afternoon soon followed by the reporter smartly dressed in a dapper blue pinstriped suit! Not the ideal choice of attire for walking through a wet and soggy wood! With the filming at the Unit concluded one very wet film crew, along with one dapper but equally drenched reporter followed Ann and me along with our three charges on the 20-mile journey to the wood.

On arrival we parked on a rough track by the wood a couple of hours before dusk and it was raining even harder! I was now seriously regretting my decision regarding the filming but it was too late for that now, we had to go through with it. They filmed the unloading of the crates each containing a badger along with the walk through the wood to the sett. The badgers were totally unperturbed by the journey and seemed quite relaxed – more than can be said for the dapper reporter as he slipped and stumbled through the wood in his by now soggy pinstriped suit and green wellies. With his brolly snagging on branches and smart suit adorned with the odd twig and leaf or two not to mention the occasional speck of mud, he was a man a million miles out of his comfort zone!! It was with some relief that we finally arrived at the sett and with filming and interviews over the crew and reporter stumbled their way back to their cars and with the rain finally easing off we scattered the badgers bedding in and around the sett entrances.

With the crew gone and the badgers seeming content in their crates, we poured ourselves a hot drink from the thermos flask and discussed the next course of action. We decided to introduce them to the sett one by one about an hour before dark. Just like Toby and company, they immediately began to explore the holes and drag bedding underground. Despite the weather and the extra burden of a film crew it went well and by the fourth night all three badgers had completely taken over the sett and were spending more time out foraging and exploring the woodland before returning just before dawn to vanish underground and sleep away the day. It was all going to plan but little did we know that all was about to change very quickly and very unexpectedly! As with Toby, Millie, Kippy and Cassie we had marked them in order for us to identify them more easily in the field. By day five, all was going well and everything appeared to be heading to a successful reintroduction. Then it happened!! In the early hours of day six, I was deep in the wood when I spotted the distinct black and white striped face of a badger coming towards me.

I shone my torch towards it and as it came level with me, it paused for a second and I recognised Spike. He then trotted off at a rapid pace along another narrow woodland path followed very shortly by a second badger. It too paused for a moment before taking the route that Spike had followed. At first, I thought it was one of the sows but quickly realised that we had an unmarked badger in our midst! I watched as the second badger trotted off down the path that Spike had taken and vanished into the darkness. Then I heard rustling coming from within the undergrowth some way down the narrow path followed by loud crashing and then the unearthly sound of badgers fighting. It was now all too obvious what was happening, a wild boar badger had picked up Spikes scent and followed him into the wood from the neighbouring field.

My first reaction was to stay where I was and let them sort it out but it all too quickly became obvious that a serious battle was taking place with loud growling, snarling and spitting sounds filling the night air intermingled with the cracking of branches as they jostled and charged through the undergrowth. By now, my hair was beginning to stand on end at the commotion: the sound was horrendous and I was becoming increasingly worried about Spikes safety. He could easily be seriously injured or even killed! I now felt that I had no choice but to try and intervene and set off running towards the sounds of the fighting.

As I entered a small clearing I spotted them, Spike and the wild boar locked in combat. I ran up to the pair of them hoping that with my arrival the wild badger would release his grip on Spike and run off, but he didn't! He completely ignored my presence; I just stood there transfixed as I watched the two of them literally fighting at my feet, two growling and snarling black and white entwined bodies rolling around in combat. Spike was definitely getting the worst of it; he was on his back with the wild one on top of him. I had to do something and in sheer desperation grabbed a branch and began to jump up and down like a demented dervish banging it hard on the ground making as much noise as I possibly could until finally they separated.

Spike just lay there completely exhausted whilst the wild

badger merely moved off a few paces before turning to stare straight at me and for one horrible moment, I thought I was next on the agenda. Suddenly Ann came running down the path and as she did so, the wild badger slowly, without a hint of panic or fright, turned and ambled off into the darkness. Ann went over to Spike and picked him up and by some miracle he didn't appear to be injured but he was shaking with fright and panting heavily through exhaustion. With Ann now at the scene and holding Spike, I attempted to follow in the direction that the wild badger had taken but soon found myself in total darkness with no alternative but to retrace my steps back to Ann and Spike.

We now had one massive dilemma! Do we carry on with the release knowing that we had a wild boar in the vicinity that would undoubtedly come back for another assault on Spike and this time seriously injure him or worse, or do we abort the release? We decided to abort and I drove Spike home to the safety of the enclosure and then with a quick turnaround drove the twenty miles back to the wood.

By the following day all three badgers were safely back home and I felt particularly sorry for the two sows they were doing well and would, in all probability, have been okay but that would have left Spike on his own in captivity and, with him being a single boar, a successful release was greatly reduced. It was a massive quandary and one that we could have done without.

With all three back home, we decided to search once again for another release site and another attempt at getting them back to the wild. They had shown beyond doubt that they could be successfully released if only we could find a decent site! The following day we searched the wood in daylight but could find no trace of badger activity other than from our own three. When I attempted to follow the path that the wild boar had taken, I was alarmed to discover that if I had continued to try to follow him in the dark I would have gone over a 20-foot drop! We never did discover where he came from. All we could say for certain was that he wasn't living in the wood, but what was certain is that he would definitely have returned for another go at Spike.

The big question was why wasn't he afraid of us? Why did he not run off when Ann approached as any normal wild badger would have done? Also when he eventually let go of Spike why did he pause and turn to stare at me for a few seconds before nonchalantly ambling off into the darkness? His reactions towards us were not that of a wild badger, he showed not the slightest hint of being afraid of us. It's a mystery and one that we will never know the answer to.

One of the major problems with any badger release is the strong possibility of territorial disputes, particularly for a boar, hence it being absolutely imperative that everything is done in the early stages to try and avoid such contact. Unfortunately this proved to be a classic example of despite doing all the groundwork and liaising with the local badger group, the unexpected can still arise and jeopardise the release.

Search as we may, no suitable release site materialised and the weeks turned into months. The badgers seemed happy enough and appeared to have settled well back into their large enclosure but Spike was maturing and becoming noticeably more aloof around me. It wasn't something that particularly worried me, but I was aware that he was maturing and that I didn't have the bond with him that I had enjoyed with Toby. The crunch (no pun intended) came one evening. We had been out for an evening meal returning home around 10 pm when I suddenly realised that I hadn't fed the badgers.

With rapidly fading light I pulled on my green Hunter wellies, got the bucket of food from the Unit and set off for the badger enclosure. The enclosure had two doors with the first leading into a small enclosed area with two large wooden sleeping boxes connected by a 12-inch diameter drainage pipe with a second pipe leading from the boxes into the main outdoor enclosure. The food was to be tipped from the bucket into a large round plastic feeding dish situated in the main section of the enclosure accessed by a second door. With bucket in hand, I entered the small enclosure closing the door behind me and dropped the catch to prevent it from opening accidently. I then slid back the bolt on the second door and as I opened it to enter the main enclosure the two sows who had heard me coming came bounding over to greet me and, in their enthusiasm, slipped past me into the small enclosed area.

I now had both sows running around my feet. Normally this wouldn't have been a problem as they would merely follow me back through door but as I made my way towards it, Spike appeared and instinctively I knew that I was in trouble. I had just presented the badgers with something that was out of their normal routine. It was late, almost dark and Spike sensed that I wasn't totally in control of the situation. With the sudden appearance of Spike the two sows went back through the door into the main enclosure. Normally I would have followed and tipped the food into their feeding dish but Spike was heading towards me and I immediately sensed from his body language that I was in trouble. I had crossed a boundary and I was about to pay the price!

As he passed through the partly open door into the small enclosure he charged towards me and launched an unrelenting attack. I instinctively jumped back as he tore at my jeans just below the crotch. (Ouch!). I tried to feel for the door catch but couldn't find it and not daring to take my eyes off him as he was constantly lunging at me. I was hopping about on my right leg whilst trying to fend him off with my left foot as he tore into my wellie. I was shouting for Ann for all I was worth. She heard the din but assumed that it was coming from the country park and totally ignored me!

I managed to grab the bucket with my right hand that I had put on the floor prior to the attack and attempted to fend him off with it but he managed to clamp his jaws onto my thumb and amidst growls of rage proceeded to chew upon it. I eventually yanked my thumb from his mouth, which by now was merrily pumping blood all over the place. I was still hopping around on one leg whilst attempting to fend him off with the other as he continually lunged at me in his unrelenting attempts to sink his teeth into another part of my anatomy. The longer the attack went on the more incessant he became as he lunged forward emitting a low menacing growl.

Feebly I tried once more to feel for the door catch with my, by now, rather tattered and blood spurting thumb! But to no avail. I was becoming desperate. It was only a matter of time before I was going to be seriously injured. I shouted and hollered for all my worth until after what seemed an eternity Ann finally appeared!

She looked visibly shocked and stunned for a few moments until my scream of "Open the blasted door!" shook her into action.

She yanked at the door but to no avail shouting, "I can't, it's locked from the inside!"

Spike just kept coming at me relentless in his endeavours but by pure luck and the grace of God, I finally managed to knock the catch up and the door was released. But, I still had to get out and with Spike securely attached to my left leg it wasn't going to be easy! Eventually Ann managed to open the door just enough for me to hop half way out on my right leg whilst she closed the door shut on my left leg and Spike, who was by now merrily spitting out bits of blue denim from my jeans and green rubber from my wellies! Finally he succumbed to the pressure of the door and let go. I seized what was possibly my one and only opportunity of escape and hopped out whilst Ann slammed the door shut!

I was free at last! I must have looked like someone who had just gone a couple of rounds with a grizzly bear! My jeans were ripped, my wellies were in tatters and my poor thumb was merrily pumping blood all over the place.

Needless to say, I spent a few hours in Accident and Emergency having my thumb put back together with internal stitches to put the hanging out bits back in and external ones to close the flap up! (And Mike Jackson thought Toby was tough!)

But there was more to come, Spike hadn't finished with me just yet! I still had three badgers to care for including

Spike who now made it quite clear that if he ever got a second chance a sore thumb would be the very least of my problems. It became a game of catch me if you can. I would go into the small enclosure and very quietly try to open the second door before he realised I was there and very quickly attempt to bung a large log into the pipe leading from the boxes to the main enclosure to stop him getting out. The log also had a length of rope attached to it that could be pulled from outside of the enclosure to free the pipe. With the pipe well and truly bunged, I would dash into the main enclosure doing what I had to do as quickly as possible whilst listening to a very demented Spike in the pipe trying to remove the log for all he was worth. As soon as I was safely on the outside I would pull on the rope to free the pipe. This was very much a joint effort in respect that as I pulled he was pushing!

As soon as the log was out, he would shoot out of the pipe with the velocity of a cannon ball and charge at the wire in an attempt to get hold of me. What was even more unnerving was that when I was in the small enclosure by the sleeping boxes, he would try to lift the large heavy hinged lids in an attempt to get out and attack me. I eventually placed a metre long concrete kerbing stone on each lid to add more weight and he was still able to lift them a good two inches. My hair stood on end at the thought of him catching me again, I know for a fact that I would have been very seriously injured.

We obviously had a massive problem on our hands; any attempt at release for Spike was now totally out of the question. He had become a very aggressive, dangerous animal and even Ann wasn't safe from his constant frenzied charges at the wire. All of this this was by no means normal; in fact it was very abnormal behaviour for a badger.

I had heard stories of this happening occasionally with hand-reared, tame and sexually mature male badgers but had never before experienced it first-hand. Sadly, he was just one very mixed up individual and it was only a matter of time before he would find the opportunity to attack me again. We just couldn't risk it and decided that the kindest end would be euthanasia. At least with Spike gone we could concentrate on the two sows who were behaving perfectly normal and still releasable. However, fate took a hand once again with the decision taken from us when one morning, upon entering the small enclosure and fully expecting the usual din as Spike tried to lift the box lids, all was silent!

I carefully peeked through the inspection window of the first box and could just make out the form of two badgers that appeared to be sleeping side by side in the straw and a third badger standing up in the second box. Badgers often fall into a deep sleep and just lie there snoring away but it was too quiet. I very cautiously removed the kerbing stone and with baited breath slowly lifted the lid of the box. I was very aware of the fact that I could be making Spike's dream come true and leaving myself wide open for another frenzied attack that would undoubtedly leave me seriously injured and hospitalised.

But as I slowly lifted the lid of the box with the two badgers they didn't move. I realised that it was Spike and one of the sows and cautiously put my hand in to touch them; they were both warm and soft, but dead! I was dumfounded! Why had they died, and even stranger, why the two of them together? There were no outward signs to indicate a problem and they were in good bodily condition. That afternoon I took them to the Pathology Dept. at Leahurst Veterinary Field Station for a post mortem examination and the results were very strange indeed.

It concluded that both animals had died of acute heart failure and asked the question as to whether they were siblings. If so, could both possibly have been born with an inherited malfunction of the heart? They were not related and Spike was, without doubt, a very mixed up individual but the two sows had always been fine. It was very sad but it did solve the dilemma regarding Spikes future and the one remaining badger was eventually returned to the wild.

A couple of years later I was asked by a well-known badger sanctuary if I would take on another problem boar badger that, like Spike, had been hand-reared, was tame, had reached sexually maturity and now displaying signs of aggression. Needless to say I declined and recommended euthanasia, the advice was ignored and I was told some months later that it had in fact attacked and quite seriously injured the sanctuary owner and was put to sleep.

Under normal circumstances badgers are not aggressive, they are quiet, unassuming creatures but a captive male badger that's been hand-reared and reaching sexually maturity with testosterone pumping around his body can, very occasionally, become a psychologically mixed up individual resulting in a very unpredictable animal. At least Spike was predictable; he just wanted to kill me!! But another tame adult boar badger was about to enter my life that was just the opposite of Spike. He would be a fun loving, mischievous individual that would be a joy to be around. His name was Basil.

The story began a couple of years earlier when Ann and I visited the now defunct Bridgemere Wildlife Park in Cheshire. It had been a pleasant day out until we came across a small shabby enclosure and were appalled to see three badgers huddled together under a paving slab raised up on three breeze blocks on permanent public display. They were living in conditions totally alien to their natural instincts and the enclosure was filthy. We took their plight up with the Wirral and Cheshire Badger Group who in turn contacted the Nature Conservancy Council. Under the 1973 Badgers Act a licence was required to keep badgers in captivity and the park had been issued with a licence to keep all three by the N.C.C.

Unfortunately, the fact that they were being kept in abysmal conditions didn't seem to warrant revoking the licence however, on the 20th November 1989 I received a telephone call from a Dr Manson of the Nature Conservancy Council who explained that he had been trying to get hold of me for the past couple of weeks. He wanted to know if we could assist him in the confiscation of the three badgers from Bridgemere Wildlife Park. Apparently, it was now under new ownership after having been sold as a going concern along with all the animals, which, of course, included the three badgers. It transpired that the new owners had not applied for a licence to keep them. At last the long overdue decision was finally made to confiscate them. I explained to Dr Manson that we had been in the Gambia for the past three weeks and that yes we could help with the confiscation and as such arranged to meet him along with the parks manager at the Wildlife Park at 10.30 am on the morning of the 7th December 1989.

It was a cold, damp, foggy morning as we loaded the van with animal carriers lined with fresh clean straw, graspers and anything else we might need. We had no idea if the badgers were tame, young or old - apparently no records of their history had been kept which I thought rather strange considering that a licence had been issued to the previous owners. The drive took about an hour or so, a little longer than anticipated due to the fog but we eventually arrived and drove through the main gates and along a tarmac road passing various enclosures and cages holding a variety of animals until we arrived at the main office.

Dr Manson was already there and in conversation with the parks manager who, with formal introductions over, proceeded to inform us that there were in fact only two badgers, one having died some months previous. He asked us to follow him through the park to the badger enclosure and after a short drive, we pulled up outside the still very shabby looking rectangular pen. Once again, the first thing we spotted was the two badgers curled up together under the paving slab. It was just as we remembered, squalid and basic with no access to water for drinking or bathing.

We asked the manager for some background information regarding their history and if they were tame. He replied that he had no information whatsoever and with regards to them being tame, his response was that no one ever went in with them with food being shoved through a hatch. He went on to say that he thought the sow was about nine years old and the boar about four - they were in fact both males! As he unlocked the door to the enclosure one of the badgers came out from under the slab, ambled over, and proceeded to climb up the wire.

"Thought they weren't tame?" I asked.

He replied with "They're not; he always comes over to the wire at feeding times!"

Great, I thought, this is going to be fun! A boar badger that's not afraid of people and not used to being handled! I was still waking up in a hot sweat after my encounters with Spike and I had no particular wish to repeat the experience! But we had to get them in the carrying boxes one way or another. Whilst pondering over the predicament I wandered over to the far corner of the pen to be followed on the other side of the wire by the badger. At this point Ann took the opportunity to get herself and an animal carrying box into the enclosure. She placed the box on the floor with the door open and stood slightly to one side of it. The badger decided to wander over and investigate, he quietly walked up to Ann, sniffed her wellies then the box, climbed inside, sat on his bum and proceeded to pile mounds of straw up under his belly.

Ann closed the door and with a rather smug self-satisfied expression on her face said, "Well that's that one sorted!"

The second badger was far more timid and had to be lightly sedated in order to get him from under the slab and boxed. The journey home was uneventful with only the odd scratching, rustling of straw and snuffling sounds coming from the boxes.

Once home I checked the enclosure that we had prepared for them. It was much larger than the one they had at the park and came with a dark, cosy sleeping box full of straw which they entered by going down a large drainage pipe. It was warm, cosy and clean, the enclosure also had a large shallow bath for them to drink and bathe in if they so wished. All our previous badgers loved to wallow in water, particularly on a balmy summers evening.

Before settling them down in their new enclosure they were examined and found to be infested with lice; the sedated one also appeared to be quite old whilst the other, although younger, was also not in the best of condition.

After the formalities of routine health checks and delousing, we carried the boxes into the enclosure and decided that the first one out would be the one that had voluntarily climbed into the carrying box as he seemed the more confident and outgoing of the two. We opened the door and stood back as he cautiously emerged from beneath his mound of straw, sniffed the air, quietly walked out of the box and proceeded to inspect everything around him and if met with his approval, scent marked it. He then wandered over to Ann and me who were duly scent marked before ambling over to a pile of fresh straw. He then proceeded to gather up as much as he possibly could under his belly before finally shuffling backwards down the pipe with his prize.

This was the individual we christened Basil and as far as he was concerned, he was home. With Basil well and truly settled we opened the door of the second box to allow badger number two out. This one was far more cautious and only after much deliberation and sniffing of the air did it eventually decide to leave the security of the box. Step by cautious step he gradually emerged to take in his new surroundings whereupon he soon discovered the pipe and quickly vanished down it to join Basil. They settled in very well and it was joy to watch them in the evenings as they emerged from their sleeping quarters to feed, dig the odd latrine or two and just generally chill out in their new home. Within a couple of weeks, they were looking much healthier and happier. We soon discovered that Basil had a spark of mischief in his eyes and always seemed to be grinning. At this point, we didn't go in with them too often other than to keep their quarters clean and to ensure that they had ample food and clean water. They were content with their own company and we were happy with that.

On the 5th January 1990 I went into the enclosure and as I lifted the lid of the sleeping box to check that everything was clean and tidy I discovered that the older of the two had died in his sleep. A post-mortem stated that the animal was in good bodily condition but with badly worn teeth with some incisors missing that hadn't appeared to have caused the animal any problems. It concluded by saying that he died of a heart attack and senile changes in the kidneys. He had simply died of old age! Sad, but at least his last few weeks of life were not spent in those appalling conditions that he'd endured for God knows how many years.

That left us with just Basil! We couldn't expect him to live out the remainder of his life in solitary confinement and decided that it was time to really get to know this individual with the sparkling eyes and mischievous grin. We began to go in with him on a daily basis and on the very first occasion that we did he wandered over to greet us and very quickly left us in no doubt whatsoever that we had one very tame and very good natured badger in our midst!

His enclosure ran parallel to the front garden which still had the badger proof fencing around it from the days of Toby, Millie, Cassie and Kippy; it also had a door that opened out into the garden and one evening we decided to allow him out of his enclosure for the first time. As I slid back the bolt and slowly opened the door, he ambled over and just stood there on the threshold for a few minutes as if mesmerized. He looked up at me as if to say 'can I really come out?'

After a few words of encouragement, he cautiously crossed the threshold to set foot on the grass. Probably the first grass he had felt under his feet for a long time - he sniffed it, glanced up at me one more time and that was it - he was in seventh heaven!! He bounced around all fluffed up and stiff legged just like Toby used to do and then went bounding off into some dark corner only to come running back a few moments later to excitedly sit on our wellies and scent mark us. The expression on his face was a joy to behold and I think that every blade of grass must have been scent marked that night! That became an almost nightly event for many years to come with his sense of fun and mischief developing even more as time went by. He never once showed even the slightest hint of aggression and constantly amazed us with his adorable character.

Our favourite game was 'hide and seek' and yes I know, he was an animal and animals are not generally considered to be capable of such emotions as a sense of fun, or anything else for that matter that's generally regarded as being purely the exclusive rights of us *homo sapiens*! Anyway, nobody had bothered to tell Basil and as far as he was concerned he liked to play games just for the fun of it!

He would amble around the garden sniffing the undergrowth and generally doing badger things when suddenly he would vanish as if beamed up! That was my cue to go looking for him; I would walk around the garden calling his name, occasionally catching a fleeting glimpse of him as he sneaked away under another bush to hide in the shadows. Finally, he would come dashing out of the darkness all fluffed up and excited, grinning the face over before bounding off to vanish once again. That was my cue to climb up to a bough of a large poplar tree.

Once he considered that he had given me ample time to scale the tree he would suddenly appear once again to go charging around the garden frantically looking for me as I watched his antics from above. He would occasionally stop to sniff the night air and even pause briefly at the base of the tree to gaze up at me before continuing his search. Eventually after umpteen laps of the garden he would come running up to the tree for the final time, stand on his hind legs with his front paws reaching up against the trunk to give me that grin of his.

That was my cue to climb down whilst he ran off to hide once more and so it went on until he became bored and decided on a new game. One of his favourite tricks was to come bounding up to you, suddenly throw himself onto his back with eyes closed and legs in the air. The first time he did it we thought he'd popped his clogs! But no! It was just another one of his party tricks! And they say animals don't have a sense of humour! Accuse me of being anthropomorphic if you must but I have had too many animal experiences not to believe that they are sentient beings with feelings and emotions. Like some of the badgers before him, Basil gained a bit of a reputation and occasionally found himself in the spotlight and posing for the odd picture or two. Generally this would be for some article or other highlighting the illegal persecution of badgers and like others before him, became a TV star.

Ann & Basil in the garden

It was February 1990 and I got a call from Central Television explaining that they had a TV programme called 'The Earth Dwellers Guide' and that Kim Wilde, daughter of the sixties pop idol Marty Wilde, who at the time was a pop star in her own right, would be presenting this particular episode. They also explained that she was an animal lover and despised the barbaric and illegal pastime of badger digging and baiting and thought that her meeting Basil as part of the programme would be an ideal way of highlighting the issue. We knew that Basil wouldn't mind in the slightest and as I was coming up against these thugs on an almost weekly basis obviously agreed to the filming. Anything that highlighted the cruelty of badger digging and baiting by these mindless morons had to be worth doing! It was explained that they wanted to film Kim talking to me about badgers in general and the illegal persecution of the species with Basil in shot as much as possible. A filming date was fixed and it was arranged that the crew and Kim would arrive around 7.00 pm.

About a week before filming, I got a phone call from the producer saying that Kim would like to come over to meet Basil and talk over a few details with me in preparation for the actual filming and so it was arranged that she would come over on a particular evening.

We hadn't told anyone of this arrangement and on the chosen evening Kim Wilde just happened to be sat in the living room drinking coffee when there was a knock at the door followed by a voice saying, "It's only me," as one of Ann's friends walked in and duly sat herself down opposite Kim.

Now Ann's friend was an avid Kim Wilde fan and up to this point hadn't appeared to notice that she was in the same room as her idol. I poured her a coffee and thought that I had better be polite and carry out the introductions but before I could summon up the words, Ann's friend appeared to go into a trance with eyes and mouth agape just staring at Kim.

She then began to mumble some almost incoherent words to the effect of, "My God you're Kim Wilde!" in between spluttering out droplets of coffee.

I seized upon the moment to carry out the introductions in the hope that it would possibly jolt her back to some form of normality. It appeared to work, at least momentarily, and we carried on with the topic of the actual filming. However, Ann's friend seemed to be finding it difficult to focus on anything but her idol and began to glaze over once again and thankfully, after almost emptying her coffee over the carpet, decided that she had better make a retreat whilst she still had some inkling of normality about her and stuttering her farewells headed for the door.

A few evenings later, the filming took place with Basil behaving impeccably and Kim getting the message across 'that badgers are brilliant creatures and badger diggers are nothing but cowardly bullies and should be castrated at birth.' (At least that's what she meant to say!)

What she did say was that, "every year 10,000 badgers die lingering and agonising deaths at the hands of these morons who are a peculiar breed of individuals who enjoy seeing these harmless and lovable creature's torn limb from limb by their dogs."

The one and only occasion that I ever saw Basil take a dislike to someone was the time that 'The News of the World' rang me explaining that they had a guy working undercover infiltrating badger digging and baiting gangs in order to gain secret footage that would eventually be used in a story and could this guy meet Basil? They went on to say that the only badgers he had ever seen were ones caked in dirt and blood and fighting for their lives! Obviously I said yes and it was arranged that he and a reporter would arrive one evening. I was introduced to the guy but told that his real name couldn't be revealed or any photographs taken because if his true identity came to light, his life could be in danger.

He was a stocky bloke in his mid-thirties and seemed a decent sort of a chap. He told me about a few of the incidents he'd been involved in which, having infiltrated these gangs, meant that he was having to take part in the proceedings i.e. digging and baiting. I took him into the garden and introduced him to Basil. I immediately noticed a change in Basil who seemed to take an immediate dislike to him and when the guy bent over to stroke him, emitted a low warning growl. Whether or not he could sense something about him or on him I don't know, but he certainly wouldn't let him touch him!

Basil lived on for another few years before old age caught up with him and he faded away. At least he didn't die in the squalor of his old enclosure at Bridgemere Wildlife Park and we like to think that the years he spent with us were happy ones. We were certainly much richer for having known him!

Chapter Nine
A Student from Helsinki: A Saker Falcon in the Depths of an Iranian Ship and a few Scaffold Songs Raise Money for a New Wildlife Unit

Over the years many creatures passed through the doors of the Wildlife Rehabilitation Unit, some common and some not so common and we have had experiences that we could never have dreamt of all those years ago in Dunsop Bridge. It didn't seem that long ago that I was patrolling the moorland around the Forest of Bowland and striving to become a full-time ranger. Now, here I was, only a few short years on and not only managing my own section of a Ranger Service but greatly involved in the care and rehabilitation of wildlife plus being invited to lecture far and wide.

Ann and I had just recently returned from the Isle of Wight where I had been guest speaker at the islands badger group AGM and was now preparing to drive up to Inverness to speak at a wildlife rehabilitation conference. Before travelling down to the Isle of Wight, I had been invited to present a paper at the British Veterinary Nursing Association Annual Congress at The National Agricultural Centre in Warwickshire. The event was well attended with two lecture theatres in constant use throughout the two days with delegates being given a choice of subjects covering a wide range of topics relating to the care of animals. My lecture was scheduled from 4.00pm to 4.45pm and entitled 'Wildlife Nursing and Rehabilitation.'

At 3.45pm I was relaxing over a coffee when a rather flustered congress organiser tracked me down to ask if I could make a slightly earlier start due to the fact that the theatre was already full to capacity with around two hundred people taking up every available seat. At the time, Ann was attending another lecture scheduled to end at

3.50pm resulting in her having to be quietly ushered in and stand at the back to listen to her hubby spouting on about wildlife nursing and rehabilitation. A spin off to my presentation was that my paper was published in 'The British Veterinary Nursing Journal' and subsequently read by the curator of the Avian Department at Helsinki Zoo, Finland.

A couple of weeks later he contacted me explaining that the zoo often took in sick or injured birds of prey to be cared for in their veterinary department but were finding successful rehabilitation difficult and would it be possible for me to train a member of his staff? It was arranged that Andrea Kurten would spend a month in the UK during which time I would endeavour to teach her the basic ins and outs of successful raptor rehabilitation. As luck would have it, I had the ideal candidate for her to begin her lessons in the form of a wild female peregrine falcon recovering from a broken wing. At the end of her four week crash course, she was familiar with, and confident in putting into practise, the general procedures used in successful raptor nursing and training prior to a bird entering a soft release and monitoring programme. On her return to Finland, she kept in touch and told me how she was putting her new found skills to good use.

Every year peregrines bred on the tower of Hamilton St. railway station in Birkenhead and inevitably a youngster would end up chasing a pigeon into the Mersey Tunnel Ventilation Shafts and, unable to find its way out again, I would be called to the rescue of, by this time, one rather dishevelled and sorry looking specimen of a peregrine!

One of the most amusing calls was from a guy explaining that for the past week he'd been watching a very large owl sitting on top of a telegraph pole and due to the fact that it hadn't moved was adamant that it must be sick or injured and could I rescue it? I thanked him for his concern but explained that the owl in question was in fact not a real owl but a large plastic decoy of the type used to deter pigeons and seagulls. Presumably feeling a little foolish and embarrassed by this, he hung up!

I got a call one day from Merseyside Docks and Harbour Board to say that an Iranian ship the 'Iran Vahdat' had docked in Liverpool and the captain had informed them of a bird of prey on board requiring urgent attention and could I help? Some 40 minutes later, I was through the Mersey Tunnel and driving onto the docks to be met by one of the port inspectors who informed me that once on board, we would officially be on Iranian territory and expected to follow certain protocols, one of which was the taking of coffee with the captain.

We were met by the first mate who escorted us on board skirting around an assortment of ropes, chains and other maritime paraphernalia including a number of the crew gathered around a converted oil drum barbecuing kebabs! Eventually we entered a door leading into a long narrow passageway before finally being ushered into a small room and asked to take a seat. Some ten minutes later, another crew member, giving off a rather strong aroma of engine oil, body odour and cigarette smoke, arrived to escort us to the inner sanctum of the captain's quarters and office. He was a large, swarthy black bearded man sitting behind a large desk with an ornately framed picture of their Islamist leader the 'Ayatollah Khomeini' looking down upon him. He seemed a pleasant enough guy as in broken English; he invited us to take a seat and offered us sweet strong coffee served in small beautifully decorated porcelain cups.

After about thirty minutes of politely sipping coffee and responding to his various questions, he finally summoned a crew member. They exchanged a few words in Persian after which the crew member vanished to return a few minutes later with a second person. The captain proudly explained that this man was called Gholam-Reza Sarebani and was a very brave man and that whilst the ship was passing through the Suez Canal, Gholam had spotted a bird floundering in the water tangled in wire and rope and risked his life by diving 40 feet from the stern to rescue it. Once safely back on board he and another crew member knocked together a makeshift cage from scraps of wood and string and placed it in the engine room where it was fed on scraps of cooked chicken from the galley.

Once the captain had completed his in-depth account we were led down a labyrinth of narrow corridors, hatches and steep stairways into the depths of the ship until at last we entered the engine room. We were immediately hit by the stifling heat, noise and overpowering smell of a combination of diesel, engine oil and grease. Gholam indicated for us to follow him to a far corner of the room where on the floor in the crudely made wooden cage was a very sad looking Saker falcon.

The Saker is a large bird of prey that lives in semi-desert regions and spends its winter in Asia, Iran and China, but this bird's wanderings appeared to be well and truly over. It was in a sorry looking state with dirty, dishevelled and broken feathers and badly undernourished. Its dull sunken eyes stared at me with an equal look of total despair and fear as I carefully lifted it out of its small ill-fitting cage. Its breastbone was sharp and protruding, its legs were badly swollen and its feathers were soiled and broken. Gohlam with a broad smile tried to explain in very broken English that they had looked after it very well and it had been fed only the best scraps from the galley. His faith in my ability to save the bird was over-whelming but I didn't have the heart to tell him that the prognosis looked pretty dire!

I gently placed it into my carrying box and we made our way back up the metal stairways and narrow passageways until we were once again back out on deck. The captain was waiting to bid us farewell and after warmly shaking our hands, left us to say our goodbyes to Gholam and what appeared to be every other member of the ship's crew! Finally, after endless hand-shaking we were led off the ship and I headed off home with my very sick falcon.

Once back at the unit I examined it more thoroughly after which I felt even less optimistic about its chances of survival. It was in a state of shock, firstly from its ordeal in the water then from being subjected to some three weeks of confinement in a small wooden cage, kept in a very noisy alien environment and probably eaten very little during its time on board. It was a miracle it was even still alive!

It wasn't Gholams fault; he had, after all, saved the bird from certain death by drowning and had done all he possibly could have under the difficult circumstances.

I treated it for shock and got some nourishment into it and the following day took it to be examined by Brian Coles the specialist avian vet. Nothing appeared to be broken and he prescribed a course of antibiotics plus a lot of constant care and attention. Over the following few days I painstakingly hand fed it and administered the antibiotics.

On day three Gholam came to visit. He was convinced that it would recover and all would be fine, but once again, I didn't share his optimism although I hadn't the heart to tell him so. His ship was due to sail in a few days and I felt that he deserved some sort of recognition for his act. I contacted the RSPCA informing them of his heroic deed and asked if they would consider giving him some sort of award. As a result, just prior to him sailing for home, he was presented with a framed letter of commendation in both English and Persian and put forward for an RSPCA bravery medal.

Despite numerous visits to the vets and a lot of careful nursing the Saker died. A creature can only endure so much before it passes the point of no return and despite all the best efforts in the world, will slowly fade away. I was becoming increasingly frustrated with the lack of funds and decent facilities and the Saker falcon's death, even though neither had played a part in its demise, only added to this frustration. It bothered me that occasionally we could have people visiting the Unit that had previously only read about it, or seen snippets on television and as such, had a preconceived idea as to what to expect.

Andrea from Helsinki Zoo was a typical example and I couldn't help but wonder if she expected something far more professional and better equipped than a small second hand shed and a collection of aviaries and pens scattered around what had been our garden. Possibly an even bigger frustration was the fact people often assumed that I had staff and volunteers tripping over themselves 24 hours a day, seven days a week, busily feeding and cleaning.

Due to the fact that the only official member of staff was me assisted voluntarily by Ann, it required very careful management to stop the Wildlife Unit from becoming full to the point where it would be impossible to devote the time required to treat each individual. I had a good number of ranger staff, but the Unit was not part of their brief and they were not expected to become involved. There were exceptions of course, with Mike Jackson being the most obvious one in helping out with the badger release and occasionally one or two others, but they chose to become involved because of their personal interests. The prospect of improving things both from a financial, equipment and accommodation point of view seemed very slim indeed. The council were looking at making savings and streamlining services, including the Ranger Service and as such it was not the most appropriate time to ask them for more money! It wasn't beyond the realms of possibility that the Wildlife Unit's existing budget could be lost; it was only a small annual amount but it was a lifeline!

Thankfully, circumstances intervened in that my old boss Wilf Watson decided to take retirement, which in turn gave the council the opportunity to re-organise the service and they offered me the newly created post of Wildlife Officer but still retaining some Head Ranger responsibilities. It gave me much more time to devote to wildlife matters rather than people and the Units budget was safe, not increased! But safe! At least one hurdle had been crossed but it didn't solve my frustration with lack of funding and facilities. The second-hand shed that served as the main treatment area was beyond its best and we were in desperate need of a replacement. The problem was that the budget only covered the daily running costs and nothing more; if I needed anything above and beyond, I had to rely on the generosity of the public or raise the cash myself through talks etc. But help was at hand in the form of a good friend and ally.

I was having coffee at his house one day and having a bit of a whinge about lack of funds for a new treatment facility. After pondering over this for a while he asked that if any funds were to become available what sort of figure did I have in mind. I explained that in the ideal world it would be new (no more second-hand cast offs) larger than the present facility and fully equipped with purpose built hospital cages plus fridge and freezer etc. Basically everything required to efficiently run a small wildlife hospital.

His next question was, "How much would that cost?"

I think I came up with a figure off the top of my head of around £7,000.

Then without the slightest hesitation my friend said, "Right, let's see what we can do," and began to prepare a plan of action.

He contacted a local Wirral newspaper, 'The Wirral News,' who in turn began a fundraising campaign. A couple of weeks later we were once again chatting about how well the campaign was going with a few hundred pounds already having been donated.

Pausing for a moment he said, "I suppose I should do something, what do you think?"

I responded by saying that he already had, it was he who got the campaign off the ground in the first place.

Then, as if suddenly hit by a bolt of inspiration said, "I know I'll do a gig! I occasionally perform with a group of lads known as the 'Chip Shop Boys,' they do a few Blues Brothers numbers and I can do a few Scaffold songs such as Lily the Pink, Liverpool Lou, Thank U Very Much and Gin Gan Goolie, what do think?"

He was obviously on a roll and before I could answer, followed on by adding, "We could have an auction as well, if you can drum up a few prizes and I'll ask our kid and a few other people to see if they will donate anything.

I was gobsmacked!

My friend was Mike McCartney, entertainer, musician, songwriter, author, photographer and formerly Mike

McGear of the Liverpool chart topping trio, 'The Scaffold' and, last but not least, younger brother to Paul.

I had visions of him on the phone saying, "Hey our kid, I'm doing a charity gig and auction for Mal Ingham and his Wildlife Unit down in Thurstaston, got anything you can donate?"

The prizes rolled in with Mike donating signed copies of his books including Remember, *The Recollections and Photographs of Michael McCartney*, consisting of Mike's historic photographs of himself and Paul living in 20 Forthlin Rd. Liverpool and the early days of the Beatles. The actor Lewis Collins of the TV series 'The Professionals' donated a jacket worn in the series plus many other items from people that Mike had cajoled into donating.

Mike McCartney & the Chip Shop Boys doing a gig to raise funds for the new Wildlife Hospital Unit.

Mike and the Chip Shop Boys put their heart and soul into the evening ensuring that it was a success with them performing Blues Brothers numbers and Scaffold hits with Mike taking charge of the auction during the interlude. On more than one occasion I found myself uncontrollably sticking my hand up to bid for an item only to be told by Mike to stick it back down again because I wasn't allowed to bid! Within a matter of weeks the magic target of £7000 had been reached!

The new Wildlife Hospital Unit

I purchased a brand spanking new log cabin fully equipped with all the necessaries and at long last, we had a decent and professional treatment room. We had an official opening ceremony attended by various council big wigs and of course Mike to cut the ribbon and declare the new Unit officially open. Reporters and photographers attended from 'The Wirral News' and various other newspapers to cover the story. The new Unit served us well over the coming years and not only helped tremendously in the care of innumerable species of wildlife, but also played host to quite a few celebrities during the filming of various wildlife orientated TV programmes. I always found it a rather odd experience that on occasions I found myself rubbing shoulders with people that I had only previously seen on the telly.

One such person was Professor David Bellamy. The council were looking for a well-known conservation orientated TV personality to give a presentation in Birkenhead's classical style Grade II listed Town Hall.

Proceeds from the ticket sales were to go to a local Children's Environmental Watch club and they asked if I knew of anyone that may be willing to do it with David Bellamy at the top of their list.

At the time, he was at the height of his popularity, being on TV and in the media virtually every week plus being an avid and outspoken advocate on global conservation issues. I agreed that David would be the ideal speaker and attract a lot of media publicity for the event. Unfortunately, the ball was then well and truly thrown into my court to contact his agent and hopefully book him. When I posed the question, "why me?" the response was, "well you are the Wildlife Officer and you have a few contacts in that area and as such the best person to get the ball rolling."

In truth, I didn't have a clue how to sort it! Thankfully, my predicament was unexpectedly resolved one evening whilst Ann and I were having dinner with friends and I happened to mention that I needed to try and contact David Bellamy's agent regarding the talk.

Much to my surprise and relief they immediately responded with, "Oh don't bother going through his agent he and his wife are friends of ours, just leave it with us."

True to their word, they telephoned a few days later saying, "We've spoken to David, he said to pass his telephone number on and for you to give him a ring."

That evening I dialled the number, his wife answered and explained that David was going to be away for the next couple of weeks but to ring again on his return and hopefully I should catch him at home. Two weeks later I rang again and immediately recognised the distinctive voice of the man himself. He explained that he had a very busy schedule ahead but if I gave him a couple of dates, he would try to fit it in and would be in touch to confirm ASAP. A couple of weeks later we spoke once again, a date was fixed and upon enquiring about his fee he very generously said that he would waver the fee due to the fact that the proceeds were going towards a children's environmental club.

The talk was widely advertised with tickets selling like

hot cakes. David was due to begin his presentation at 7.00 pm with him arriving around 6.15 pm and, as such, I needed to be there around 4.00 pm to ensure everything was in place and to carry out a few final checks on equipment etc. The place was empty apart from me and the caretaker who was tasked with showing me where David's dressing room and projector room were located plus the control for the lights etc. With guided tour and instructions over with, I proceeded to set up the projector and ensured that his dressing room was comfortable and supplied with any refreshments he may need.

Finally, after checking everything umpteen times and satisfied that all what needed to work worked, I checked my watch, it was 6.15 pm. Suddenly the silence was broken by footsteps ascending the stairs and the arrival of the man himself.

His large frame came striding through the door and with a beaming smile and an extended hand said, "Malcolm I presume?"

I escorted him to his dressing room and made coffee whilst he ran through the content of his presentation.

Once satisfied he handed me two slide carrousels to take to the projection room and as I left, I asked him how he would like me to introduce him.

"Whatever comes to your mind son, whatever comes to your mind," he replied.

At that, I made my exit to make one last final check on the projector and to load the first slide carrousel. With projector loaded and remote control working, as it should, I made my way back to the dressing room. By now the place was filling up fast with multitudes of people milling around, some chatted in groups whilst others made themselves comfortable in their seats.

As I crossed the main hall I was accosted by half a dozen senior council members including the Chief Executive, the Director and my immediate line manager David Cooling, who seemed to be sweating profusely and appeared to have developed a nervous twitch as he grabbed my arm and led me away before whispering, "Has he turned up yet?"

I couldn't help myself as I glanced at my watch and replied, "No, not yet, he's cutting it a bit fine!"

To which he replied, "He is coming isn't he?"

As I was doing well I couldn't help myself as I spurted out, "Said he was, hope he hasn't forgotten, perhaps I should have gone through his agent after all!"

It took all of my will-power to retain a serious expression and not burst into hysterical laughter as the sweating and twitching became visibly worse as he looked around at the, by now, very full town hall and then towards his lords and masters. They smiled and motioned him over and with face contorting uncontrollably, hands tightly ringing together and back slightly stooped; he smiled weakly back and made towards them. He reminded me of a character out of a Dickens play humbly about to plead with his master for clemency. At that point I made my way backstage and to David B's dressing room.

As I entered he said. "Are we ready to go?"

"Yes," I replied, "it's a full house, whenever you're ready."

Briskly jumping up he announced, "Okay, off you go, I'll come on stage from the left."

As I made my way to the stage, the lights went up, the curtain came back and I paused for a second before striding out to begin my introduction. As I made my way to centre stage I glanced down at the front row of seats reserved for the Mayor and Mayoress, Chief Executive, Director, invited guests and last but not least, my line manager Mr. D. Cooling, who by now was looking quite pale and fidgety. For a moment, I actually thought I saw a wink of encouragement but then quickly realised that it was nothing more than an involuntary eye twitch brought on by the stress of the evening.

After saying a few words, I concluded the introduction with, "Ladies and gentlemen, will you please put your hands together for Professor David Bellamy."

With an outstretched arm, I looked to my left whereupon

he appeared from the right amidst much laughter and applause and, to my enormous relief, at the flick of the remote slide number one appeared on the large screen and he began.

The evening was an enormous success culminating with him leaving the stage to chat to people, sign autographs and pose for a few press pictures and I was congratulated for organising such a successful event. Unfortunately, my line manager continued to retain certain conditions seemingly brought on by the stress of the evening, particularly the wringing of hands and the subordinate inclinations when in the company of more senior beings. The eye twitch became a more permanent feature, which from a positive note at least, proved to be a constant reminder of a magical evening!

Wildlife never ceases to amaze me. There is always something new and intriguing just around the corner and sometimes, to some people at least, may even seem a little far-fetched! One such episode involved a young male tawny owl that came into the Unit many years ago as a so called orphan having been found sat on the floor at the base of a tree during the day. This is perfectly normal for a young tawny owl and should have been left well alone for as dusk fell mum would have continued to feed and protect it. But like many others in similar circumstances it was assumed to be in need of rescue, picked up and taken home by some well-meaning person.

Tawny owls are very easy to hand rear but if done incorrectly will, like many other species, become imprinted and unsuitable for release. We got round this problem by severing direct human contact once the chick was able to feed itself if presented with food. It was then transferred into a very large natural aviary with a soft-release hatch attached to a feeding board on both the inside and outside. After a few weeks the owl was accustomed to taking food off the inside board and one evening around September when the wild population were not quite so territorial and any young tawny owls in the area were becoming independent, we opened the soft-release hatch. This allowed the owl to make its first tentative flights into the wild but return to the feeding board for food.

It's a process known as hacking back, an old falconry term for a gradual return to the wild or soft release. The aviary was his home and a place of security and at first a little reluctant to leave deciding instead to sit on the feeding board looking out or to fly onto the house roof and back again. After a few nights, he became a little bolder and would venture farther into the country park and surrounding woodland but as time went on would spend the day roosting away but returning nightly to the aviary for food.

As the weeks passed he began to return less frequently as he became more adept at catching natural prey. On some occasions we wouldn't see him for a week or more returning only occasionally for food if the weather was particularly bad, or just to sit in a tree in the garden and look for mice. Time went on and the weeks turned into months and the months into years. By now he had claimed his own territory which included the garden and the Wildlife Unit and he'd also found himself a mate. During the winter months we would see very little of him but come spring he would suddenly appear again knowing full well that we would once again begin to place food on the board for him. We knew that he had a mate due to the fact that he only returned for food during the breeding season when he had a family to feed. Then one year he brought her back and the two of them would fly around the garden or sit in the trees or on the house roof, their heads bobbing from side to side as they gave off their food calls.

The following year we decided to make a determined effort to discover where their nest site was. We knew it couldn't be too far away because of the frequency of their nightly visits but he seemed to have an uncanny inclination as to what we were up to! Once he'd taken food off the food board he always flew off in the same direction heading for an area of woodland known locally as the Dungeon. It was about a mile from the Unit and seemed the ideal place to begin our search. His routine never varied, and every night during the breeding season, would suddenly appear in the poplar tree in the garden (the one I would climb whilst Basil my badger would pretend to look for me) whereupon he would stare down at us through the living room window. This was our cue to put food on the board. As soon as he heard the front door open, he would fly from the tree onto the house roof ready to swoop down and take his prize to fly off in the general direction of the Dungeon with the food tightly gripped in his talons.

The plan of action was for Ann to be in the park a few hundred yards or so from the house and as he took the food, I would relay a message to her on our two-way radios that he was heading in her direction but, more often than not, she wouldn't see him! We discovered that if he suspected we were watching he would detour off in another direction. One evening I radioed to Ann to say that he was on his way and I would meet up with her on the old camp site not too far from the Dungeon and directly on his flight path. When I arrived, she was sat on a bench below a small tree with the owl perched above looking down at her!

One of the most unusual events occurred one evening. We had walked down the Wirral Way into the Dungeon area and immediately heard the sound of young tawny owls food calling. There seemed to be two or three of them sat high up in the branches and as an adult landed in the tree, the youngster's calls became louder and more urgent. Had we really discovered his nest site at long last? They were definitely young tawny owls and we had seen an adult but could this be simply another breeding pair? As if knowing what we were thinking the adult flew towards us to perch in a low branch directly above us and looked down as if to say, 'and what are you two doing here?' That was all the proof we needed, they were his youngsters!

We made our way back down the Wirral Way to the sounds of the birds on the estuary and talked about how pleased we were to have finally found his nest site and upon returning home who should be on the house roof waiting for his grub? You guessed it! He'd followed us home.

Chapter Ten
Muffles and Velvet
A Walk on the Wild Side
Hamish the Scottish Wildcat
And a Beached Whale

As mentioned previously, many varied and unusual species of wildlife have passed through the Unit over the years with most returning to the wild, but a few have lived out the remainder of their lives with us. I have spoken of old Basil the badger who was one of those special characters of the animal kingdom that it was a privilege to have known, but there have been others. One in particular will always be remembered with special fondness, a fox called Muffles!

I first met her whilst at the RSPCA's Stapley Grange Wildlife Hospital in Nantwich, Cheshire. I had taken a kestrel along for treatment and was about to leave when the vet asked if I wouldn't mind taking a look at a young fox. He proceeded to take me outside to a small enclosure. As I entered, this half-grown female fox of around five months old came sauntering up to me and as I knelt down, she proceeded to climb onto my knee. She had a look of mischief in her twinkling eyes and, like old Basil seemed have an air of confidence and friendliness about her. Very little was known about her other than that she had been collected from a Police Station by an RSPCA Inspector.

After a few minutes the vet said, "What do you reckon, could you take her?"

I explained that it was plainly obvious that she had been hand-reared from a young age and was totally humanised making any thought of rehabilitation out of the question and as much as I liked foxes, I didn't particularly want a resident one at the Wildlife Unit.

A couple of days later he rang me with his first words being, "Malcolm, what are we going to do about this young fox? I know that she's not a candidate for rehabilitation but if you can't take her she will have to be euthanized, we are a hospital not a sanctuary."

He'd just played his trump card, psychological blackmail!!

I had to admit that there was something special about her and that she had been playing on my mind a little. Eventually I relented and promised to collect her within the week. To be honest I had virtually made up my mind to take her anyway and would have been devastated to have rung only to be told I was too late. Ironically the previous Head Ranger to Wilf Watson, a major somebody or other had been a keen huntsman and constructed a large enclosure to accommodate foxhounds. It was about forty foot long by twelve foot wide and six foot high with a wire roof. It wasn't too dilapidated and with a few minor repairs and alterations would make an excellent enclosure for a young fox. I installed a couple of warm and comfy sleeping boxes connected with large drainage pipes and two raised platforms for lounging about on. An added advantage was that it opened out onto quite a large area of land secured by badger proof fencing. Intended to keep badgers in, not out! This would allow her some freedom from the confines of her enclosure to play and romp around during the day in a fairly natural environment.

The week flew by and at last everything was ready and on the 11th August 1996, I drove down to Nantwich and brought her home. She proved my instincts to be bang on! She was mischievous, fun loving and gentle and we christened her Muffles!

Some three years later in 1999 the unit and I featured in a thirty-minute Granada TV programme entitled 'Walker's Wild Side' hosted by TV personality Anna Walker. Over the period of a week, they filmed me at the Unit caring for, and releasing various animals. They even set up infra-red cameras to film badgers at night leaving their enclosure to forage on the area of land by Muffles enclosure. They decided to end the documentary on this piece of land with

Anna Walker sat on a bale of straw talking to camera with Muffles in shot. Unfortunately, Muffles had other ideas and took the opportunity to show off and chase around like a greyhound. The producer being a little perplexed by this asked if there was any way of keeping her in shot without physically having to hold on to her.

Muffles in the grass

One her favourite pastimes was to dive into a large pile of straw scattering it in all directions and so I decided to place a mountain of the stuff next to the bale that Anna was sat on. It worked a treat! Muffles took flying headlong leaps into it sending straw flying in all directions as she pounced and frolicked around with that silly foxy grin of hers and, with the camera rolling, Anna began her closing commentary. Muffles was in her element, she loved every minute of the attention and behaved impeccably! With the exception that is, of pinching the script out of Anna's back pocket and taking great delight in shredding it!

Obviously, by the time these things are edited you never really know what will or will not be shown, but when finally televised, it ended with Anna in fits of laughter talking to camera while a demented fox with a mischievous grin pounced into a pile of straw and shredded her script! Magic!

A couple of weeks later I got a call from a lady in Liverpool who explained that she had seen the programme and asked if I would like another tame fox! The thought had crossed my mind that it would be nice for Muffles to have a companion but that's as far as it went, nothing more than a thought. All too often captive foxes spend their life in a totally unsuitable enclosure with no mental or physical stimulus to keep them occupied. As a consequence they spend their days constantly pacing up and down or are shy timid creatures living in limbo, not happy in a captive world and yet not able to survive in the wild. Muffles was neither, she was a happy outgoing individual with a zest for life who, albeit captive, lived in a reasonably natural environment with a lot of space and other stimuli to keep her both mentally and physically occupied. I decided that if I ever did acquire a companion for Muffles, it would have to be another vixen of a similar nature and totally happy within a decent captive environment.

As a kid living in Clitheroe, one of my regular stomping grounds was Clitheroe's ancient Norman Castle, not because of any deep seated interest in history, but to visit a captive fox. In those days in the castle grounds by the museum the council had a tiny aviary housing an assortment of budgerigars and an equally small enclosure housing a captive fox. I can still vividly the remember my feelings of mixed emotions ranging from utter captivation at seeing such a beautiful animal at close quarters, to extreme sadness at its circumstances as it constantly paced up and down in its tiny wire cage. The poor creature was expected to live out its life in those tiny, squalid conditions purely as an added attraction for visitors. That memory of my very first encounter with a fox and the mixed emotions it stirred within me are as real today as they were all those years ago and as such the last thing I wanted was a physiologically mixed up animal.

The lady explained that the fox was a female, about four years old and very tame. So far, so good!! Apparently, it had been her husbands who had sadly passed away a few months previously and she could no longer keep it.

I decided there was nothing to lose by at least driving over to take a look for myself. Now Liverpool is a big city and even though I'm familiar with the tourist areas and have fond memories of visiting the Cavern Club on Mathew Street in the 1960s, driving around Liverpool's urban sprawl is another matter entirely! Anyway armed with an address and rough directions, (no satnav in those days!) off I went through the Mersey Tunnel and more by luck than navigation, I eventually found the street consisting of rows of Victorian terraced houses. I pulled up outside the house to be met by a pleasant elderly lady, who led me through the house and into what had been a large back garden. It was now a sea of concrete with a high solid timber fence all around it and in the middle of all this stood a shed with a small wire run attached.

She explained that this was where the fox was kept and as we approached, it came running to the wire to greet us. She slid the bolt back on the door and as I entered, it came running over and rolled on her back for a tummy rub. She was obviously very tame, good natured and appeared to be in good condition albeit a little overweight. I decided there and then that Velvet as she was known, would make the ideal companion for Muffles and we were soon on our way back through the tunnel and her new home.

In order for the pair to get used to each other prior to actually making physical contact, I decided to temporarily split the enclosure in two with Muffles on one side and Velvet on the other. As soon as Velvet was let free in her section of the enclosure Muffles was at the wire bouncing up and down in excitement, ears back, tail wagging from side to side and grinning the face over. After a few days with Muffles less overpowering in her excitement, I decided that the time had come for them to actually meet face to face. Rather than just remove the wire separating the two, I decided to allow Velvet onto the adjacent secure piece of land and she made her first tentative steps over the threshold onto the green, soft grass.

At first, she wasn't quite sure what to make of the stuff, obviously not having seen, smelt, or touched it for a very long time. By this time Muffles was bouncing around all excited at the prospect of being allowed to meet her new companion nose to nose. With Velvet now exploring the expanse of greenery beneath her feet I decided to let Muffles out. She came bounding out like a greyhound out of a trap and playfully began to chase Velvet here, there and everywhere. Poor Velvet didn't quite know what to make of this demented creature that looked like one of her own but seemed to have boundless energy and was obviously a lot fitter. When she could stand the chase no longer she collapsed into a panting heap whilst Muffles bounded around enticing her to get up and play.

From that moment on, they lived and played together for many years but the two were very different, not only in character but visually. Velvet was much darker and more reserved whilst Muffles was your typical textbook handsome red fox with an outgoing mischievous nature. But the one quality both had in abundance was their gentleness. They loved human company, particularly children. In the company of grown-ups, they would exuberantly charge around and play but when in the company of children they much preferred just to sit gently by their side and be stroked whilst staring up at their young admirers with their foxy grin and sparkling eyes.

During the week prior to wandering over to my office in the Visitor Centre I would go through my routine of cleaning, feeding and treating the various species of wildlife in care at the Unit with my last task being to spend some down time with my foxes. They were both very pleasant individuals but I had a very special relationship with Muffles. On entering their enclosure, she would emerge from her sleeping box to welcome me with her foxy grin and tail wag. I would walk over to their platform and rest my arms on the highest section whereupon she would climb up to gently tug at my hair before eventually settling within my arms. I stroked her, she would gaze back at me with those large friendly dark eyes whilst licking my hand. She was an attractive animal with a beautiful shiny henna red coat and soft velvety ears tinged with black and a thick bushy tail.

Velvet

We kept free-range chickens for many years and one of my fondest memories of Muffles was of the day I walked down to the enclosed patch of land with the intention of letting her out for a run around. The gate leading onto the area had been open all day allowing the chickens to grub around in the grass and nettles and as such, my first job was to ensure that they were all rounded up and evicted but unknowingly, I missed one! I opened the door to the fox enclosure confident in the fact that all the chickens had been evicted but no sooner had Muffles done her statutory three laps when she bounded into a thick clump of stinging nettles to emerge with a squawking chicken in her mouth!

I immediately shouted, "Muffles put it down!!"

She instantly spit it out with an expression as if to say, 'How did that get there?' The chicken, none the worse for its experience, shot off clucking and squawking with legs a blur and wings flapping with me in hot pursuit and once cornered gave it a quick check over and ejected it through the gate. Muffles came bounding over to me with the odd feather or two protruding from her mouth and looking all apologetic. I gave her a good fussing and cursed myself for not checking properly in the first place.

It was an amusing sight to see on a bright sunny day half a dozen chickens laid on their side by the fox enclosure sunning themselves whilst Muffles and Velvet would be doing the same on the other side with no more than a quarter of an inch of wire separating them.

There is no doubt that the fox is an opportunistic hunter, it has to be to survive. They are intelligent, captivating animals and I have a great fondness for them. They are one of the most attractive and enigmatic species of our native wildlife and yet one of our most maligned and persecuted. The fox is reviled and endeared in equal measure but despite all that is thrown at him, old Reynard is a born survivor and long may he remain so.

Muffles and Velvet lived on for many years and were excellent ambassadors for their species never once showing anything but friendliness, gentleness and playfulness to all who had the pleasure of meeting them.

One day in 1998, I was asked if I would allow a five-year-old girl who at the time was very poorly with a congenital heart defect to meet Muffles. The little girl's immunity system was very low and as a consequence wasn't eating properly or enjoying life. Of course, I said yes and she arrived accompanied by her big sister. Muffles behaved impeccably, she was gentle and attentive and the little girl loved every second of the foxy attention. Many years later, January 2019 to be precise, some twenty years on, the big sister contacted me once again to say that:

> *"Meeting Muffles all those years ago changed my sister's life! I saw her change quickly, it was unreal to see and I never thought it possible! I will never be able to thank you or the beautiful Muffles*

enough. My sister is now twenty four years old. She isn't in great health but from that day on animals have always played a big part in lifting her spirits."

To hear that all those years on brought a lump to my throat and brought it home to me just how animals can play such a vital role in helping people, particularly children overcome many difficulties.

Both Muffles and Velvet were special, but Muffles had that special quality that made her different, she wasn't just a tame fox, she was magical and knew just how to cast her spell! But nothing lasts forever and in February 2010 Muffles passed peacefully away followed by Velvet a few short weeks later. They were almost 15 years old! A ripe old age for a fox whose life expectancy in the wild is anything from twelve months to five years if they are lucky. They had a good life and gave a lot of pleasure and thankfully were spared the horrors of the hunt or terrier men that, had they been in the wild, would have taken great pleasure in ensuring they faced a terrible death.

Over the years, we had hand-reared many orphaned animals from weasels to stoats to red squirrels. The National Trust has a reserve at Formby on Merseyside with a good population of red squirrels and occasionally we would be asked to hand-rear orphaned kits. Once fully weaned they would be transferred to a large enclosure at Formby before being soft-released back into the reserve.

On one occasion the squirrels were the stars of the BBC programme 'Rolfs Amazing World of Animals' with filming at the Wildlife Unit at Thurstaston and the NT reserve in Formby. The final filming took place a few weeks later in front of a studio audience at the BBC Studios in London. This involved me being introduced onto the stage by the presenter and engaging in general chit chat about the show and red squirrels. The most nerve-wracking part, for me at least, was not so much being on live television but being powdered and dusted in the make-up room before being escorted to the Green Room to await my cue. Ann had the easy bit; she was escorted to a nice comfy seat in the audience!

To say that butterflies in my stomach were doing triple somersaults would be an understatement. I suppose the nearest thing I can relate it to, is being sat in an aeroplane with a parachute strapped to your back waiting for the of the aeroplane's engine revs to drop as you approach the drop zone and the inevitable shout by the jump master of 'number two in the door,' (I was always number two!). Then shuffling forward to a gaping hole and looking out into an abyss waiting for the command to jump! They both get the adrenalin pumping to about the same degree and no matter how many times you do it the feeling is always the same, butterflies, trepidation and finally elation. Whether it is the silence of floating effortlessly in the sky or of the buzz at the sound of applause from an audience, they both have one thing in common! Euphoria!! Particularly when it's over!!!

The Unit always attracted a fair bit of media attention with articles in Cheshire Life, the Wirral Globe, Heswall News, Liverpool Echo and Daily Post plus a few nationals and, as mentioned briefly in chapter three, even 'Hello' magazine!

I remember once being in the studios of Radio Merseyside whilst giving an interview about hedgehogs and the many threats they face from bonfires, strimmers, slug pellets and harsh winters etc. They had asked if I could possibly take a hedgehog into the studio and as the saying goes, never work with children or animals! It grunted, snorted and when not rolled into a tight ball perforating my hands with its needle sharp spines, insisted on exploring the studio. Despite the listeners not being able to actually see the hedgehog I was at least able to give a running commentary on its antics, which due to the amount of phone-in questions went down well.

One of the fascinations of being a Head Ranger/Wildlife Officer and running a Wildlife Rehabilitation Unit was the fact that you never really knew what the day had in store for you. As a Head Ranger, my job was fairly predictable. It generally consisted of managing staff, controlling budgets and promoting the Ranger Service. In complete contrast to this was my other role as a Wildlife Officer, which often meant that the unpredictable was a telephone call away and could see me confronting badger diggers or caring for some rare species of animal or bird.

One such telephone call came one day that ended with me caring for, of all things, a Scottish Wildcat. The guy at the other end of the phone explained that a pure bred young male Scottish Wildcat had been bred in captivity at the Scottish Wildlife Park and was about to be transferred to another establishment in southern England. He went on to explain that his new enclosure wasn't quite ready and was there any chance that in the interim he could be housed with us for four or five weeks? As luck would have it, I had a very large empty enclosure that, with a few alterations, would make an ideal temporary wildcat enclosure. I decided on a three dimensional design with raised walkways and platforms and a couple of cosy secluded dens and quickly got to work.

A week later, a large van arrived with a sturdy wooden crate in the back containing our temporary guest. He was magnificent! He was much larger than your average domestic male tabby with a thick coat (pelage) and that gorgeous thick, bushy tail with its distinctive black rings. As I peeked in at him, he arched his back and spit at me - the epitome of wildness! We carried the crate into the enclosure, opened the crate door, and he shot out like a bullet from a gun and vanished up a seven foot conifer tree. Food and water had been provided, his dens were full of clean straw and so decided to leave him to recover from his journey in peace.

The following morning I noticed that some food had been taken but I couldn't see him anywhere then I spotted two large eyes transfixed on me from behind some branches on one of the upper platforms. I left him alone for three or four days just briefly popping in to top up his drinking water and provide fresh food. Gradually he got used to the routine and became a little less wary even to the extent that he would slink out of his hiding place and onto one of the raised walkways. He looked magnificent and had an aura of wildness about him that enthralled me. A week went by and I decided that the time was right for me to go in and do a general clean-up. Unfortunately, he was using the farthest corner of the enclosure for his toilet, which meant that I had to walk under the walkways with my bucket and shovel.

Before entering, I checked on his whereabouts, he was in his usual spot high up on a far platform hiding behind some conifer branches. Fine I thought, in all probability he will stay out of sight whilst I do what I have to do. How wrong I was! I entered the enclosure ensuring that the door was securely closed behind me and proceeded to walk to the far corner. I had probably only gone a couple of yards when he appeared above me on one of the walkways, albeit very cautiously. I looked at him and fully expected him to slink back out of sight, wrong again!!

I spoke a few words of endearment to him and slowly made my way forward. I was just about to walk under the walkway when he came forward once again constantly staring at me with those big green eyes. I decided to call his bluff and carried on, he came even closer but this time looking much bigger and more intimidating with his coat all fluffed up and erect and hissing loudly. I took another step forward, he came even closer and was now directly above me hissing loudly. One of us had to give in and it was now becoming obvious that it wasn't going to be him and as I didn't particularly fancy having a hissing, spitting wildcat on my head I slowly retreated backwards and out of door. That was lesson number one! I wasn't dealing with a badger or fox now; this fellow was a different ball game altogether and required a much more subtle approach. I solved the toilet issue by putting a hatch in the wire that separated his enclosure from the one next door and sliding in a large wooden litter tray filled with a couple of sacks of cat litter and bingo, he used it! Problem solved! All I had to do was go next door unlock the hatch and clean the tray without invading his space.

As the weeks went, by he settled in very well and seemed quite content, the secret being not to invade his space; if you did, he would let you know about it in no uncertain terms! Six weeks went by without hearing anything regarding his transfer to his new home. I decided it was time to chase it up only to be told that they were closing down and could we keep him. As I was becoming quite fond of him, it wasn't really an issue and as now a permanent resident, decided he should have a name and christened him 'Hamish'.

Hamish the Scottish Wild Cat

Over time, we built up a mutual trust and respect and he became much more relaxed around me, even allowing me to provide his den with clean straw whilst he quietly watched from some high vantage point. He even got into the habit that when he heard me approaching he would come out into the open and walk along a walkway that took him onto a raised platform next to the wire where he would stand totally relaxed whilst I spoke to him and gave him a treat.

The months turned into years and it concerned me that as a pure bred male Scottish Wildcat and registered in the species studbook, he should not be spending out his days with me. He would be far more valuable in a captive breeding programme but despite making enquiries I constantly hit a brick wall.

Eventually I got a call from a guy on the Isle of Skye on the West coast of Scotland who asked, "Malcolm, have you still got your wildcat?"

I replied that I had, to which he said, "What are you going to do with him?"

I explained that I would have liked him to go into a captive breeding and release scheme but had got nowhere with my efforts to find one. He explained there was a guy starting up such a scheme in the Highlands of Scotland who knew of Hamish and that he was very keen, if I was agreeable, to take him as a stud male. He assured me that he would be living in an enclosure much bigger and more natural than the one he had at the moment and that he would have a good life. After more enquiries and seeing photographs of the breeding enclosures, I decided that it would be the best thing for him and arrangements were made for him to travel to Scotland.

The people from Skye were coming down to England for a long weekend and it was arranged that on the day of their return I would attempt to have Hamish ready to go. The plan was that I would entice him into my large cage trap and transfer him to their carrying crate on the day of the journey to Scotland. On the day in question, we placed the cage trap baited with rabbit into Hamish's enclosure. We checked half an hour later and there he was sat in the trap totally unconcerned. We popped a blanket over it and carried it into the Unit. I rang them to say that we had him and a couple of hours later they pulled up outside. We carried the travelling box into the Unit and put it next to the trap with both doors facing each other. The doors were opened and Hamish quietly and calmly walked from one to the other without the slightest hint of stress or anxiety. It was difficult to believe that it was the same hissing, spitting animal that arrived some eight years earlier. With him loaded up and seemingly content, off he went. I was sad to see him go, but his new home in Scotland seemed a much better place and that's what mattered. He was going into a captive breeding scheme where he would be with his own kind at long last and helping to save his species from extinction in his homeland.

I eventually received a report on how he was settling in and all seemed well but about a year later, I got an e-mail to say that he had been moved farther north into another breeding scheme and then the sad news that he had died! Despite making enquiries, I never did discover what he actually died of but he was no longer a youngster and in all probability his death would have been age related. I hope at least that he died peacefully and enjoyed his remaining time back in his native Scotland.

The unexpected arrived once again when I received a call from the Visitor Centre at Wirral Country Park saying,

"Malcolm can you get down to the beach ASAP?"

"Yes, what's the problem?"

"There's a beached whale on the foreshore!!"

"There's a what?"

"There's a beached whale, a member of the public has just been in and reported it."

Now this was a new one! I have dealt with seals, porpoises and seabirds; I have been in the Manchester Ship Canal with a dolphin, been in the main ventilation building for the Mersey Tunnels rescuing trapped peregrine falcons and been into the depths of an Iranian ship rescuing a Saker falcon - but never a whale!

Anyway, off I went into the park, walked across to the cliffs and down to the beach and there it was - a freshly dead twenty-foot whale. It had severe lacerations along its body and was bleeding badly from its dorsal fin and mouth. I immediately contacted the pathologist at the Liverpool University Leahurst Vet School on Wirral explaining that I was on the beach at Thurstaston with a freshly dead whale and would he be interested in doing a post-mortem? Cetaceans were his speciality i.e. whales, dolphins and porpoises.

He immediately responded with, "Yes I am, I'll ask them to get the PM room ready, can you have it down here in an hour?"

He then put the receiver down leaving me wondering how on earth I was going to get a twenty-foot whale off the beach and seven miles down the A540 to Leahurst.

After a couple of frantic phone calls, a local contractor arrived with a tractor towing a low load trailer followed by an even bigger tractor with a winch. Within thirty minutes, the whale was loaded and covered with a large tarpaulin and was off down the A540 to Leahurst. Within an hour and a half of my call, the whale was being winched off the trailer and into the PM room, albeit with a little head scratching on the logistics of winching a twenty-foot whale through a fifteen-foot high door!

A week later, the PM report arrived on my desk stating that it was a Bottle-Nosed Whale with injuries consistent with having being caught up in large commercial trawler nets and died of internal injuries. It had obviously been completely disorientated having travelled down the Dee Estuary to become beached and die.

But humour has to be found in some of the saddest events and as usual Mike Jackson put his artistic talents to use once again by coming up with a sketch to match the occasion!

It depicted me with a stethoscope on the whale and Ann asking, "Can you do anything for it Malcolm or should I put a pan of chips on?!!!"

Mike Jackson's sketch

Chapter Eleven
On the Trail of a Big Cat
Confronting Badger Diggers
And
Time to Hang Up My Boots

My role as a Wildlife Officer was anything but predictable. I was constantly a telephone call away from working alongside the Police, RSPCA Special Operations Unit or The National Wildlife Crime Unit. You never knew what sort of job would turn up next - it could be anything from birds of prey to badger related crime.

Undoubtedly one of the strangest came when I got a call from the then Merseyside Police Wildlife Crime Officer Andy McWilliam to ask if I could accompany him to a flat overlooking Bidston Golf Course. Apparently an elderly couple had reported seeing a very large cat resembling a lion walking across one of the fairways. This wasn't my first experience of assisting the police in tracking down a big cat sighting with everything from lynx to a black panther having been previously reported - but never a lion!!

Andy and I duly arrived at the flat to be met by a pleasant elderly couple who immediately went on the defensive stating, "We know you don't believe us but it was over there."

They guided us through the living room towards the French windows that led out onto a balcony directly overlooking the fairway.

"That's where we saw it," pointing to an area by a bit of rough some fifty or so metres away. "It was pawing a dead woodpigeon around on the ground like a cat with a mouse, I videoed it all from the balcony, come back inside and I'll pop it in the telly."

"You got it on video?!!!" We exclaimed in unison!

"Yes, sit down, sit down," the elderly gent insisted in his eagerness to shatter any doubts that we may have been harbouring.

We plonked our backsides on the couch and waited with eager anticipation as he popped the cassette into the recorder explaining that the quality wasn't very good as he was shaking uncontrollably at the time. The cassette clunked, whirled and made a few other strange noises before settling down to flash a few seconds of jumpy, out of focus footage onto the screen. I can only say that what we saw was strange! The quality was very poor but there was something there and judging by its size compared with its surroundings, it looked big and its colouration appeared similar to that of a lion. It had a long tail the head was large and flat and its body language was that of a big cat.

After watching the footage a few times all we could say was that it looked like a large cat of some description, unfortunately however, due to the very poor quality it was impossible to be conclusive and we would need to speak to people on the course to determine if anyone else had seen it and, with that, we thanked them and left. We then made our way to the clubhouse to speak to the Secretary to let him know that we would be on the course and talking to members.

Upon entering the building we immediately received some very odd looks from a few well healed elderly ladies sat sipping their mid-day gin and tonics when one of them remarked in a rather posh mouth full of marbles tone of voice, "Excuse me constable should you two really be in here?"

We explained that we were on our way to the Secretary's office to which she retorted, "What on earth for?"

"Someone's reported a lion on one of your fairways!" Andy replied.

She looked at him with a rather bemused expression before replying with, "Reported it for what?" Before teetering off back to her gin and tonic.

The Club Secretary upon hearing the reason for our visit treat us with equal disdain and almost fell out of his chair laughing.

"Well, I suppose you had better be off and look for your lion then, and mind the balls as you cross the fairways!"

We checked the area opposite the flat where the video footage was taken; we looked for tracks or anything else that may have collaborated the story but found no trace of anything that remotely resembled a lion other than a very friendly tabby cat. The couple were, without doubt, very genuine in thinking that they had witnessed a big cat sighting and both came across as level-headed intelligent people who were visibly worried about being ridiculed. However, this wasn't my first or last encounter with big cat sightings.

About a year before, a local councillor came in to the Visitor Centre one day to say that on the previous evening as the sun was setting he had seen what he described as a very large cat like animal skirting the boundary of a field. Six weeks later a group of campers reported seeing something similar walking along the side of a hedgerow early one morning.

Probably the most dramatic of all was when the police rang me to say that a householder had reported seeing a very large cat in his garden and could they send a patrol car to take me there? The patrol car duly arrived and we set off at some speed to the scene. On arrival, I was surprised to see a number of police cars already there with a fair number of officers milling around and thinking to myself that they were obviously taking this report seriously. The house was a large detached property with a large garden bordering farmland. I was introduced to the householder who, I was told, was a successful businessman and not one to fantasise about such things.

As we approached the house, a middle-aged gentleman came striding towards us. He appeared a little distraught and nervous and said, "I know that nobody believes me but I'll show you where it jumped over the hedge from the garden and into the field, it left some tracks."

He then proceeded to lead me into a far corner of the garden saying, "It was there when I saw it; it was just walking towards the lawn and when it saw me it ran over to the hedge, jumped into the field and was gone."

He then grabbed hold of my arm and guided me to an area of bare soil and pointing to it said, "Look down there, see those tracks?"

Sure enough imprinted into an area of soft damp soil were indeed tracks. I immediately decided they were not the tracks of dog, fox or badger and were indeed feline but not from your average run of the mill moggy! They were far too big for your average domestic moggy but also far too small for your average big cat i.e. - black panther or whatever. I came to the conclusion that the most logical explanation was that they may have been from a breed of large domestic exotic cat that was becoming increasingly popular as pets in the UK at the time. Two weeks later the RSPCA were called to the same area following a second sighting of a very large cat up a tree but when they got there, it had disappeared!

The newspapers quickly picked up on the story and I was asked for my opinions as to whether or not Wirral did indeed have the odd black panther or lion roaming its countryside. I have never personally seen any conclusive evidence to prove that big cats are out there - but neither do I have conclusive evidence that they are not! I keep an open mind. Some people may see a large dog or an unusual breed of domestic cat or even a fox that, in the fading light of dusk or early morning mist, may convince them that they have seen something out of the ordinary but not all by any means. There are far too many big cat sighting in the UK for them all to be mistaken identities. Remember the couple at Bidston Golf Course and their video footage? They gave me a copy of the video and I've watched it many times over and even though the picture quality was poor, the body language of the animal was that of a big cat, the way it moved, the way it held its tail, the shape of the body and the large flat head. I have observed big cats in the wild on many occasions in Africa and I have to say that it had all the right attributes to that of a young female lion! I took the video to

Chester Zoo where the curator of big cats viewed it and came to the same conclusion, but a lion roaming free on Wirral? Highly unlikely! But the question remains, what did they see?

As mentioned in previous chapters, badgers have been a big part of our lives for many years and I have been fortunate enough to have had many unusual and fascinating experiences because of them, but I have also seen the dark side of being involved with badgers. I have been in the witness box for up to three or four hours at a time under cross-examination whilst acting as expert witness for the prosecution in badger digging cases. Many times, I have had to watch over and over again videos of these cowardly thugs carrying out their sadistic pleasures while explaining to the judge what is happening.

To watch an animal that you know so well as a species and have great affection for being subjected to such torture is difficult at the best of times, but to watch it and remain professional and unemotional is doubly so. The sheer fact of knowing that if you get it wrong these thugs will walk out of court laughing all the way to the nearest pub and be out badger digging again at the first available opportunity keeps you going. The look of absolute astonishment on their faces when found guilty and given a custodial sentence is worth every second of relentless cross-examination by the defence lawyer who would love nothing better than for you to begin to crack at the seams and lose control. I take great satisfaction in the fact that, on the numerous occasions I've acted as expert witness in badger digging and baiting cases, we have won and seen at least some justice done for the badger.

I shall never forget one particular instance when acting as expert witness and advisor for the prosecution, both the defence lawyer and expert witness made an enormous blunder. The case was its third day and for the past two days, I had been in court advising the prosecution on various evidential issues but on this day I was called to give my evidence as expert witness. I had been in the witness box for about two hours with the defence lawyer going over various points time and time again like a dog with a bone to the extent that the judge intervened on a couple of occasions to remind him that I had answered sufficiently and could he please move on!

Eventually the court convened for lunch and the judge took the usual precaution of reminding me that I was still under oath and not to speak to any other witnesses during the recess. Ann had been in the public gallery throughout the three days and on this particular day, rather than go to the café around the corner for lunch, I thought it wise to stay in the court building and have a coffee and a sandwich in the main public area. Towards the end of the lunch break, Ann and I were sat talking when the defence's expert witness, a Dr Leachy, walked by to enter the courtroom. As he passed by, he gave us a rather strange look and just before entering the court paused to stare at us one last time. The next minute the defence lawyer appeared and also began to observe us for a few minutes. I remarked to Ann that they must be up to something but I had no idea what. With lunch over, I was back in the witness box and the judge reconvened the court.

The defence lawyer stood up to commence his cross-examination. I awaited his further questions but he just stared at me for a few seconds before addressing the judge with, "Excuse me Sir but I have something very serious to report regarding Mr. Ingham."

"And what might that be Mr. Ross?"

"Sir, during the lunch recess I saw Mr. Ingham discussing the case with another witness for the prosecution!"

The judge looking across at me asked, "Is that true Mr. Ingham?"

"No sir, I have discussed the case with no one, witness or otherwise." I replied.

The judge then said to the lawyer, "Mr. Ross, do you see this witness in the court room?"

"Yes, sir, I do."

He was then asked to point out the witness to which he turned and pointed to Ann who was sat in the public area of the court saying, "There she is; Mrs. Brocklehurst who I believe is a witness for the prosecution from the local badger group!"

At which point the judge with a wry smile said, "Mr. Ross, that is Mrs. Ingham, Mr. Ingham's wife who is not a witness in this case, is she not?"

"No sir, I believe she is not," was the rather embarrassed reply.

The look on his face was a picture! He could only apologise for making such a ridiculous mistake and I gained quite a few brownie points which he failed to claw back. Needless to say the defendants were found guilty and given custodial sentences. Another amusing incident during the trial was when Dr Leachy, upon taking the stand, began to state his very long list of credentials with regards to his role as expert witness for the defence, including a degree or two from a university in the United States. He was, at the time, very well-known not only for acting as expert witness for the defence in badger related crime but also for his rather eccentric attire consisting of a clergy dog collar and a rather large crucifix dangling from his neck, it was also rumoured that he had attained some of his credentials by rather dubious means.

It was on the second day of the trial and I was sat with the prosecution lawyer. Dr Leachy had just concluded his evidence for the defence and the court had convened for lunch when he wandered over.

Andy McWilliam, who had been sat at the back of the court, came forward and leaning towards him said, "Excuse me, Dr Leachy, the degrees you were awarded from that university in the USA."

"Ah, yes officer, what about them?"

"I've got a degree from that very same university!"

"Is that so and when did you study in the US constable?"

Andy, with his usual dry wit, replied with, "Oh, I didn't study for it; I bought it off the internet!!!!"

Leachy's face turned every shade of scarlet as he huffed and puffed his way out of the court room!

I have not only acted as expert witness for the Police and the RSPCA Special Operations Unit but have also been on many warrant raids, particularly with the National Wildlife Crime Unit on bird of prey related offences.

Generally speaking, the people involved in wildlife crime are more often than not also involved in other crimes such as drug dealing, robbery and violence etc. In my experience, this tends to be particularly true of the badger digging and baiting fraternity with our paths having crossed on many occasions. To say that I'm not their most popular individual would be putting it mildly. I have been spat at, called all the names under the sun and threatened with a spade on more than one occasion. In a gang with their mates around them they are all mouth and bravado - on their own it's a different matter entirely. Here you see the real side of these cowardly cruel, sadistic thugs, they are just like any other bully, and they don't like it if someone fights back!

When called out to badger digging incidents Ann always insisted on coming along and had the annoying habit of taking photos which, for obvious reasons, they tended to object to and as such I often found myself having to watch her back as well as my own.

One such incident involved two known badger diggers who were spotted digging a fox earth on council land. When I arrived, two police officers were on the scene talking to them. Fortunately, they were spotted and reported before they could do any serious damage and as a consequence the only offences committed fell under local authority bye-laws, i.e. removing turf and in pursuit of wildlife etc. It wasn't deemed to be a police matter but before leaving the scene they gave me the diggers names and addresses and advised them to get into their van and head back to Liverpool.

Unfortunately with the police out of the way they had other ideas with one in particular becoming threating and proceeded to push and shove me. I advised him to stop being silly and do as the police asked and leave. He became more belligerent and unfortunately, the situation escalated with one thing leading to another which culminated in him locking himself in their van but forgetting to wind the window up. Somehow, my hands found themselves on his clothing attempting to pull him out through the open window whilst he shouted for his mate to hit me with a shovel. Thankfully, his mate ignored the request much preferring to get into the van and drive off.

Actions such as this are not to be recommended under any circumstances and potentially the outcome could have been very different but it can be difficult to remain in control when confronted by these thugs and particularly so when they expect you to be intimidated by them. I have always regarded threats by these people as merely bully-boy bravado but there was one particular incident that the police took very seriously, so serious in fact that I was under police protection for a couple of months.

It came about one day when I responded to a call saying that a number of men with dogs and spades were in the vicinity of a known badger sett on private land and could I attend? I was advised that the police were on their way and should be on the scene by the time I arrived. Twenty minutes later, I was making my way across a couple of fields towards the badger sett and could see two police officers talking to a number of men with dogs. As I approached, one of the officers came towards me to inform me that the sett hadn't been tampered with and the only offence appeared to be trespass. He went on to explain that all they could do was see them off the land and as I made my way a little closer he advised me not to.

When asked why, he responded with, "They seem to know you and we don't want any trouble."

I did as requested and watched as the police took their details when one of the diggers moved away a little and began to talk on his mobile phone making it quite plain that I that I was the topic of the conversation all the while looking across at me and grinning until the officers finally moved them on.

I thought no more about it but two days later I got a call from the ranger at Eastham Country Park who, upon unlocking the gates to the courtyard, found graffiti daubed over the walls about me and signed the 'badger diggers.' I immediately asked her to contact the police but she said there was no point as she had painted over it because it was very nasty! She refused to tell me what it said only saying that I didn't want to know!

I advised her that if it happened again not to destroy it but to ring the police, and guess what? Two days later more graffiti! This time the police photographed it, took samples of the paint and asked me about any incidents I may have been involved in recently. I mentioned the incident with the diggers and the mobile phone call etc.

They got the details off the attending officers and I was called in to Bromborough police station to be interviewed by an Inspector after which he said, "We have enough to carry out a warrant raid on their properties, but we can't promise a result, it very much depends on what we find."

I was happy with that and to be honest I just put it down to typical badger digger mentality, scrawling obscenities and threats on a wall was just about their level. The raid went ahead and evidence was found including videos of themselves badger digging resulting in their arrest. Apparently under interview they made threats as to what was going to happen to me which the police felt could not be ignored resulting in me being given a rapid response telephone number that if rung, would have sirens and blue flashing lights speeding to my rescue. Occasionally a patrol car would drive slowly by the house of a night time and on more than one occasion I would be walking across the car park at Thurstaston to have a patrol car suddenly appear and stop to ask if everything was okay. Two of the men were given custodial sentences and ultimately the police protection ran its course and I heard no more about it.

A few years after the badger in the garage prank I was set up once again by the boys in blue when attending a conference at the Police HQ in Liverpool where a detective constable and myself were jointly giving a short illustrated talk on Wildlife Crime. I thought it a bit odd that Andy McWilliam, the forces Wildlife Crime Officer at the time, and the DC seemed unusually concerned that I had to be there and not have to cancel due to some unforeseen circumstances, which I thought a little odd as the DC could easily have given the presentation without me. Anyway I arrived at the conference and after a coffee and a mingle with other delegates I sat myself down on the front row just in time for the Asst. Chief Constable to begin his official opening of the event.

At the closing of his opening speech on the topic of tackling the scourge of wildlife crime he said, "I have just one more duty to perform before we begin, will Mr. Malcolm Ingham please come forward."

I was gobsmacked!

I hesitantly left my seat and moved forward as requested whereupon he warmly shook my hand, said a few kind words and he presented me with a 'Merseyside Police Certificate of Recognition' stating 'For the outstanding contribution and assistance he has given to Merseyside Police in the fight against Wildlife Crime over many years etc. etc.' As I thanked him and posed for a couple of photographs I couldn't help but notice Andy and the DC sat on the front row with smug grins all over their faces!

When asked to attend a warrant raid you never really know the full details until you arrive at the Police station for a briefing along with the team of officers executing the raid, it can be anything from illegally kept birds of prey to badger digging or baiting.

One incident I attended with Andy resulted from a drugs raid having taken place in a large detached Victorian property in Liverpool. In the process of searching the place, the police discovered large aviaries in the grounds containing various birds of prey including peregrine falcons. My job was to catch each one up for examination, identification and photographs. As it was a crime scene I had to pass through the police barrier tape and sign in.

As I was being led through the house and into a large overgrown garden where the aviaries were situated the detective said, "Have you ever seen a cannabis farm?"

"No, I haven't,"

"Follow me," he said looking furtively around, "but don't touch anything."

He led me through a door, up umpteen flights of stairs and finally through a trapdoor leading into a large attic. It was amazing! It was like some giant enclosed greenhouse with heat lamps, water systems and rows upon rows of cannabis plants.

Apparently, the house belonged to a well-known drug dealer who, by this time, had been incarcerated in a police cell and as it transpired was also making money out of dealing in illegal birds of prey. The aviaries were nothing more than solid rectangular wooden boxes measuring some eight foot by eight foot with a wire roof and the only way in, for me at least, was through a narrow feeding hatch by the floor. They were designed in this way to ensure that the birds had maximum seclusion for breeding purposes. I had to literally crawl on my belly through the hatch, catch up each bird and then pass it through to Andy to be boxed and recorded. The aviaries were filthy, the floors were a stinking quagmire of guano and rotting remains of uneaten food with nettles so tall, they were touching the roof. By the time I had finished I had nettle stings in every conceivable place and was covered in foul smelling sticky bird poo. It was, without doubt, one of the filthiest jobs I've been on, even the soles of my boots disintegrated some two weeks later!

On another occasion, I was asked by Andy, who by this time was working for the National Wildlife Crimes Unit as an Investigative Support Officer, if I could assist in a raid at premises in North Wales. I had to report to a particular Police Station and attend a pre-raid briefing along with police officers and a DEFRA (Department for Environment, Food & Rural Affairs) Inspector. As it transpired the raid was to be carried out on a Bird of Prey Centre and once again my job was to go and catch up numerous birds including fifteen European Eagle Owls. Knowing that I would be handling very large birds of prey, I had asked the police to ensure that they had plenty of very large pet carrier type boxes to put them in as I caught them up. Unfortunately, they turned up with four small cardboard cat carriers!

Now a European Eagle Owl is a very large powerfully built bird and with the best will in the world, you will not squeeze one into a cardboard cat carrier. This meant that with up to six or more of these massive birds in each aviary, I was left with no alternative but to catch one and restrain it whilst the DEFRA inspector scanned it for a microchip, took ring numbers, photographed it, and checked to see if it was on his list of birds listed to be on the premises. Once that was done I would release it back into the aviary whilst I caught up another one.

Sounds simple enough but generally speaking one European Eagle Owl looks very much like another which meant that I had to ensure that I wasn't catching the same bird twice. I entered the first aviary which had a steeply sloping grass floor with six very large owls stood on the floor at the back watching me intently. I looked at each one trying to identify them individually and then with net in hand I slowly started to make my up the slippery grass incline. As one of them took off I swooped it up in my large catching net and carried it back down to the door at which point the DEFRA Inspector would enter, carry out his checks, and make a hasty retreat before I released it in the hope that I could distinguish it from its mates.

And so it went on until all the birds in the first aviary were done. All I had to do now was to repeat the performance with the ones next door, but I had a problem; my catching net was rapidly disintegrating! As mentioned before, European Eagle Owls are very big powerful birds armed with long sharp talons and combined with the force of flying into my net, coupled with their sharp powerful claws ripping away at it; it was beginning to fall apart.

Anyway, I entered the second aviary and began to slowly walk towards my chosen quarry ready to scoop it up mid-flight. It was a very large female with big enormous bright orange eyes and long dark sharp talons. She watched me intently as I crept forward then she was airborne with her great bulk and six foot wingspan no more than a metre above my head, I swooped with the net and she was in, got you!! Then she was out having flown straight through it leaving me with one very sorry looking net in complete tatters. From then on it was a case of stealthily creeping towards them whilst whispering sweet words of endearment until close enough to be able to rugby tackle my quarry, whereupon I would carry it to the door for the Inspector to do his bit once again. On that day, I caught up a total of twenty birds from European Eagle Owls to a Great Grey Owl and Buzzards, all in a day's work!

I often reflect on how fortunate I have been and often think back to the day when I was advised by my School Careers Officer to dismiss any ambitions I may be harbouring to work within conservation and wildlife. How many kids accepted his negative advice as gospel and missed out on what could have been? From being told that I had no hope whatsoever of working within conservation, I had become a Ranger, a Head Ranger and Wildlife Officer. The years had flown by, the Wildlife Rehabilitation Unit had gained what the media termed as an international reputation and I had handled over a hundred different species of wildlife. I had lectured throughout the UK from Inverness to the Isle of Wight, written technical papers and been on telly. But time was rolling on and thoughts of retirement were beginning to become more frequent and lingered just that little bit longer.

The ranger service was changing! Financial cuts, bureaucracy and certain negative elements within middle management who cared little or nothing about wildlife and conservation eventually gave me the required impetus to finally hang up my boots and a move to sunny North Wales.

And so it came to pass – we bought a cottage with a

large garden and a patch of woodland where I could reflect on my past life and potter - or so I thought!!!

Within a matter of weeks, I found myself rescuing a badger from a snare, followed by monitoring the local wildlife: from polecats to willow tits to buzzards. Now, eight years on, I sit on the conservation committee of the North Wales Wildlife Trust plus acting as expert prosecution witness for the North Wales Police Rural Crimes Team and the RSPCA Special Ops Unit.

In Feb 2017, I was expert witness in operation Manhattan - a joint Police and RSPCA SOU badger-baiting raid on a farm in Blaenau Ffestiniog in the heart of Snowdonia National Park following on from an RSPCA covert operation. The police picked me up from home at 6 am for a briefing at Blaenau Ffestiniog Police Station prior to the raid at around 8 am. I arrived back home at 5 pm to soak away the stench of the day in a hot bath, it was without doubt the worst case I had been involved in in all my years of confronting these people.

The case went to court in Llandudno in Feb 2018 where, once again as expert witness, I was cross-examined by two defence lawyers. I had to calmly and methodically watch horrendous video footage of a badger being ripped apart by dogs as a gang of thugs, including a hunt master and hunt terrier man, kicked and punched the badger whilst encouraging the dogs to worry it. Terrified foxes were also discovered kept in filthy cages and awaiting the same fate.

They received 22 and 20 weeks custodial sentences respectively plus costs and an eight-year ban on keeping dogs. Not a lot considering the shocking cruelty they were inflicting, not only on badgers and foxes but also on the dogs who, when not being encouraged to rip wildlife apart were kept in filthy squalid conditions. Since that case I have given expert witness evidence in court in Carlisle, gathered evidence at badger digs in both North and South Wales with two court cases pending as I write.

Thankfully, the police take a far more proactive role in wildlife crime than twenty years ago with many forces now having a dedicated Rural Crimes Team. North Wales Police pioneered the concept forming a dedicated team of experienced officers to fight rural crime ranging from farm theft, stock rustling and sheep worrying to poaching and illegal persecution of wildlife including badger digging and baiting.

On a lighter note, we have badgers wandering through the garden and woodland on a nightly basis. We sit in the comfort of our conservatory watching badgers coming up close for their treat of peanuts and watch a sow and her cubs romping playfully around on the lawn.

I utilise trail cameras for monitoring the secret lives of badgers and otters, often recording rarely seen footage of the secret and complex lives of these fascinating nocturnal creatures. This has resulted in a large database of otter movements from following an otter bitch and her two cubs for nine months all the way through to dispersal, their trials and tribulations and the death of a young otter crossing a road. The panic as a sow badger inadvertently knocks one of her cubs off a log bridge and into the stream causing a full-scale rescue by other clan members.

Wildlife never ceases to amaze and enthral me; I find it just as fascinating now as I did as a kid in Clitheroe.

I get the same tingling thrill when I catch an otter passing by one of my trail cameras or discover their footprints in the mud or their spraint on a rock as I did when I spotted my very first one all those years ago. I can't imagine a life without wildlife! It's full of surprises, constantly providing me with intensely interesting, dramatic and often amusing events - from an otter bitch playing with her cub to badgers mating, fighting, playing or just generally chilling out. They all provide me with fascinating stories to tell.

But, that's for another time - so much for hanging up my boots!

.